Good Girls,
Good Food,
Good Fun

MEGHAN K. WINCHELL

Good Girls,
Good Food,
Good Fun

THE STORY OF USO

HOSTESSES DURING

WORLD WAR II

THE UNIVERSITY

OF NORTH

CAROLINA PRESS

CHAPEL HILL

© 2008 The University of North Carolina Press
All rights reserved

★

Designed by Heidi Perov
Set in Janson and URW Grotesk
by Keystone Typesetting, Inc.
Manufactured in the United States of America

The paper in this book meets the guidelines for permanence and
durability of the Committee on Production Guidelines for Book
Longevity of the Council on Library Resources.

The University of North Carolina Press has been a member
of the Green Press Initiative since 2003.

Library of Congress Cataloging-in-Publication Data
Winchell, Meghan K.
Good girls, good food, good fun : the story of USO hostesses during World
War II / by Meghan K. Winchell.
p. cm. — (Gender and American culture)
Includes bibliographical references and index.
ISBN 978-0-8078-3237-0 (cloth: alk. paper)
1. United Service Organizations (U.S.) 2. Soldiers — Recreation — United States —
History. 3. World War, 1939–1945 — War work — United States. 4. World
War, 1939–1945 — Women — United States. 5. Women — United States —
Social conditions — 20th century. I. Title.
D810.E8W56 2008
940.53082 — dc22   2008017085

Portions of this work appeared in " 'To Make the Boys Feel at Home':
USO Senior Hostesses and Gendered Citizenship," *Frontiers: A Journal of
Women Studies* 25, no. 1 (2004): 190–211, reprinted here by
permission of the University of Nebraska Press. Copyright
© 2004 by Frontiers Editorial Collective.

A Caravan book. For more information,
visit www.caravanbooks.org.

cloth   12 11 10 09 08   5 4 3 2 1

*University of North Carolina Press books may be purchased at a discount
for educational, business, or sales promotional use. For information, please
visit www.uncpress.unc.edu or write to UNC Press, attention: Sales
Department, 116 South Boundary Street, Chapel Hill, NC 27514-3808.*

For Guy

Contents

Introduction 1

★ ONE ★

To Make the Boys Feel at Home:
Senior Hostesses and Gendered Citizenship 12

★ TWO ★

The Loveliest Girls in the Nation 44

★ THREE ★

Wartime Socializing 76

★ FOUR ★

Nice Girls Didn't, Period:
Junior Hostesses and Sexual Service 106

★ FIVE ★

Courtship and Competition in
the USO Dance Hall 135

Conclusion 171

Appendix:
Interview/Questionnaire Template 177

Notes 179

Bibliography 221

Acknowledgments 239

Index 241

Illustrations

I.1. USO fund-raising poster 8

1.1. "I Gave My Son" 22

1.2. Private First Class Larry
Wakefield 27

1.3. Coffee and donuts at the San Francisco USO 34

1.4. Mrs. Alfred Scott and a soldier at the
Phyllis Wheatley YWCA USO 36

1.5. Sewing service at the USO 40

2.1. Nancy Brown, Hollywood Canteen
junior hostess 46

2.2. Front of West Adams Los Angeles Area
USO identification card 50

2.3. Back of West Adams Los Angeles Area
USO identification card 51

2.4. Betty Ward, director of the Miami USO 52

2.5. "Willie Gillis at the USO" 54

2.6. "After the Ball Is Over" 64

2.7. Two junior hostesses and a sailor sharing a soda 69

3.1. Ping-Pong at the Miami USO 90

3.2. More Ping-Pong at the Miami USO 91

3.3. Junior hostesses and soldiers playing games at a
Boston area USO club 97

3.4. "Loose Lips Might Sink Ships" 98

3.5. USO certificate 104

4.1. "Wholesome Kids" at the Miami USO 126

4.2. "She May Look Clean — But" 129

5.1. Dancing at the Miami USO 140

5.2. Square dancing and the Paul Jones 142

5.3. Anne Rodriguez dancing with a sailor at
the USO in Honolulu, Hawaii 143

5.4. Jitterbugging at the Miami USO 145

5.5. Margaret and Roger Fredrich's wedding portrait 169

C.1. Miss America Phyllis George on a
USO tour in Vietnam 174

Abbreviations & Acronyms

ASHA   American Social Hygiene Association

BSSC   Boston Soldiers and Sailors Committee

CDHC   Concord Dance Hostess Committee

GSO   Girls Service Organization

JANCWR   Joint Army and Navy Committee on
Welfare and Recreation

NAACP   National Association for the
Advancement of Colored People

NCCS   National Catholic Community Service

OCWS   Office of Community War Services

OPA   Office of Price Administration

SDC   Stage Door Canteen

USO   United Service Organizations

VD   venereal disease

WAC   Women's Army Corps

YMCA   Young Men's Christian Association

YWCA   Young Women's Christian Association

Good Girls,
Good Food,
Good Fun

Introduction

Rosie the Riveter remains the ubiquitous symbol of World War II's female patriot. In the popular imagery of the "Good War," Rosie arguably stands second only to the courageous soldiers raising the American flag at Iwo Jima. Today, the War Department's depiction of Rosie peddling a "We Can Do It!" attitude, with her pouty lips, enviably long eyelashes, and oversized muscular biceps, graces posters, note cards, magnets, coasters, and even pot holders. The proliferation and endurance of this image might prompt one to conclude that immediately following President Franklin Roosevelt's "A Day That Will Live in Infamy" speech, hordes of American women rushed to the shipyards, seized riveting guns, and went at it. In truth, the majority of American women did not enter the industrial labor force during the war. They found Rosie's image daunting. Many of these women were like junior USO hostess Nancy Brown. She surmised that hostessing at the Hollywood Canteen "was what I could do. I really was not Rosie the Riveter. I was not one of those women who could go out there and work on an assembly line." Instead, Nancy worked as a secretary, and in her view hostessing "was the ideal way to do my part in the war effort."[1] She was not alone.

Historical scholarship has shown how the state and media mobilized women into "men's" roles, including soldier and industrial worker, during World War II,[2] but little work has been done on the ways in which quasi-state organizations such as the USO mobilized them to perform "women's" work that did not challenge gender norms. USO hostesses extended private acts of nurturing and caretaking to the public sphere and performed them in USO clubs and canteens. In doing so, they made their usually private work visible and rendered unpaid yet vital services as mothers and sweethearts to the state and the military. This gendered labor helped to humanize the military experience for servicemen. This study reveals how tens of thousands of USO hostesses like Nancy conducted work that helped to maintain the role of the virtuous woman in this time of crisis.

In the United States, women who volunteered at USO clubs offered wholesome recreation to millions of enlisted soldiers and sailors outside camp in their off-duty hours. It is likely that many servicemen spent their entire wartime experiences in the vicinity of a USO club, because of the 16 million who served in the military, 25 percent remained in the United States throughout the war.[3] The USO grew quickly to meet the recreational needs of soldiers and sailors. Prior to the U.S. entrance into the war, six of the organizations that had provided assistance to U.S. troops during World War I — the Young Men's Christian Association (YMCA), the Young Women's Christian Association (YWCA), the Salvation Army, the Jewish Welfare Board, the National Catholic Community Service (NCCS), and the Traveler's Aid Society — combined to form the United Service Organizations (USO) for National Defense early in 1941.[4] By September 1941, civilian volunteers were lending their time and talents to 89 USO clubs. One year later, the USO was opening two new clubs or service programs every day, with a total of 967 in operation.[5] At its height in 1944, the USO operated 3,035 clubs and canteens that assisted 1 million people in the United States each day.[6] The USO, therefore, played a central role in constructing the wartime experience for servicemen as well as for women who volunteered as hostesses.

The USO was a broad-based organization that attracted middle-income and wealthy volunteers, just as it advanced the social and cultural agenda of those who considered themselves to be part of the elusive middle class. "Middle class" as a distinct category is slippery and difficult to identify. Persons who both earned and aspired to earn middle incomes and those who identified with them created a middle-class culture that dominated the United States from the late nineteenth century onward.[7] Professionals and managers made up the core of this modern middle class. These white-collar workers held a variety of positions, from clerical to managerial. Whether their income put them in the middle or not, they considered themselves of the middle class by virtue of working in offices as opposed to factories. A middle-class image also included a husband/father who earned a family wage, along with a wife/mother who managed the home and raised children. When mothers who considered themselves middle class worked outside the home for pay, it was often to earn the money needed to maintain the family's status within an inviting consumer and leisure culture. Members of the middle class were likely to be white and native-born. They also benefited from public school education and valued college degrees, even if they themselves did not obtain them. Middle-class principles included respectability, public decorum, and "good character." "Acceptance of [these values] signified 'middle class' and implied success," according to historian Jay Hatheway. Such acceptance by those who did not meet the economic qualifications for "middle class" broadened the reach and influence of middle-class norms.[8] Individuals who held decision-making power in USO clubs across the country fell into this broad outline of middle class, either ascribing to themselves such status or holding firm to the white-collar employment most closely associated with it.

Though both men and women volunteered for the organization, women's labor provided the foundation for most USO activities and kept the clubs open throughout the war. For this reason, this book is an examination of junior and senior hostesses within the United States, not of the USO organization as a whole or of its subsidiary, USO Camp Shows, Inc.[9] The USO counted on the volunteer efforts of more than 1.5 million Americans by the end of the war in 1945.[10] In April 1942, USO president Harper Sibley revealed the importance of women's work to the USO project when he acknowledged that "the men of the United States believe in the USO, but it is the women of the USO that are the heart and soul of the USO. . . . The people who make these clubs so attractive to the men are the women."[11] Indeed, to servicemen the sheer presence of women in USO clubs afforded a welcome counterpoint to the masculine army and navy. When she began chairing the Women's Committee of the USO, Mrs. Maurice T. Moore revealed, "We have found that women are desperately, pathetically eager to do what they can to win this war."[12] Moore's description of women's passion to end the war with victory suggests that in her view they would take pains to keep their male loved ones safe.

Government officials attempted to channel that kind of passion into outlets that maintained historic notions about respectable women's roles in wartime. According to Robert P. Patterson, the undersecretary of war, it was the obligation of "American mothers and American families" to make sure that servicemen found healthy "companionship and hospitality" while they were off duty.[13] This rhetoric implied that women, senior hostesses in particular, possessed the ability to prevent men from engaging in illicit sexual relationships, if those women selected proper feminine companions for servicemen. This idea, of course, denied men's role in choosing their own partners, sexual or otherwise. Moreover, when the USO and the military personalized the troops and its war-making campaign by calling on "mothers" to care for "sons," these organizations made it difficult for women to criticize the very war that was taking those men from them. The practice of personalization reveals the uso's role in marshaling necessary home front support, particularly female, for the war.

Political scientist Laura Balbo's theory of "emotional work" best illuminates the function of hostesses for the wartime state. According to Balbo, women's daily efforts to convert "resources" into usable "services" are essential to upholding capitalism in general. Wartime magnified this form of gendered labor. For example, women's work within the capitalist welfare state includes cooking and cleaning as well as being the human link to day care centers, welfare agencies, doctors, and other service providers. Women perform emotional work as they embody this human link — as they transform state checks into hot meals or discuss a child's development with preschool teachers. While Balbo focuses on the role of low-income women in the welfare state, her theory applies to uso hostesses in a number of ways. They cared for servicemen as if they were personally connected to them, just as they would have cared for their own families. In essence, they performed emotional work for the military and followed Mrs. Moore's suggestion to "prove in every way" that they were "behind our fighting men." Balbo contends that "women's work is invisible, though its worth is known to all; it is not even considered to be work, for the words which are used are love and self-denial and care for the needs of others." In retrospect, few hostesses described their uso service as work. In fact, most former hostesses in this study emphasized the patriotic nature of their volunteerism, occasionally complained about aching feet, and most often spoke about their service as expected and fulfilling, thus illustrating Balbo's argument that their emotional work was invisible, even to them. This invisibility does not negate women's agency in choosing to volunteer as hostesses and in reaping pleasure from their wartime contributions. Finally, uso hostesses coped with "service work" by coming together to perform it, just as Balbo argues women do within their families on a regular basis.[14] Many women had already honed the skills necessary to uplift the morale of individual servicemen when the federal government issued a call for those skills.

Charles P. Taft, assistant coordinator of health and welfare for the Office of Community War Services (ocws), defined the uso project in an address to the Central Atlantic Area ymca Convention in Atlantic City, New Jersey, on 17 May 1941. He claimed the organization provided "friendly service to our men at arms." In the speech, he opposed critics who might suggest that it was unnecessary to raise $10,765,000 to entertain servicemen who received a monthly allotment. To the critique that servicemen ought to be "he-men, able to defend the rest of us" without civilians to "hold their hands or try to save their souls," he responded that hundreds of communities were experiencing "soldier and sailor indigestion." The million and a half men in military training camps at the time flooded local communities that were unprepared to deal with their numbers. According to Taft, communities eagerly accepted military camps and war industries as economic catalysts but did not have the means to entertain or contend with so many servicemen and defense workers who visited town in their off-duty hours. The USO's purpose was to offer those individuals "intelligent recreation . . . participation in worthwhile, leisure time activities," fueled by "real community hospitality." Taft acknowledged that women would organize and staff most USO programs and would work closely with representatives from the federal government.[15]

Taft's speech highlights the major elements of the USO as a new national organization, including its desire to entertain and emotionally support servicemen and its reliance on volunteers. The USO responded to communities' appeals for assistance in housing and hosting servicemen, while it used its power as a quasi-state agency to focus civilian energy toward supporting instead of questioning the war effort. In its major publicity campaigns the USO personalized the plight of lonely soldiers and sailors who needed the moral guidance of home while the military ensconced them in its impersonal, morally suspect world. It was this public concern and tangible appreciation for the serviceman that would make it possible for him to survive the war with his spirit intact and facilitate his transition back into civilian life. Ultimately, a specific kind of woman who embodied the USO's version of American womanhood would ensure this transition.

The national USO relied on and reified the assumption that white middle-class women were inherently sexually respectable and feminine, thereby strengthening a good girl/bad girl dichotomy. Working-class sexual ideology was similar to that of the middle class in that working-class parents often safeguarded their daughters' chastity, particularly in immigrant families. The key difference between middle- and working-class sexual ideology in the first half of the twentieth century was that members of a broad middle class attempted to define and circumscribe the sexual behavior of all women, not just those in their immediate purview. The working class, conversely, did not situate itself within a reform culture that dictated social practices to others.[16]

Sexual prescription served both as a mark of class status and as a qualification for USO service in which senior hostesses groomed "good girls" to represent the USO alongside a federal crackdown on female prostitution and the arrest of thousands of so-called pickup girls suspected of passing venereal disease (VD) to servicemen. Servicemen's propensity to contract (and spread) VD at a time when penicillin was not yet in use posed a real and serious threat to the military. Both pickup girls and USO hostesses negotiated a sexual double standard that made them responsible for men's sexual misconduct. This double standard allowed men to pursue sexual intimacy free of social, though not physical, consequences, while women endured the physical and social repercussions and responsibility for their own sexual choices. Nonetheless, within this context, junior hostesses built on the examples of middle-class college students from the 1920s and white-collar working women of the 1930s to expand the sexual choices and actions of respectable single women, thereby transforming the definition of a good girl.[17] Junior hostesses and servicemen operated within a larger sexual landscape that included VD, promiscuity, and alluring pinup girls, all of which were informed by class- and race-based notions of sexual respectability.

Massive population shifts led to inadequate off-duty housing and recreation options for servicemen in civilian communities. When the United States mobilized for war, the War Production Board oversaw private factories' conversion from consumer goods to military hardware at the same time that 16 million people gathered to serve in the armed forces. These developments caused the movement of millions of Americans from their hometowns to cities that offered war work or housed U.S. troops.[18] The population of Norfolk, Virginia, was 250,000; but it increased by 126,000 military personnel and war workers nearly overnight, and the community did not have enough recreational or even dining options to host them early in the war.[19] The national USO established local clubs to organize leisure activities in towns, like Norfolk, overrun by war workers and servicemen on the move. The USO Field Plans Committee responded to population shifts by developing a set of key questions or issues to determine whether or not a city was in need of a USO club. Those issues included whether or not the Office of Production Management had labeled the community a "Defense Impact Area," or a military or naval area; how much the population of the area had increased as a result of these designations; and how developed the town's existing recreational infrastructure was.[20] As the USO moved into towns where it was needed, the organization began to recast servicemen who represented wartime population shifts, and the anxieties that accompanied them, from potential menace to innocent patriots.

The public held contradictory perceptions of servicemen throughout the war. The anonymity of their uniforms could erode servicemen's sense of individuality and their social connections. At the same time, that anonymity could threaten civilians' control over their families and communities. USO agencies and fund-raisers believed that servicemen needed healthy recreation to keep them out of trouble and to sustain their humanity. John D. Rockefeller, chairman of the National Sponsoring Committee of the USO, appealed to the neighbors, friends, and parents of servicemen when he argued that "in the service, these sons of ours are only Private Jones, or Seaman Smith, — to us they are our pride and joy."[21] The USO attempted to personalize the monolithic "servicemen" to the public, to single out each man from the crowd as a "son" and to celebrate his individuality. It was a volunteer's task to maintain men's moral connections with home. Similarly, fund-raising spots for radio emphasized that servicemen were "human. They [were] of our own kind, our own people. They [wore] a uniform which sometimes [was] described as marking them as more American than the man who [did] not. But this [made] them nonetheless the active fun loving Americans they were before they put on that uniform." The USO asked for funds to maintain the humanity of the individual wearing the uniform and not to allow that uniform to obscure the person he used to be and, in essence, truly was.[22]

The 16 million individuals who found themselves surrounded by supposed immorality and potential combat relied on the USO to alleviate the boredom, loneliness, and tension of military life. Servicemen expressed a desire simply to spend time in "friendly" towns where civilians made eye contact with them and spoke to them.[23] They also searched for various forms of entertainment to fill their off-duty hours. As statistics from a 1944 national survey of USO services illustrated, 30 percent of white soldiers and 44 percent of African American soldiers described the USO as "absolutely essential," while 51 percent of white and 47 percent of African American soldiers described the USO as having "great importance" to them.[24] The majority of soldiers depended on and endorsed the work of USO volunteers. By September 1942 an average of 4.5 million visited USO clubs on a monthly basis.[25] These numbers increased greatly as the war progressed. For example, in July 1944, 22,740,431 people visited USO clubs.[26] Servicemen responded to the USO in great numbers, and it served as their most popular alternative or complement to bars and their surroundings.

I.1. uso fund-raising poster (courtesy of United Service Organizations, Inc.)

★ ★ ★

Patriotism mandated support and gratitude for those who were to fight the war. At the same time, the democratic rhetoric of the U.S. government during the war years conflicted with the prejudice and discrimination that was commonplace in American society and institutionalized in the military itself. As a civilian institution operating within local communities, the uso was an important site for the enactment of racial conflicts and accommodations. The uso's policy to integrate its clubs only where public sentiment would allow integration and not in all situations, for example, suggested to many black servicemen and civilians that the organization, and by extension the American government, did not value their contributions to the war effort. Furthermore, local USO clubs' discriminatory treatment of Hispanic women in the Southwest and Jewish volunteers in the Southeast opened debates about who was eligible to represent the USO as hostesses and which servicemen were worthy of USO hospitality.

Racial conflict within USO clubs, or the efforts of black men and women to gain equality in the United States through USO service, challenged the organization's image of womanhood. For example, various African American groups applauded the USO's policy of racial integration and equality but disapproved when the organization did not enforce it uniformly. According to the USO *Manual of General Policies,* the USO's purpose included providing all necessary services for black troops, although USO organizers on the national level believed that programs and USO clubs needed to be segregated in some communities. The USO's policy was to offer assistance and include black servicemen in all programs but not to break the barriers of racial segregation and limit discrimination.[27] It likely chose this path to avoid complaints from local communities that disdained interference from national organizations with regard to community control over race relations. The problems that the USO faced included how to make available equal recreation facilities where small numbers of black troops existed, how to serve black troops in towns with small black populations, and how to deal with towns where "community attitudes" prevented integration.[28] One of the key problems that African American servicemen faced was a direct result of the military's reluctance to station them together in large numbers. As a result, the military scattered small cadres of black servicemen throughout the country, so it was difficult for the USO and in-camp facilities to provide them with a wide variety of recreational options. The USO's efforts to surmount these difficulties remained limited throughout the war, as the organization focused instead on recruiting white hostesses to entertain white servicemen.

African American troops and hostesses posed a problem for the USO because the organization fashioned a race-specific ideal of American womanhood for which it presumed white servicemen were fighting. Dominant notions of race and female sexuality informed the recruiting process of many USO clubs as well as the behavior of police and the military throughout the war. Such ideas held that, as a race, African American women possessed a sexuality that was dangerous and uncontrollable. For instance, in the southern United States, white authorities did not make it easy for black men and women to volunteer for the USO. Georgia police arrested black women who were on the streets after dark en masse, despite the women's social connections or reasons for being in public at that hour. Humiliating experiences such as this caused the wife of one African American USO-Traveler's Aid director to fear for her safety as she went to work in the evenings.[29] African American organizations attempted to counter these negative stereotypes by taking advantage of the positive reputation of the USO and its hostesses, thereby participating in a problematic campaign of racial "uplift." The National Urban League argued that volunteers from African American neighborhoods who participated in USO functions "learn[ed] social graces" as a result. In this case, leaders of the National Urban League hoped that African Americans from all classes would model USO notions of middle-class propriety. They believed that by becoming active in the USO, African American men and women could prove to white members of the community that they were responsible citizens worthy of equal treatment.[30] This tactic exemplifies persistent efforts by middle-income African Americans prior to World War II to "uplift the race" by altering the conduct of black men and women in an effort to end white racism.[31] Within this context of white racism and racial uplift, USO volunteerism for black junior hostesses became both a notable attempt to redefine American womanhood and an adoption of the race-based power structure that limited their opportunities.

Ultimately, American society deemed social discord rooted in race, class, sexual behavior, and regional differences particularly critical throughout the war. Analysis of the USO affords an opportunity to assess the institution's relationship to these social divisions. This book is organized around the volunteer work and social activities of senior and junior hostesses, while also highlighting the experiences of servicemen within USO spaces. Chapter 1 examines the USO senior hostesses who transformed the activities they performed in their homes on a daily basis into a public fulfillment of their obligations to the wartime state. Chapter 2 illustrates how the USO's process of selecting junior hostesses inextricably connected class, race, and femininity, while Chapter 3 adds to the story of junior hostesses by uncovering the reasons why they chose to volunteer for the organization. The next chapter argues that the USO recruited reputable young women and advertised their pure sexual image because it relied on them to domesticate servicemen and prepare them to return to their homes and to family life. Hostesses, soldiers,

and sailors made the uso dance hall a key site in which to confront or circum-
vent existing conflicts over race, class, gender, and sexuality. The book's last
chapter reveals that it was within dancing and dating that the unavoidable
clash between the uso's need to entertain a democratic army and its preference to recruit a specific type of junior hostess occurred.

Throughout the book I rely on a combination of oral interviews, published
sources, and archival research in government documents and the collections
of uso member agencies to address issues of sexuality, citizenship, and wom-
en's volunteer service during the war. Published sources reveal the image that
the uso created for itself, while government documents establish the links
between this private, nonprofit organization and the military and federal government. I conducted oral interviews with or administered questionnaires to
approximately seventy former hostesses, who supplied me with rare firsthand
testimony about their experiences as junior or senior uso hostesses.[32] These
women volunteered for uso clubs in various parts of the country and relocated
to the Phoenix, Arizona, area at some point after the war. These interviews,
along with published sources, help to provide a geographically balanced account of uso clubs. For narrative purposes I refer to the women who shared
their memories with me by their first names throughout the text. As they do
all sources, historians must approach oral histories with a critical eye. In this
case, former junior hostesses recounted and assessed their memories of the
uso approximately fifty-five years after living those experiences. This time
span likely colored some women's perceptions of certain events and experiences, making them more positive or negative as a result. At the same time,
distance from the events of the early 1940s also granted them the benefits of
hindsight and a mature ability to assess their contributions to the war.

This account of the uso and its volunteers enhances the characterization of
the wartime period as one filled with conflict and challenge to a single American identity. It reveals the organization's effort to portray a racially harmo-
nious and stable home front with regard to sexual conduct. The gendered
volunteer work of senior and junior hostesses also helps to explain women's
so-called return to domesticity after the war. While they will likely never
displace Rosie the Riveter on souvenir shop postcard racks, uso hostesses
merit investigation for several reasons. Mostly, they stabilized dominant gender roles in the midst of expanding work and career options for women at the
same time that they subtly manipulated and, in the end, reshaped their own
"good girl" identities.

To Make the Boys Feel at Home
Senior Hostesses and Gendered Citizenship

In 1943, Helen Scheidel and her sister Marge attended USO dances at Mayor Kelly's Servicemen's Center in Chicago, once a month on Saturday nights. As a single eighteen-year-old, Helen represented the typical junior hostess, famous for jitterbugging across the dance floor with fresh-faced soldiers and sailors. Helen and the other junior hostesses at the center "tried to not let someone sit by themselves" and eagerly listened to servicemen's stories about their homes and families. Helen recalled that when a soldier or a sailor seemed especially anxious or distraught, however, she and her peers were "not mature enough to talk about their problems" with them. What they needed was someone "to take Mama's place." Helen and Marge referred these "boys" to senior hostesses, because they were there "to do serious talking."[1] Mending shirts, baking cookies, and "listening" were hardly revolutionary undertakings for middle-class women in the early 1940s in the same way that joining the Women's Army Corps was.

Senior hostesses, usually married women over age thirty-five, clocked hundreds of thousands of hours at the USO, where they not only served as informal counselors but also sewed insignias on servicemen's uniforms, baked sweets and made sandwiches, and chaperoned male soldiers' and sailors' interactions with junior hostesses. Their activities did not threaten the patriarchal order or existing gender or sexual norms. Women's domestic work and emotional labor in USO clubs, however, were important. In her assessment of the modern welfare state, political scientist Laura Balbo details the invisibility yet necessity of women's unpaid "emotion work" such as cooking, "counseling," and "mothering" in upholding a capitalistic society. Sociologist Arlie Hochschild takes the idea of "emotional labor" into the public sphere to argue that feminized service professions require women to "feign" happiness and enthusiasm in order to perform their duties successfully.[2] Similarly, senior hostesses engaged in emotion work by censoring their feelings while working in USO clubs to shield the servicemen in their care from anxiety created by the war. They donated their domestic and emotional labor to the military and the wartime state for personal and patriotic reasons. In doing so, they performed private tasks, previously reserved for their families, for strangers in a public setting.

While the Great Depression magnified the importance of women's domestic skills for a short time by highlighting their ability to tighten the household budget, women's household labor regularly went unnoticed unless it was absent. Historians have given female volunteers, senior hostesses in particular, much the same treatment. Senior hostesses completed work for servicemen and servicewomen in USO clubs that women had always done, and this helped to erase its historical significance.[3] For example, historian D'Ann Campbell concludes that women's volunteer work for the USO and the Red Cross did little to affect the prosecution of the war. Instead, their volunteer efforts served to make elite and middle-class women feel good about answering the government's call for women's wartime support. Campbell more thoroughly discusses women's volunteer work for the Red Cross than she does for the USO, and this might have prompted her to conclude that senior hostesses' work had little real value.[4] When the USO creeps into popular memory, furthermore, it is junior hostesses like Marge and Helen Scheidel who represent the organization, not their older married counterparts who kept the clubs functioning throughout the war.

Senior hostesses reinforced their primary peacetime roles as mothers and caregivers[5] and made their services as such available to the military, thereby performing a gendered form of citizenship. According to historian Linda Kerber, liberal citizenship entails a set of reciprocal obligations in which citizens repay the state for a general sense of security and basic provisions with their service and deference. During World War II, the state expected men to take up arms in the nation's defense but contributed to the "popular understanding [that] defin[ed] women as fulfilling their civic obligation within their homes,"[6] even as it encouraged some women to work as welders in heavy industry. Historian Lizabeth Cohen's argument that the consumer role of women grew during the war dovetails with Kerber's notion that the state preferred women's wartime contribution to be an extension of their gendered familial obligations. For example, the Office of Price Administration (OPA) complimented women who followed strict rationing guidelines and who monitored other women's use of ration points. Women who used their "purchasing power" for moral ends, whether as paid government employees or volunteers for various OPA committees, increased their "active public role" as supporters of the wartime government and of the war itself.[7] Likewise, senior hostesses felt privileged and obligated to volunteer their time to an organization like the USO that was assisting the 16 million young men, maybe even their sons, in uniform. These women converted public clubs and canteens into "feminine" spaces by infusing them with the behaviors, amenities, and cuisine of home. As they nurtured American "boys" in the armed services, senior hostesses implicitly consented to the loss of their own sons. By replicating the sentiments and structures of home, these women performed a vital task for the military. Their actions tacitly encouraged young men to sacrifice their careers and perhaps their lives for a civilian world from which they were physically, and even emotionally, disconnected.

WHILE THE GOVERNMENT spending that accompanied the U.S. entrance into World War II brought the country out of the Great Depression, the war did not end older ideas rooted in the 1920s about women's function within families and within the workforce. Depression-era middle-class women who were not impoverished by the economic crisis met their family's needs by making "small economies" that stretched a husband's paycheck to cover basic expenses. Many middle-class women entered World War II having already honed the skills necessary to save money and to follow the rules of rationing set out by the OPA. These skills would prove useful as they baked treats for servicemen, and for their own families, as USO senior hostesses. Those who chose to work during the Depression and were able to find feminized jobs such as secretarial positions did so to provide the better-than-average standard of living to which the family had become accustomed in the 1920s. By 1941, married women workers in particular had also dealt with a barrage of negative publicity accusing them of taking men's jobs and sending them the obvious message that they ought to stay out of the workforce.[8] From the National Economy Act of 1932, which required workforce reductions to begin with employees who had a spouse in the civil service, to restrictions on married teachers to articles in *Ladies' Home Journal* that reminded women that their husbands' careers were more important than their own, women learned that questions about their femininity and commitment to marriage accompanied work for pay. While women's participation in the labor force increased marginally in the 1930s, a large number of middle-class women remained out of the paid labor force.[9] It would be the women who had learned to live within a tight budget during the Depression and who had a conflicted relationship with paid labor who would form the most obvious volunteer pool for the USO in 1941.

World War II prescriptive literature generated by the media claimed that it was the responsibility of women to contribute to the war effort through volunteerism, including domestic activities sponsored by the USO. Prior to the Japanese attack on Pearl Harbor, most women's magazines reflected their readers' isolationism. Afterward, however, periodicals such as *Ladies' Home Journal* endorsed U.S. involvement in the war. These magazines and other prescriptive literature helped women who had feared the dangers of war join home front mobilization efforts.[10] In her 1943 advice book *Arms and the Girl*, Mary McBride argued, "The intangibles of morale have always been women's peculiar concern."[11] The USO *Bulletin* attempted to harness women's caretaking work for the war when it advised local clubs to enlist women in its projects, because "maintenance of morale can be largely a housekeeping job."[12] The National Catholic Community Service (NCCS) believed that women could uniquely contribute to the USO because "all of them have a prayer in their hearts, either consciously or subconsciously."[13] In its view, women possessed an innate spirituality necessary to lift soldiers' spirits. Many women agreed with this sentiment and responded by offering their time to the USO. When Hattiesburg, Mississippi, opened a USO club for white servicemen in 1941, it had 14 senior hostesses. By 1942, 1,022 senior hostesses were volunteering there, and these numbers reached their peak in 1943 with 1,824 senior hostess volunteers.[14] Volunteer work appealed to women who did not have young children at home or who could afford to hire someone to watch their children in their absence.[15] At the same time that opportunities were growing for women in industry and in the armed services, many middle-class women continued to find their niche in volunteerism. One-quarter of American women volunteered their free time to various relief agencies throughout the war.[16] This decision to volunteer was in keeping with American women's history of volunteerism. Throughout conflicts including the Revolutionary and Civil Wars as well as World War I, many women in the United States offered material and emotional comfort to servicemen that augmented the inadequate supply of both provided by the military.[17]

For African American soldiers, the absence of these comforts was pronounced. According to its policy, the USO made its services available to all soldiers and sailors regardless of race.[18] It attempted to do this, however, within a national culture that segregated the military and public places throughout the country either by law or custom. Historian Megan Taylor Shockley illuminates the ways in which local white communities shortchanged African American soldiers by not providing them with adequate USO facilities. African American clubwomen raised money to expand USO services and facilities for black servicemen in Detroit and Richmond.[19] Individual women also volunteered to improve conditions for black service personnel. Mrs. Mallie B. Williams responded to the USO's request for volunteers and asked the National Association for the Advancement of Colored People (NAACP) for information to help her create a USO club in Jacksonville, North Carolina. She had previously volunteered for a USO club in Massachusetts and recently had moved to Jacksonville. She observed that African American servicemen there "badly" needed a club. Williams believed that it was "the colored peoples [sic] fault here why they haven't been entertained and treated as servicemen should be treated. The white [sic] have a USO and I feel sure that we should have one." Williams implied that the African American community in Jacksonville had not taken the initiative to form a club, as she was doing. Cash shortages within the local black community and black women's need to work for pay, more than lack of interest in servicemen's well-being, might also have explained the absence of a USO club for black marines in Jacksonville. As were thousands of women throughout the country, Williams was "eager to give [her] service" to soldiers and sailors through the USO.[20] The national USO depended on the service of women like Williams to fill the gaps it left as it cheated black servicemen of the comforts it afforded white men. As senior hostesses, black middle-class clubwomen seized the opportunity to transform their volunteer work into a bid for full citizenship rights. Black women found power in assisting the USO because they could then use their work to justify making claims for full citizenship from the government.[21] Rather than erase race from the home front, the USO's inadequacies, along with black women's responses to them, made race and racial conflict more visible.

Women and men within the black community also transformed USO clubs, such as the South Broad Street USO in Philadelphia, into places for interracial growth. African American volunteers operated this club for black soldiers and sailors, but several white people also volunteered at the club. This confirmed that interracial cooperation was feasible and "extremely profitable in the development of understanding and growth."[22] Black women proved their loyalty to the government by offering their unpaid labor to the war effort in an act of "responsible patriotism." They trusted that this would compel the government, in turn, to award them full equality.[23] At the same time, black senior hostesses seized USO volunteerism as a means to form ties to the white community and further dismantle racism through interracial assistance.

Some white women also worked to end racism and provide adequate recreational services for black troops, including elite white women who motivated other people to make USO spaces available to all servicemen in places where acute racism existed. City councils throughout the country allocated property and buildings for local USO clubs to purchase for use by black and white troops. Some all-white city councils such as the one in Tucson, Arizona, refused to give approval for African American USO clubs to erect buildings and operate recreation centers for black soldiers. The other USO clubs in this desert city also refused admittance to African Americans, thereby creating a shortage of entertainment options for them. The city of Tucson feared that the existence of African American soldiers or civilians in the community would discourage white eastern tourists from visiting, so it did as little as possible to make life "comfortable" for black residents, such as integrating housing or granting them full access to city swimming pools.[24] When the city rejected a proposal to build a USO center for black servicemen, a local newspaper printed an open letter from Ada McCormick, a prominent white Tucsonan. McCormick chastised the city council members who denied black soldiers "any comfort station outside of a saloon." McCormick referenced the council's concern that soldiers from all-black Fort Huachuca, located approximately ninety miles away, would flock to Tucson to use the club. She argued that this fear was unrealistic, given their time constraints and lack of transportation. Instead, the club would serve the small number of black servicemen stationed in Tucson. As for the apprehension that black soldiers would deter tourists, McCormick contended that "a Negro in uniform [was] a fine and touching sight" in Bermuda, Havana, and Hot Springs and also would be in Tucson. While McCormick's tone was paternalistic, she staunchly supported the creation of a club for black servicemen. She forced Tucsonans to ask themselves, "IS WHAT I AM DOING HELPING HITLER OR HELPING AMERICA?" Within a week after the paper published her letter, the city began funding a USO club for black soldiers.[25] McCormick successfully used her influence in the community to shame the city council into establishing a separate club for black servicemen. Her actions illustrate how a woman could use servicemen's needs for USO clubs to spur interracial dialogue that in this instance achieved results.

As the previous information attests, USO volunteering was both a class-based and racialized endeavor. Middle- and upper-income white women who paid domestic servants to do housework for them had a tradition of contributing to philanthropic work.[26] While this tradition made it possible for some white women to volunteer for the USO, the economic need to work as a domestic servant in a labor market with limited options for women of color precluded many black women's desires to do the same. In 1943, the National Urban League contended that 80 to 90 percent of black women worked as domestic servants, and "as a result, many women and girls who might otherwise be USO volunteers [were] working in the homes of white women (who would otherwise not have the time for volunteer USO work themselves)."[27] One USO club confronted these facts. The Fayetteville, North Carolina, USO held an interracial meeting of local women's leaders during which they discussed new job opportunities for black women that the war opened, as well as their continued role as domestic workers in white women's homes.[28] Such a meeting exemplified the opportunities that USO and wartime volunteerism offered for cooperation between women of various backgrounds, yet it did little to alleviate black women's financial strains. Ultimately, the meeting exposed volunteering as a class- and race-based privilege made possible for a number of white middle-class women by black women's domestic labor in the Upper South.

The image of the USO as a respectable and useful organization depended on the behavior and dedication of its volunteers. The national USO reminded all hostesses that "the USO service [would] be judged by their abilities." Each USO club used general guidelines from the national USO and the desires of the community in which it operated to "formulate local standards for USO senior hostess groups." The USO *Manual, Community Conducted Operations*, suggested that USO committees select senior hostesses on the basis of their "personal integrity, social responsibility, tolerance and unquestioned loyalty to the United States."[29] If potential senior hostesses did not volunteer for the USO as part of an existing organization, the national USO asked them to supply two references. In practice, it does not appear as though clubs enforced this policy on the local level, as scant evidence of verification exists in the historical record. Senior hostesses required junior hostesses to provide references but did not ask their peers to do the same. Rather, senior hostesses referred one another on an informal basis such as by word of mouth, since most volunteers knew one another. For example, when it added senior hostesses to its ranks, the Women's Committee of the Philadelphia Stage Door Canteen (SDC) preferred that committee members "suggest their friends rather than calling strangers from the files."[30] This less formal approach attests to the trust various women within the community had in one another to uphold the positive image of the canteen. The national USO wanted local clubs to keep track of their senior hostesses and ruled that "only registered senior hostesses may participate in social activities for members of the armed forces."[31] Many clubs kept lists of senior volunteers in an effort to manage USO functions and to staff the clubs. The USO did this for the sake of convenience, whereas senior hostesses themselves updated lists of junior hostesses in a direct effort to limit or encourage the young women's attendance at USO events based on their conduct and respectability.

The USO encouraged women from all class backgrounds to volunteer for the organization, but the unpaid nature of the work made it more amenable to women who did not work for wages full time. Middle-income and elite women had more free time than working-class and poor women to donate to the USO.[32] During the war years, 37.2 percent of women between ages thirty-five and forty-four, and 21 percent of women over forty-five worked for wages outside the home.[33] The USO Manual clarified its general selection advice by indicating that senior hostesses should come from diverse "social and economic groups," reflecting the pervasive discourse of the day that in order to win the war, Americans from all facets of society would have to cooperate and participate. The national USO suggested that councils look for senior volunteers in those organizations that were dominated by middle-class women such as "women's clubs . . . business, professional . . . groups, school and college faculties." It also, however, suggested that councils recruit volunteers from working-class unions and industrial organizations.[34] Local USO clubs usually staffed their canteens in shifts of several hours at a time, making volunteering most appealing to women who had large blocks of free time in the mornings, afternoons, or late evenings.[35]

Women who volunteered for the USO as senior hostesses often concurrently were involved in religious organizations or women's clubs. In fact, the national USO stated that churches, community groups, and "other responsible organizations" might provide senior volunteers.[36] Joella Miller's husband was away from home in the navy during the war. At that time, she was a member of the

Junior League and the Alumni Club of Phi Beta Phi. Joella chose to spend time with servicemen at the USO because her "friends were doing it," it was "patriotic," and the "young men were extremely grateful for having a little time with the women." Joella came from the same economic background as most female volunteers. Born in 1907, she taught school for a year before she got married in the early 1930s. She had to be "very economical" during the Depression but was able to raise her children and not work for pay during the war years. She made time to volunteer at the Phoenix USO club once a week.[37] Helen Campbell's background was similar to Joella's. Both women were financially stable, and they already had experience as volunteers through church or women's groups. Helen earned a degree in elementary education from Northern Arizona University, married a private in the army in 1942, and taught school in Winslow, Arizona, throughout the war. She was an active member of the Mormon Church who made sandwiches for soldiers as part of USO canteen work. It gave her a "good feeling . . . to help" the servicemen. After teaching all day, Helen drove to the Winslow airport,[38] while Joella found child care for her children and dedicated one day a week to the USO. Helen's and Joella's choice to become senior hostesses was an extension of their family, community, and social responsibilities.

The USO assumed that all senior hostesses would be trustworthy women, based on their age and marital status. The national USO did not require that senior hostesses meet a certain age requirement, but it declared that their "maturity [was] an asset."[39] The USO included as senior hostesses' primary duties chaperoning, receiving guests, providing refreshments, and monitoring club libraries and game rooms.[40] A hostess ought to have been out of the dating game herself if she was going to command respect from the junior hostesses and servicemen she chaperoned, because the basic purpose of her chaperoning was to make sure that young female volunteers and male servicemen did not become intimately involved inside USO clubs. The Austin, Texas, Junior Hostess Club, for instance, preferred that senior hostesses be mothers of junior hostesses so that they might take a special interest in chaperoning USO dances.[41] According to courtship customs of the time, these women would naturally want to protect their own daughter's reputations,[42] and the USO hoped they would extend this motherly tendency to all junior hostesses. The USO considered married women to be appropriate authority figures, but it did not require senior hostesses to be married or junior hostesses to be single.

The process of selecting senior hostesses is important because it illuminates the USO's efforts to enforce dominant ideas about women's sexual respectability with regard to age, whether those women be married or single. It also reveals the USO's central project of maintaining a coercive influence over ideas about the sexual behavior of young people on the home front.

Many women chose to volunteer for the USO as senior hostesses because they felt emotionally obligated to support the work their sons or husbands were carrying out in the military. Given the sensitive and sometimes lonely context of war, USO service had the potential to bring women closer to their male loved ones in spirit. As senior hostesses immersed themselves in USO activities, they could comfort someone else's son or spouse in the same way they hoped someone was comforting theirs. According to one soldier's letter reprinted in the USO Bulletin, GI's "let the women sew on [their] buttons — they act[ed] as if it were a privilege to do so." He went on to posit that senior hostesses performed these domestic tasks because they "hope[ed] someone else [was] doing [them] for their sons."[43] Fashion writer Ethel Gorham advised married women to fill their time with volunteer work because "every moment of idleness will make [a husband's] absence more painful."[44] In some cases, women volunteered at USO clubs to ameliorate the pain of losing a family member. For example, a New York woman who lost her son in combat dealt with her "emptiness and loneliness" by volunteering her labor in a local USO kitchen.[45] USO work provided women with female and male companionship and, in its ideal form, lightened women's emotional load by distracting them from their personal concerns and fears. Female volunteers in NCCS-USO clubs rarely discussed their "own griefs or misgivings concerning [their] loved ones, — instead [they were] concentrating [their] efforts on making other people happy, and relieving their minds of worry in various and sundry ways."[46] Time spent volunteering at the USO helped women sublimate their own fears about friends and relatives at the same time that it deterred them from questioning their government's participation in the war itself. Such questions would have seemed to senior hostesses to be an attack on the very men and women whom they were coming into contact with in USO clubs. Senior hostesses successfully stifled their concern that the troops would meet violence and death, and they buried those worries beneath a preoccupation with servicemen's lack of nutritious sandwiches, birthday cakes, and darned socks. This approach was a healthy one for many women with relatives in the

God gave His Son willingly. Mary Harding found that that is the only way to give.

1.1. "I Gave My Son," illustration by Daniel J. O'Brien, in *The War Cry*, 3 July 1943 (Salvation Army War Services Subject Files, 1939–1950, Salvation Army Archives and Research Center)

★ ★ ★

military and government work, given the seriousness of the Axis assault on the United States and the minimal likelihood that the United States would not prosecute the war fully.

As they used USO work to put their own problems aside, senior hostesses performed the emotional work of mothering by guiding young soldiers and sailors through their problems and fears in informal counseling sessions. Paul McNutt, director of Defense Health and Welfare Service for the Federal Security Administration, believed that servicemen "want[ed] — unconsciously perhaps, but often quite desperately — to keep hold of their private and personal past" and USO volunteers "must" help them do this.[47] According to a junior hostess who entertained GI's passing through one of the American Theatre Wing's SDCs, "The boys worry about a mother who is ill, a problem-child kid brother, a sweetheart who hasn't written."[48] Women of all ages listened to young men's concerns, but usually senior hostesses provided a shoulder to lean on, as a mother would for her son. For example, Elizabeth Moore praised "the mothers and the aunts and the older, pleasant, delightful people in the community who were just coming to the centers to sit around and be there for the men to talk with about their problems."[49] Moore recognized the importance of the intangible work that senior hostesses performed for servicemen. By listening to men's stories of home or passing a kind word to a stranger in uniform, these women conducted a service that neither the government nor the military could adequately perform. One serviceman thanked USO hostesses for preserving a sense of "home" for him, because spending time at the USO made him "realize that this war [was] being fought to preserve the things [he] left at home."[50] While the military made an effort to disconnect servicemen from their families in order to create a fighting force, it depended on senior hostesses occasionally to remind men of their humanity and the family and community life for which they were fighting.

The minimal amount of training that the USO offered to some clubs reveals that it implicitly expected women to provide informal counseling services for men by way of their "natural" nurturing qualities. According to the NCCS, women possessed a "sixth sense" that made them ideal listeners.[51] As wounded men returned from the war, women spent more time talking to particular servicemen about their reconversion to civilian life.[52] At a meeting in April 1942, USO directors requested that the Joint Army and Navy Committee on Welfare and Recreation (JANCWR) provide minimal training for USO volunteers, because servicemen often sought out their support concerning personal and family issues. JANCWR responded by saying that volunteers ought to be taught to distinguish between common problems and a more "complicated situation" that required referral to professionals. Horace Sprague, Red Cross assistant to the administrative services to the Armed Forces, conversely argued, "A kindly, understanding, wholesome person may be closer to the men and learn more about their trouble than a person who has had a good deal of training in counseling." Senior hostesses embodied this "kindly" person. Colonel Livingston Watrous, assistant chief of the Special Services Branch, cautioned, however, that USO staff and volunteers should not disrupt the chain of command between soldiers and their commanding officers by serving as counselors. The army expected soldiers to seek counseling from army chaplains and army hostesses in its Morale Branch.[53] The army chaplain served as a "spiritual adviser, motivator, and morale booster" for soldiers.[54] Senior hostesses were outside the military structure, so servicemen who talked to the women about homesickness and isolation could simultaneously assuage those feelings and hide them from the army or navy. These informal conversations had the potential both to benefit the military and to subvert its hierarchy. The anonymous nature of servicemen's interactions with senior hostesses provided a type of safe zone in which men could preserve their masculinity and their reputation within the military. The army and navy depended on women's unpaid labor to extend and offer an alternative to their own morale and support services, as long as those services did not breach the chain of command.

Despite the need for female counselors, the American public and the military looked suspiciously toward mothers when loneliness and homesickness developed into real problems for servicemen. Homesickness plagued men overseas who missed their homes and female relatives. Some were "obsessed" with going home.[55] A minority of army officers blamed mothers for fostering their sons' dependence on home and family.[56] This charge was indicative of a wartime fear in which mothers became subversive elements in families and society when they gained too much power over husbands and sons. Political scientist Michael Rogin contends that filmmakers wove this assumption into Cold War films. He locates the roots of this trend in the 1942 publication of Philip Wylie's best seller, *Generation of Vipers*, in which the author defines this belief as "momism."[57] One might assume that senior hostesses enjoyed immunity from attacks on their mothering skills, because their volunteer work strengthened pervasive gender norms. This was not the case. For instance, the uso cautioned senior hostesses against "misplaced motherhood" that would cause them to "possess" servicemen and control clubs.[58] When women chose a conventionally feminine form of patriotic service, the vigilant wartime culture still did not spare them from criticism. This uso warning admonished senior hostesses to avoid overmothering servicemen and told them not to see uso clubs as domains in which they could wield complete power. In 1946, military psychiatric consultant William Strecker blamed "moms" for raising approximately 2 million young men whom the military had ruled emotionally and mentally unfit for service. The existence of such a vicious opinion of mothers immediately following the war illustrates that the uso did not succeed in erasing a dominant wartime notion that all mothers were as likely to "smother" their children as they were to mother them.[59]

For the most part, throughout the war the uso encouraged a sense of contained motherliness in its clubs, especially when women could help a soldier through an ordinary bout of homesickness. According to the Salvation Army, "Servicemen appreciate the presence of these mature sympathetic women. Lonely boys, homesick boys, troubled boys with personal problems will talk by the hour to them."[60] It also believed that directors and hostesses could cure loneliness with "a smile or a kind word of sympathy."[61] While it was probably difficult to "heal" homesickness with one or two conversations, at the very least, senior hostesses helped servicemen put aside their sadness for a short time and feel comfortable in USO clubs. The navy argued that parents and communities did not adequately prepare sailors to be away from home and to live in a community of men. These types of sailors visited the USO and needed its services especially.[62] According to the Salvation Army, "Just let me talk to you" was one of the requests "senior hostesses hear[d] every evening, usually with the comment, 'You look a lot like my mother.'"[63] Indeed, servicemen often associated senior hostesses' words of kindness with a resemblance to mothers. After all, senior hostesses' abilities to smile warmly and occasionally offer a wise word or two were exactly what families and society expected mothers to do for their children. Only in this case, women were doing it for America's children.

In most clubs, visitors referred to one woman as "Ma," but each senior hostess contributed her share of "mothering" to the club's atmosphere. Servicemen and volunteers affectionately called Virginia de Barril of the Tivoli USO club "Ma,"[64] while Mrs. Israel Goldstein acted as "Ma" to visiting servicemen of the Philadelphia Jewish Welfare Board USO.[65] The reassuring presence of a devoted female volunteer added to the stability and "homelike" atmosphere of the USO clubs. Soldiers and sailors even gave women who did not have children of their own the title "mom."[66] To servicemen, any older woman who volunteered in the USO club was a motherly person. For some women, USO work wholly satisfied their specifications for wartime patriotic service. To illustrate, a "woman who look[ed] like any of a million mothers in America" managed the white USO club in Montgomery, Alabama. She "love[d] all of the servicemen who visited the club [and] enjoy[ed] doing all [she could] for them," because that was her "part in this war." For Vera Ruth Prentiss of Montgomery, being a temporary mother to thousands of servicemen was the most important donation she could make to her country during the crisis. Her choice in patriotic service was a logical and safe one that resulted in praise from the community and required few, if any, social risks on her part.[67]

Inside USO clubs, the mere "presence of ladies" afforded a direct contrast to the army's "masculine" atmosphere and promised servicemen respite from the regimentation of military life. According to one USO regional history, when serving beverages, senior hostesses "pour[ed] with a daintiness in stark contrast to the ruggedness of a mess line."[68] This description denotes how a serviceman's perception of a female presence could alter the meaning of an ordinary act. In a "mess line," men distributed food to other men without much care, but when women performed the same mundane task, it took on a "motherly" quality that reminded servicemen of "home." This example reinforces scholar Laura Balbo's contention that "unless something is added to material goods in order to link them to what a specific individual expects or wants, personal needs are not satisfied."[69] Young Private First Class Larry Wakefield "felt like [he was] in a different world" when he stepped inside a uso club, because the hostesses "couldn't do enough for you; you felt like you were at home."[70] By making friendly eye contact with servicemen or patting them on the shoulder, senior hostesses added personal touches to material tasks, thereby heightening their value.

The uso, with the support of the army and the navy, attempted to capitalize on its familial atmosphere to lure men away from brothels and into policed uso spaces. There was a general concern throughout the nation that when military service removed young men from their homes, they became "easy prey" for procurers of sex and alcohol. The military was concerned publicly with protecting and maintaining the morality of servicemen. General George C. Marshall, chief of staff of the U.S. army, argued that the army and navy could "control the physical, moral and spiritual welfare" of soldiers while they were on military soil, "but when the man [left] camp . . . troubles [began]." It was the responsibility of the uso to control this vulnerable population outside camp.[71] According to the uso, servicemen could behave as "sons," pure and good, but one must not give them too much credit for having the ability to make moral or appropriate choices when away from the watchful eyes of mothers, sisters, and wives, whom the military and uso implicitly made responsible for controlling men's actions. Moreover, General Marshall's belief that the responsibility of the army and navy for its personnel ended when they left camp boundaries distanced the military from accountability for servicemen's off-base conduct even as the military dispensed millions of condoms to servicemen visiting local communities.[72]

The U.S. military did not have broad access to penicillin until 1944, so it relied on educational programs, prophylaxis, and the control of prostitution to limit men's contact with women who could potentially infect them with venereal disease (vD).[73] In 1945, an Interdepartmental Committee on Venereal Disease meeting included representatives from the navy, the Office of Community War Services (ocws) Social Protection Division, and the War Department. Those present discussed the highest vD rates that the army had seen since World War I. Colonel Sternberg of the War Department

1.2. Private First Class Larry Wakefield, 1942 (courtesy of Larry Wakefield)

★ ★ ★

"jokingly . . . called [V-J Day] VD day" because VD rates were "up to 60" that week. With the advent of penicillin, Colonel Sternberg believed that servicemen did not use prophylaxis as often and as vigilantly as they had in the past. In light of these statistics, Dr. Snow of the American Social Hygiene Association concluded that the USO did what it could to divert servicemen's attention from prostitutes, particularly overseas.[74] The USO offered servicemen an alternative to casual sex and potential infection to protect their bodies and their spirits.

Stateside, VD was a significant problem for the armed forces, and elements of social control were involved in the relationship between senior hostesses and young servicemen. These women embodied "home" and symbolically reminded men of their mothers' disciplinary power. Middle-class women in the 1920s and 1930s read child-rearing manuals that encouraged them to provide structure and discipline for their children and to maintain a degree of aloofness in their emotional relationships with them.[75] The Salvation Army's publication *The Red Shield* illustrated, in rather contrived terms, this type of association between senior hostesses, the USO, and motherhood in the following story: A serviceman had just been listening to a senior hostess play the piano, when he said, "You have brought home and mother nearer to me tonight. Gee, how I miss my mother." The senior hostess responded with the following warning, "When you are off duty again, please don't stop where you did tonight, as drink only serves to get a man into trouble. Come to the club, where you are always welcome. I know your mother would like to think of you spending your free evenings in a USO Club."[76] From this story, Salvation Army members who were parents of servicemen could take comfort in the efforts of "Army" senior hostesses to keep their sons on a moral path. This story also reinforced the Salvation Army's long history as a temperance society.[77] Every time a senior hostess distributed a sandwich or a cookie to a male soldier, she was tacitly reminding him that "mom" was watching and would be disappointed if her son disrespected her by drinking in a tavern or soliciting a prostitute.

The USO and organizations such as the Woman's Christian Temperance Union hoped to decrease servicemen's alcohol consumption, but not everyone agreed with these moral-minded volunteers. During the war, the Conference of the Alcoholic Beverage Industries agreed to support military training programs that advised servicemen regarding the "intelligent use of liquor as a social adjunct" and to teach them that alcohol was not something to abuse. Liquor distributors were concerned that campaigns to create "dry" zones around military camps would exacerbate the illegal sale of alcohol and not help servicemen. They also advocated treating servicemen like adults and not depriving them of the "privileges which [were] enjoyed by other citizens."[78] Brigadier General Frederick Osborn agreed with the beverage industry that camps should not be dry, but he argued that the police and the government should eliminate prostitution near the camps to preserve "national morale."[79] This view had its detractors. Early in the USO's fund-raising campaign, an editorial in the *Charlotte News* criticized the USO's approach to military maneuvers. The editorial specifically addressed North Carolina

Methodists who wanted to "eliminate dives and saloons near defense camps." According to the editors, "It will take more than a donation to the USO to do the job." They went on to ask, "Just how [was] it possible to protect a million and a half soldiers from temptation? This country [was] not training monks for a monastery; we [were] training an army." This newspaper recognized age-old connections between soldiering, carousing, and sex. The editors also implied that celibate, sober men were not capable of defending a nation because they were not real men, while soldiers who indulged in alcohol and sex were.

This critique of the USO as a misplaced panacea to immoral masculinity encapsulates the tensions buried within American men and women's support of the USO and their nation's war effort. According to one USO fund-raising campaign brochure, "The USO is a vote of confidence by the private citizens of America in the armed forces and the defense workers who are doing a job for them and who must not be let down."[80] John D. Rockefeller Jr. acknowledged that no parent wanted to see his or her child leave for war, but he went on to assume that none of these same parents would "put a straw in the way of his going."[81] Rockefeller's words succinctly tie together two of the USO's main contradictions: protect your child from the immorality associated with war, and send him into battle to face that immorality and potential death.[82] For a parent to do anything less would have been simultaneously unpatriotic and selfish. Volunteer-based organizations like the USO squelched antiwar sentiment and activism because they successfully rooted their appeals in patriotic and personal terms and they enlisted civilians in the war effort.

In reality, drinking alcohol was a favorite pastime of soldiers and sailors. In an article prepared for publication in a national USO program, JANCWR reported that most enlisted soldiers avoided alcohol on their nights off, but those who did drink chose beer over hard liquor.[83] Gordon Jennings's account of hard-drinking sailors calls into question the results of the JANCWR study. Jennings volunteered for the navy in 1943 and went from being a civilian to an officer in three months. He was a "ninety day wonder" because he had completed three years of college in Ames, Iowa. Later, in 1946, he was in charge of a troop train that traveled from San Francisco to Chicago over a four-day period. Ensign Jennings did not enforce the navy's anti-alcohol rules and recalled that when the train stopped periodically, the men "ran to the taverns and bought all the liquor they could" to sustain them on their journey.[84] Historian Michael C. C. Adams asserts that the army prohibited soldiers from

TABLE 1. Ages of Men Who Visited USO Clubs

Ages of soldiers	Total USO sample (%)	White male soldiers in national agency USO clubs (%)	African American male soldiers in national agency USO clubs (%)	Army cross-section of white and African American soldiers (%)
Under 20 years	17	17	15	16
20–24 years	48	47	49	44
25–29 years	22	22	26	22
30–34 years	8	10	6	11
35 years and older	5	4	4	7

Source: *Soldier Opinion about USO Clubs* (New York: USO, Inc., n.d.), SA Papers.

consuming alcohol, and this only served to heighten its appeal. He contends that home front organizations' desires to protect servicemen from alcohol denied that the military trained these same men to become killing machines, and this behavior was more harmful than drinking beer and whiskey.[85] The USO, as one of these organizations, wished the motherly supervision of senior hostesses would lead men to choose the USO club over the tavern. This was another example of how the USO asserted domestic control in an effort to civilize a group of men who were in many regards free from society's rules and conventions.

Typical male visitors to USO clubs had distinguishing characteristics that made it easier for senior hostesses to mother and in some cases infantilize them. In 1943, the National Opinion Research Center conducted a nation-wide survey, through questionnaires and interviews, of approximately 12,500 soldiers who visited eighty-three USO clubs or who lived in one of thirty army camps. The study's objective was to construct a profile of soldiers who visited USO clubs and to discern their opinions of the clubs as a whole.[86] The study revealed that the majority of men, 65 percent, who visited USO clubs on a regular basis were under age twenty-five. This was somewhat more than the proportion of men under twenty-five in the army at that time (60 percent).[87] Table 1 details the ages of men who used USO clubs.

Since younger men tended to patronize USO clubs, it was logical that senior hostesses, who were usually at least thirty to thirty-five years old, referred to and cared for them as "boys." Senior hostesses fashioned themselves as mothers, and sailors and soldiers as children. In doing so, they gained a corollary power within USO clubs, because authority accompanied the "mother" title. Furthermore, by portraying servicemen as boys in need of motherly care, the USO, and the home front population in general, could corral and attempt to control this large and potentially frightening group of men who might turn to prostitutes, pickups, or worse, to local "good girls" for unchaperoned female companionship.

The USO counted on senior hostesses to be motherly, and it expected them to behave in a nonsexual manner. A USO visitor penned the following poem that described senior hostesses as both mature and maternal.

Let Juniors jive and get their thrills,
The Seniors have their subtler skills,
They greet, they smile, they have allure
(Not over-ripe, but just mature).
Men love to see them 'round the place,
Like Mother or like Cousin Grace.
The Service Stars they often wear
Bear loving witness why they're there![88]

This poem aptly illustrates the key components of an ideal senior hostess. She had a child of her own in the military, she knew how to listen and extract information tenderly with her "subtler skills," and she resembled "mom" or another older female relative. That senior hostesses had "allure" and were "not over-ripe, but just mature" warrants some explanation. With this statement, the poet attributed to senior hostesses a sexual maturity that the eighteen- to twenty-five-year-old junior hostesses in their midst did not yet possess. Furthermore, senior hostesses who were not "over-ripe" eschewed the desperate sexuality of "oversexed" women.

While the USO depended on junior hostesses to use their beauty and sexual appeal to entice men into USO clubs, it contributed to the construction of older women, and mothers, as asexual. As the aforementioned poem illustrates, the USO hoped senior hostesses would resemble a sexually neutral yet warm Cousin Grace. Medical literature from the 1920s and 1930s suggested that menopausal and postmenopausal women enjoyed a "heightened sexuality" perhaps because they did not have to worry about birth control. Other doctors believed that older women's sexuality was "pathological" and could manifest itself in nymphomania, lesbianism, or attraction to younger men.[89] Historian Lois Banner concludes that doctors and media associated menopause with sickness and "with a deviant sexuality from the 1920s onward."[90] According to these medical discourses, senior hostesses had the potential to be scary sexual predators, so the USO constructed them as asexual women and used rules to enforce this construction. For instance, the Concord Dance Hostess Committee (CDHC), in Massachusetts, maintained strict age limits of eighteen to thirty for its junior hostesses. To enforce this policy, it went so far as to remove from its roster one junior hostess over age thirty who also happened to be a widow. Maria Phillips[91] wanted to attend dances as a CDHC member. The club retained two other women over age thirty because the previous director "unofficially" added them to the list and they were "grand girls and an asset to [the] organization." The CDHC, led by junior hostesses, determined that it was inappropriate for Phillips to continue entertaining servicemen in the capacity of a junior hostess. The fact that the woman in question was a widow only seemed to augment the CDHC director's distrust in her.[92] Phillips had engaged in a regular sex life and might not have been sufficiently proper in her desires or behavior as a result. The CDHC's dismissal of Phillips had several implications: first, that the men with whom women would be dancing were young and, second, that the job of a junior hostess was sexual at its core. The CDHC also revealed its assumption that older women who wanted to dance with soldiers were at best socially disreputable and at worst sexually experienced, or even abnormal.

Male soldiers and sailors sometimes treated senior hostesses as sexual beings rather than as asexual "moms." One "boy" caught up with Mary Agnes Goodson, a thirty-two-year-old married senior hostess, at work one afternoon. She had met him on a Thursday night at the USO. He told her that he was "shipping out" and wanted to give her a goodbye kiss. Mary Agnes characterized herself as a "mother" to servicemen just as she was to her own two small sons. When the soldier appeared at her mother's beauty shop where she worked and asked if he could kiss her, she "thought that was normal for a son to want to kiss his mom good-bye." Although Mary Agnes, a chaperone, occasionally danced with servicemen when there were not enough junior hostesses to go around, she never saw the young soldiers and sailors in a romantic light. Consequently, Mary Agnes was shocked when the soldier did not give her a "child's kiss" but, instead, "grabbed [her], hugged [her]," and gave her a "prolonged kiss" on the mouth, outside, in front of the beauty shop. The physically intimate and public nature of the kiss made her feel "terribly" uncomfortable.[93] Mary Agnes was a Tucson, Arizona, resident whose husband worked as a civilian employee at the city's Davis-Monthan Field. The kiss embarrassed her because she did not want to mislead the soldier or damage her own reputation as a senior hostess or as a wife. For some servicemen, senior hostesses' position of authority within the club made them enticing and attractive. Senior hostesses such as Mary Agnes accepted the notion that they were asexual and that their role as senior hostesses would protect them from unwanted sexual advances.

While Mary Agnes was in Los Angeles for a beauty products trade show with her mother, she was less concerned with appearances than she was at home. She and her mother agreed to share a cab with a male sailor meeting his ship in Long Beach. A block or so later, the driver stopped to pick up an elderly couple, who joined Mary Agnes, her mother, and the sailor in the cab. Mary Agnes and the sailor carried on an animated conversation during the long ride. She enjoyed the company of the "handsome young kid" and happily responded when he kissed her on the mouth as he left the cab to join his shipmates. She "responded then [to his kiss], because [she] thought he was a sweetheart." The older couple assumed that the man was Mary Agnes's husband and commented on how sad their parting must have been. Mary Agnes gleefully responded to the stunned couple, "I never saw him before in my life!"[94] The chances that her husband would find out about the kiss were minimal. Because Mary Agnes was a married senior and not a junior hostess to begin with, she was no longer under the chaperonage of her mother. She felt liberated in Los Angeles, away from her husband, children, and the watchful eyes of neighbors in Tucson. Her mother witnessed the kiss, yet her husband, the person most entitled to monitor her sexual conduct, did not. Mary Agnes allowed herself to be caught up in the excitement of the moment. She behaved outside the context of the USO in the sexualized manner of a carefree junior hostess, not in the expected sedate manner of a reserved senior.

Many senior hostesses reinforced their identities as asexual mothers by cooking food for servicemen. Second to the "girls," servicemen often spoke most highly of the food that they enjoyed in USO clubs and canteens. For example, according to Private First Class Robert Williams, GI food was "monotonous," whereas the food at the USO "tasted like home." He proclaimed, "Those mothers were good cooks."[95] Similarly, First Lieutenant John Kelly

1.3. Coffee and donuts at the San Francisco USO
(courtesy of United Service Organizations, Inc.)

★ ★ ★

said USO food was "better than Army chow."[96] Historian Ruth Schwartz Cowan's notion that "feeding the family . . . [was] a way to encourage feelings of family loyalty and affection"[97] was prevalent in USO clubs. "Food and fellowship" were cornerstones of USO hospitality.[98] The USO advertised itself as a "home away from home,"[99] but its version of home had particular connotations. The USO attempted to re-create a homelike atmosphere where senior hostesses mothered servicemen by baking and cooking for them. This gendered division of labor represented a middle-class lifestyle in which men worked for pay and women maintained the home. Not all of the men who visited USO clubs experienced this type of upbringing. Most working-class mothers, not fathers, likely combined domestic work for their families with some form of waged labor. The USO catered to soldiers and sailors from economically diverse backgrounds, including those who were working class and poor, while it modeled the ideal middle-class home for them. On a national scale, the USO transformed women's homemade cakes and pies into symbols that it hoped would motivate men to uphold and fight for values such as stability, fidelity, and familial love. It encouraged men by its example to embrace an "American dream" predicated on middle-class gender norms.

Stories from the Salvation Army *Red Shield* emphasized both soldiers' and sailors' youth and senior hostesses' motherliness via food preparation. For instance, one "tall, ungainly soldier" told a hostess that he was afraid of eating dinner alone in the train dining car. He asked, "Please, ma'am . . . could you pack a little lunch for me like my mom used to do when I went to school? Just a couple of sandwiches would do until I can get home." The senior hostess happily made him some sandwiches as she thought of her sons who were overseas.[100] The soldier in this vignette was young and lonely, and he missed the consideration with which his mother made his sandwiches. Salvation Army and USO members replicated the syrupy tone of this tale in many articles for public consumption. Writers depicted this serviceman as particularly vulnerable and childlike. The nature of his request and the manner in which the senior hostess presumably handled it, however, were authentic and common. In this case, a Salvation Army USO senior hostess filled an emotional void for a soldier and also filled the void in his stomach.

USO leaders discouraged volunteers from distributing meals and sandwiches for free as a rule, but they also said that clubs should give away food at special events. In doing so, they made a tacit distinction between the meanings of sweets in opposition to meals. National USO policy on serving food recommended that local clubs charge a nominal fee for snack bar items such as sodas, sandwiches, and cakes. The USO did not want to overburden communities with requests for monetary and food donations for clubs. Furthermore, the "USO in *all* of its services want[ed] to encourage the sturdy American spirit of independence and self-respect." It believed that giving away food would diminish these qualities in servicemen and servicewomen.[101] Here the USO revealed the dominance of its middle-class Anglo roots. On the heels of the Great Depression and Roosevelt's New Deal, the USO did not want servicemen and -women to expect a handout from the USO. The USO *Cheers for Volunteers* pamphlet emphasized, however, that "parties [were] another matter."[102] These were the occasions during which the USO heartily endorsed the unpaid domestic labor of senior hostesses in their own kitchens or in club kitchens. Special occasions such as parties and USO dances warranted homemade cookies and cakes. Large USO clubs held dances and other parties at least on a weekly basis and frequently more often than that. Small clubs sometimes did not have snack bars, but they almost always held one dance or two each month. When one looks at the USO food policy in practice, it becomes evident that it reinforced the notion that sandwiches and meals had monetary value because they provided nourishment. Therefore, service

1.4. Mrs. Alfred Scott and a soldier at the Phyllis Wheatley YWCA USO, July 1943
(courtesy of United Service Organizations, Inc.)

★ ★ ★

personnel should have paid for them. Cakes and pies, however, represented motherly love and community appreciation, so the USO ought to have given them away free of charge, despite the labor that goes into preparing both types of food.

In the midst of government food rationing, senior hostesses baked dozens of cookies and cupcakes for servicemen. This type of domestic labor contributed to the "homelike," feminine atmosphere of the canteens and embodied the contributions of "virtuous" or traditional women to the war effort. The San Diego Women's Committee of the USO asked its female volunteers to make hard candies, cakes, cookies, and cupcakes to stock in the canteens and to serve at USO dances.[103] The San Diego clubs convinced the OPA to set aside rationed goods, including coffee, for their USO kitchens.[104] The Valdosta USO club in New Jersey held a birthday celebration, complete with cake and junior hostesses, for several servicemen and mailed photographs of the party to the men's parents. In a letter to the club, Gertrude Lill wrote to "thank you from the bottom of my heart for thinking of us Mothers and sending the picture of my Boy, it was a glad surprise." The photo that the club sent to Anna Bliss made "[me] feel that [my son was] being personally looked after" by the women at the Valdosta Club.[105] This story represents the connections between senior hostesses and mothers across the country who worried about and missed their sons. Homemakers' volunteerism for the USO illuminated and brought to a grand scale, in both numbers and public appreciation, otherwise private acts of baking, cooking, and overall "mothering."

Sweets helped to create a friendly feminine atmosphere inside USO clubs. Proud clubs kept their cookie jars teeming with homemade cookies. According to the NCCS, cookie jars were "one of the most popular features of any USO club."[106] The Salvation Army included a monthly recipe in the *Red Shield's* "Cookie Nook" so readers could add a "welcome delicacy" to their club's jar.[107] According to nutrition and food studies scholar Amy Bentley, prior to and during the war American society associated sugar with femininity and meat with masculinity. Families and communities praised women throughout the twentieth century for baking treats for their families. Women, in turn, associated baking with pleasure and their own self-identities. Wartime ration policies reduced the amount of sugar that went into American homes, so women substituted honey and molasses as sweeteners.[108] One "Cookie Nook" recipe recommended honey cookies as pleasing substitutes to deal with the "sugar shortage."[109] Bentley astutely argues that "providing . . . special, home-baked desserts symbolized and was an actual part of a woman's love and nurture for her family."[110] Mrs. Hugh B. Horn's actions confirm this theory. She baked twenty-one separate birthday cakes for soldiers at the El Paso USO club to celebrate her absent son's twenty-first birthday. She could not bake a cake for her own son who was in the military, so she used her baking skills to make cakes for other women's sons. In the process, she made herself feel better about being apart from her son on his birthday for the first time.[111] Women like Horn made USO clubs inviting places for men to visit and renew their connections with mom, her homemade treats, and civility.

The Christmas season was a difficult time for men and women in uniform who were away from their families, and senior hostesses made a special effort at this time of year to comfort them with reminders of civilian life. It was in 1942 that Bing Crosby first made Irving Berlin's "White Christmas" famous in the film *Holiday Inn*. Servicemen and servicewomen helped to make this a popular wartime song because it reminded them of faraway family and friends.[112] USO volunteers remade clubs into Christmas wonderlands at a time of year when family and home dominated servicemen's minds. The Baltimore YMCA Volunteer Hostess Club held a special Christmas night dance for soldiers and sailors who had "planned on a home-Christmas" but instead had to "spend Christmas away from home."[113] Senior and junior hostesses did their best to remake USO clubs into places where soldiers and sailors could find holiday cheer and appetizing food. A 1944 "Christmas Message from the USO" advised clubs to have tree-trimming parties, invite Santa Claus, and provide small gifts and stockings for servicemen.[114] Peggy Jane Peebler was the paid secretary for the Spokane, Washington, USO-YWCA. One Christmas Eve she received a call from a military police officer who told her that a large troop train full of servicemen was passing through town and the officers would like to "give them a little break" by stopping at the USO. Peggy Jane watched the men walk up from the train depot. They appeared to be older men who could have been husbands and fathers. The servicemen looked "miserable," "they did not know how to march," and "they had on uniforms that were too big or too little, and here they came, shuffling up the street." The volunteers who had assembled at the club "pounced on them." Senior hostesses and male volunteers took them to the food buffet and "stuffed their pockets full" of food, because they could only stay for a short time. Peggy and the others "just stopped what we were doing and did whatever we could for them." When the enlisted men left, "their step was just a little lighter." Peggy Jane noted with conviction and tears in her eyes, "We [knew] we did something for them." USO service had a lasting effect on some individuals. For years afterward Christmas was a painful time for Peggy Jane, because "I just kept thinking of those kids who were away from home. We did our best, [but] we could only do part of it" to make them feel special at Christmas.[115] This episode illustrates that some USO volunteers believed their kindness carried weight and made a difference in the lives of servicemen. This type of service was emotional at base. It was intangible, and this elusiveness made it hard to measure. The pressures the men were experiencing also heightened the importance of women's emotional contributions to their care, and yet it made them less than adequate when measured against servicemen's actual need for substantial contact with family and friends at Christmastime.

In addition to providing a festive atmosphere in which to celebrate cherished family holidays, senior hostesses in some clubs did servicemen's holiday shopping, wrapping, and mailing for them. Cultural historian Karal Ann Marling argues that women in the United States have been responsible for doing the necessary work at Christmas, such as decorating, baking, and shopping, to fulfill their family's holiday expectations.[116] Similarly, historian Elizabeth Pleck contends that as early as the 1850s, middle-class women had become the family's primary Christmas shoppers, because society understood that they were "caring, concerned with relationships, and had the time to do it."[117] In its 1944 Christmas memo, the USO made its view clear that female volunteers would perform this gendered labor for the club. It suggested that USO clubs set up a "Christmas Shopping Service." It declared, "Many of the men especially will heartily endorse this shopping service because very often their leisure time is limited and to have someone else do their shopping proves a great convenience to them." While it was true that servicemen had minimal free time during which to shop, this service was yet another example of how senior hostesses handled male soldiers and sailors as dependent offspring. Shopping could be inconvenient, time consuming, and boring for some men. Female volunteers at the USO wanted to perform these tasks for servicemen just as they likely would for husbands and sons in peacetime. The USO emphasized the gendered nature of Christmas shopping when it concluded, "Since most of the gifts to be bought are for women, the only really satisfactory shoppers are women."[118] The NCCS emphasized that wrapping and mailing committees should "select persons especially skilled in wrapping Christmas packages" and reminded USO volunteers that "men skilled in wrapping packages *for mailing* [emphasis added] should also serve on this committee."[119] In other words, women generally did a better job than men at wrapping presents in holiday paper, while men might be more adept at putting packages in boxes and preparing them for shipment by the post office. The assumptions the NCCS and USO held about women's and men's labor demonstrated the organizations' primary dependence on women for delicate "feminine" tasks and its desire to call on men when the task appeared more "masculine."

If senior hostesses were not wrapping packages for servicemen, they frequently were doing their sewing for them, and there was a lot of sewing that

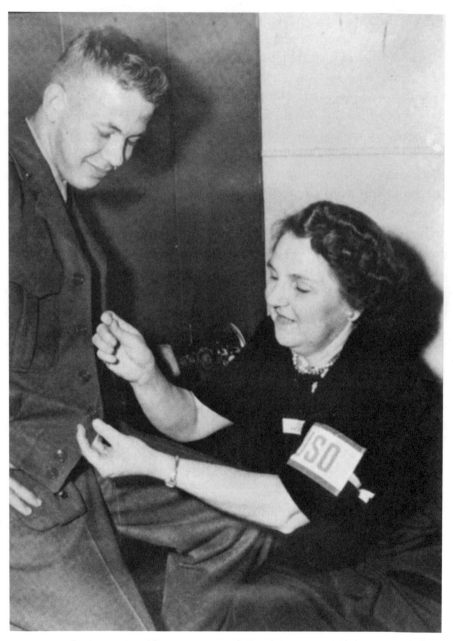

1.5. Sewing service at the USO (courtesy of United Service Organizations, Inc.)

★ ★ ★

needed to be done throughout the year. Every private first class wore one chevron and the insignia of his corps on his shirt and jacket. The number of a soldier's chevrons and badges increased and changed with rank, corps, and division assignments.[120] Field Manual 21-15 specified that soldiers keep their uniforms "clean and neat and in good repair . . . [and replace] missing insignia and buttons . . . quickly."[121] Seamen in the navy wore a minimum of two stripes on their "dress jumpers." Petty officers, next in the chain of command, wore three strips on the cuffs and between one and three chevrons on their "upper left or right sleeve." The number of chevrons and stripes on a sailor's uniform increased according to rank. Each sailor also wore a badge that represented his corps.[122] The army and navy issued a sewing kit to every private and seaman so he could affix these insignias and chevrons to shirts and jackets, reaffix buttons, and mend holes in socks. Some men used their sewing kits on a regular basis, or at least when they could not find a fellow soldier to sew for them. Private John Hoza earned extra money sewing patches on his buddies' uniforms.[123] Some did not know how to sew, and others did not want to deal with the tedium of threading a needle, embroidering patches to their uniforms, darning socks, or replacing buttons.

When it came time for sewing, soldiers and sailors longed for a visit to the USO because they usually found a senior hostess there who was happy to complete this tiresome chore for them. In its "Policies and Procedures," the national USO listed a sewing machine as one of the most important items for volunteers to acquire for local clubs. The organization also issued to clubs standard fill-in-the-blank press releases to market in newspapers women's sewing skills as part of club services.[124] Mayor Kelly's servicemen's center in Chicago advertised that a man could find a "friendly hostess to sew that new chevron on his uniform" in its USO club.[125] While she behaved as "friend and counselor," a Salvation Army USO senior hostess was also "custodian of the sewing box." She used its contents in "the replacing of a button, or the mending of a torn sleeve, or the sewing on of a proudly displayed new chevron or service stripe."[126] Private First Class Robert Williams took advantage of senior hostesses' sewing skills when he visited USO clubs. He asked senior hostesses to "mend his uniform or sew on a patch" because the "younger women did not know how to sew." According to Williams this was one more thing that senior hostesses did to make him "feel at home."[127] These senior hostesses duplicated tasks for servicemen that they performed for their own family members at home. The USO club in Rockford, Illinois, honored navy mothers whose tailoring skills made it possible for "Johnny Doughboy" to "pass inspection."[128] Historically, women had applied their sewing skills to support the military through multiple conflicts. For example, in 1780 women from several colonies raised money to purchase linen from which they sewed shirts for Continental Army troops. They refused to give General George Washington cash for the army, believing that the government would not use the money directly to assist the soldiers who needed sturdier garb than that with which the provisional government was clothing them. Not only did these women donate their sewing skills to the army, but they asserted their own power to affect military policy in the process. Additionally, white southern and northern women contributed food and clothing to Confederate and Union troops, respectively, during the Civil War. Female volunteers acted as "unofficial quartermaster corps" in the Society of Center Ridge, Alabama. In a month's time the group supplied "422 shirts, 551 pairs of drawers, 80 pairs of socks, 3 pairs of gloves, 6 boxes and one bale of hospital supplies, 128 pounds of tapioca, and a donation of $18 for hospital use." Finally, members of the National Woman Suffrage Association donated hand-knitted socks for the Red Cross to distribute to servicemen throughout Europe during World War I.[129] All of these women attempted to meet the material needs of servicemen that the state chose not to fulfill with taxpayer dollars. At USO clubs, appreciative soldiers and sailors repaid women with instant gratitude and recognition for conducting this patriotic work. Senior hostesses who sewed saved servicemen time and energy and granted an unpaid service to the military. By performing this historically feminine task, USO hostesses helped to maintain the division between male and female labor throughout the war.

DURING THE WAR, the Hillcrest USO in San Diego received a letter from the grateful mother of a soldier who thanked the female volunteers at the club for their "untiring efforts to make the boys feel at home, and all of the motherly attention [they showered] upon them."[130] Families throughout the United States appreciated the "motherly attention" senior hostesses paid servicemen. This consideration had the potential to make soldiers and sailors feel like nurtured individuals, because these women volunteered at the USO club out of concern for their well-being. Women coupled this loving supervision with more tangible unpaid labor that required their physical energy. They cooked meals and prepared snacks for millions of off-duty servicemen and servicewomen, and they mended countless shirts and pants, darned socks, and sewed emblems on thousands of uniforms. Women rendered this labor under the guise of emotional work since they were doing it out of compassion for "boys" in the service. Many senior hostesses concealed sore eyes, dishpan hands, and aching muscles with their kindness. Women's unpaid labor reduced military costs for support services, and the military depended on and would have missed middle-class women's cooking, sewing, and general domestic labor if they had not done this work for soldiers and sailors at uso clubs. Senior hostesses met their obligation to the wartime state, and more personally to men and women in uniform, by completing this gendered labor and by selecting young women to entertain servicemen as junior hostesses.

2

The Loveliest Girls in the Nation

Seventeen-year-old Doretta Cloyed graduated from Moravia High School in Iowa in 1942. Her parents, who owned and operated a farm, permitted her to join her three brothers in Washington, D.C., as long as she lived with one of them. All three of Doretta's brothers worked in the Identification Division of the FBI. While living with her brother and his wife, Doretta earned a degree in shorthand from a business school and took a job as a clerk in the manufacturing company Harry L. Grant. Ninety percent of Grant's contracts were from the federal government. Doretta was an active member of her Protestant church but found time to hostess with a girlfriend at the Washington, D.C., Stage Door Canteen (SDC). Her white middle-class roots typified those of other junior hostesses across the country.

While Doretta fit the visible mold of the ideal hostess, the SDC took the extra precaution to check her fingerprint file and required her to submit a reference from her pastor and proof of employment. This procedure, in Doretta's opinion, was to make sure that she was not a "bush rabbit, one of the gals who followed the troops when they [got] paid the first of the month." Doretta made a distinction between those women who wanted to entertain servicemen in a wholesome setting and others who might have taken advantage of them on payday. While on duty at the canteen, Doretta wore pretty skirts and blouses under her red, white, and blue SDC apron. She wore little makeup and kept her curly hair neat and fashionable. She never saw any female soldiers or sailors or black hostesses or servicemen at the canteen. Doretta surmised that servicemen preferred civilian women to Wacs (female soldiers) because "it lifted [servicemen's] morale to see a dress, or some color, something more attractive than a uniform." She enjoyed dancing and chatting with servicemen in wartime Washington because she knew she brought a "ray of sunshine" into their lives.[1] Hundreds of thousands of soldiers responded to the charm and appeal of hostesses like Doretta by returning to USO canteens on a regular basis. USO clubs throughout the country, moreover, cultivated and deployed an image of femininity and beauty in their junior hostesses to craft a specific ideal of American womanhood at a time of gender upheaval and racial tension.

As Doretta's biography indicates, the uso's process for selecting junior hostesses inextricably connected class, race, and femininity. By identifying whiteness as a feminine characteristic, volunteers at local uso clubs throughout the country ignored the advice of the national uso to select junior hostesses across class and racial lines. They made assumptions that young white women with middle-class cultural values best embodied the beauty and femininity required to meet servicemen's basic recreational desires. African American women, in turn, opposed segregated clubs while they challenged and reshaped the uso's definition of beauty to include them. uso senior hostesses and some uso directors juxtaposed their ideal of American beauty with those whom they perceived to be unfeminine women, Wacs and Waves (female sailors). Hostesses reinforced women's supportive role on the American home front by fulfilling their citizenship obligations inside uso clubs, even while some of them challenged uso standards of femininity and wholesomeness by flouting dress codes, for instance. The ideal junior hostess enhanced her physical attractiveness to men by dressing in pretty clothes and conducting herself with composure. Most junior hostesses valued their good looks and their own sex appeal. This examination of uso standards of femininity and beauty changes our understanding of the context that produced Rosie the Riveter and the female soldier by bringing to the forefront the uso hostesses who helped to offset the explosive potential of these options for middle-class women.[2]

THE USO SHAPED its junior hostess ranks by employing a variety of class- and race-based selection processes that presumed middle-class white women were innately feminine and sexually respectable. Elite men and women operated and selected hostesses for SDCs in cities like New York, Hollywood, Philadelphia,[3] Washington, D.C., and San Francisco. The Hollywood Canteen asked the managers of Douglas Aircraft if they would select young women who were "socially and morally and physically appropriate to work as volunteers." Chief Engineer James Edwards chose three of his secretaries, including eighteen-year-old Nancy Brown. The Hollywood Canteen granted Nancy security clearance to entertain soldiers and sailors after senior hostesses such as the actress Marlene Dietrich interviewed her.[4] Similar to the Hollywood

2.1. Nancy Brown, Hollywood Canteen junior hostess, 1943
(courtesy of Nancy and Sumner Blake)

★ ★ ★

Canteen, the Philadelphia SDC recruited from upscale department stores such as Lit Brothers to ensure a high caliber of hostesses.[5] In the 1940s, middle-class white women dominated higher-level clerical work, and department store managers exclusively employed white women as sales clerks. Working-class women had access to "low level" clerical work after 1920, but middle-class women had higher access to secretarial jobs requiring more skills. Clerical work often put working-class women on a path to financial independence and social respectability within the middle class.[6] By relying on the judgment of white-collar managers to determine who among their female employees was respectable, the USO excluded most women of color and blue-collar workers from prime hostessing slots at the SDCs. The USO welcomed black women as hostesses at the smaller, less wealthy clubs it operated for African American servicemen, but generally it did not integrate clubs in major cities.

While SDCs found hostesses within department stores and company secretarial pools, other USO clubs drew from college sororities to shore up their core of middle-class hostesses. For example, Radcliffe organized a group of hostesses and sent their names to the YWCA of Cambridge, Massachusetts, for its USO dances.[7] Seventeen-year-old Bettelee Zahn volunteered for the San Francisco USO with several of her sorority sisters from Stanford.[8] Female college students, who comprised nearly 50 percent of those registered in American colleges and universities in 1940,[9] were the appropriate age for USO hostesses and usually had free time to volunteer. Many other women, like Nadine Thomas of Washington, D.C., heard about the USO from their friends and decided to join.[10] Word of mouth on college campuses and through offices accounted for a large number of junior hostess volunteers. After she graduated from North Dallas High School in 1943, Beverly Littlejohn and one of her girlfriends signed up to hostess at weekly dances at the USO in downtown Dallas. They also danced with servicemen at USO dances at Camp Wolters in Mineral Wells, Texas, one Saturday each month where according to Beverly, "about 22 of us would arrive and be greeted by about 800 men."[11] The urgent and obvious need for dance partners for thousands of servicemen caused the USO to rely on its hostesses to bring their friends to sign up for duty. This practice helped to solidify a reputable group of hostesses as one presumably respectable young woman invited another one.

Catholic churches and synagogues gathered hostesses from their congregations, and YMCA and YWCA clubs drew on preexisting connections with older teens to find volunteers. This practice was in line with national USO standards for junior hostesses, which, as with senior hostesses, encouraged clubs to recruit women from "different social and economic groups."[12] The USO expected junior hostesses to entertain and converse with a "democratic" military filled with men of all social classes.[13] The YMCA of Baltimore organized older teens into a Volunteer Hostess Club.[14] Sisters Helen and Marge Scheidel joined Mayor Kelly's Servicemen's Center in Chicago and the Catholic Diocese of Chicago USO through their Catholic Daughters of America club, while the Jewish Welfare Board in Philadelphia recruited Jewish hostesses from area synagogues to entertain servicemen during its USO functions.[15] The prewar relationships these women had with established community groups proved that they were respectable and dependable.

While not all of these hostesses were exclusively from the middle class, they all had at least one appropriate social connection, such as a pastor or priest, to facilitate their admittance to the uso. The national uso set reference standards at "two . . . from persons other than relatives, including one character and one business reference." It stated that the uso follow up on and keep a record of contact with those references and keep such investigations private.[16] uso clubs took references seriously. For example, in order for Anne Luckow to hostess at the Catholic-sponsored uso in Rockford, Illinois, she had to get a letter from her monsignor. When Anne arrived at her first uso dance, the senior hostess at the door was "rude" to her because the club had not received her letter. The woman pointed to the corner and said to Anne, "You go wait over there with those girls." Anne surmised that the woman at the door believed she and the other women in the corner were "questionable characters." The senior hostess refused to admit Anne that evening. Unlike those hostesses who attended college full-time, Anne had an unstable economic background. The Depression hit the Luckow family hard in the 1930s. Anne took a job at a newspaper office; she lived with her parents in Freeport, Illinois, and paid the mortgage and utility bills for them. She supported her family because her father was out of work and her mother was a homemaker.[17] After Anne's first experience at the uso, the volunteers located her letter in their files, and she and her friends went to the club every Saturday night and Sunday afternoon from 1941 until the end of the war. Anne's family did not enjoy middle-class economic status, but her connections with the Catholic Church afforded her the respectability and character references that the uso required. Her attendance at these dances expanded the uso's narrow definition of femininity to include working-class women, providing a male referee could vouch for their respectability.

Local uso clubs desired hostesses who possessed sexual respectability and positive social reputations, so its organizers searched for young women from their own class and racial background whom they presumed naturally embodied these qualities. Dominant notions surrounding white female purity and African American women's supposed "deviance" have their roots in an American legal system that made interracial sex illegal, thereby marking black men's and women's bodies as both abnormal and "hypersexualized."[18] White uso senior hostesses acted on these prevailing and erroneous notions and subsequently reinforced them with their class- and race-based selection process for junior hostesses. A significant number of white women who volunteered for the uso either worked in clerical or sales jobs or attended school; their mothers were homemakers while their children were in grammar school, and their fathers maintained steady employment.[19] While education is an imperfect marker for class status, the fact that numerous hostesses performed their white-collar jobs in the daytime, as opposed to taking on less respectable evening work, and their fathers earned enough money to support their families shows that many hostesses came from economically stable backgrounds. Those backgrounds included fathers with blue- and white-collar jobs along with those who were farmers and ranchers, members of the "old middle class."[20] Whether reaching for inclusion in the middle class or already established as a solid member, most junior hostesses and their parents subscribed and adhered to middle-class notions of sexual respectability and physical comportment. This adherence, as well as their references, race, and class background, made them acceptable to the uso.

In numerous uso clubs, senior hostesses conducted brief interviews with junior hostesses, examined their applications, and checked their references to guarantee that they were proper young women from moral backgrounds. The national uso described this interview as the proper time to "obtain personal impressions and information for use in selection."[21] Senior hostesses likely observed young women's carriage, manner of speaking, and level of deference in these meetings. The Girls Service Organization (gso) in Baltimore, Maryland, had a fairly rigorous selection process requiring junior hostesses to complete a telephone interview and a personal interview, provide two references, complete an application, and then undergo a two-dance "orientation" period before becoming full-fledged hostesses.[22] That orientation period at the Philadelphia uso Labor Plaza was actually a probationary period during which senior hostesses made the final judgment as to whether or not the women were "suitable for junior hostesses."[23] The uso Women's Committee selected hostesses for the Philadelphia uso clubs.[24] Ethel Hutchinson and Laura Servais looked into the backgrounds of applicants for the Concord Dance Hostess Committee (cdhc) to ensure that they would be "favorable" members.[25] The Hattiesburg, Mississippi, uso relied on "six local women [to] go over each application independently and pass on or reject the girls."[26] The national uso named honesty and patriotism as its most basic standards for hostesses, but all clubs interpreted these vague standards in their own ways.[27] The selection process worked both to sort hostesses according to social connections and to keep up the appearance of respectability for the uso.

2.2. Front of West Adams Los Angeles Area uso identification card
(courtesy of Marilyn Hale)

★ ★ ★

The legacy of World War I, specifically families' fears that venereal disease
(vd) and the immorality that they believed plagued military training would
corrupt their sons, shaped the uso's plan to overcome vd in the 1940s by
providing chaste companions for servicemen.[28] One uso member organization, the National Catholic Community Service (nccs) addressed the need for
wholesome recreation. The nccs worried that as thousands of servicemen
crowded into camp towns, instead of finding uso clubs they would encounter
"those who [lay] in wait to lead them astray."[29] In essence, the army removed
men from civilization and civility during the week and then released them on
the weekends to communities that tempted them with sex and alcohol. The
coordinator of Health, Welfare, and Related Defense Activities came to the
somewhat obvious conclusion in 1941 that "men on leave [were] much more
likely to take advantage of wholesome recreational facilities if the vicious
resorts [were] closed and the exploiters of prostitution and other vices [were]
prevented from carrying on their illegal trade."[30] The uso hoped to reduce
servicemen's use of prostitutes and alcohol. Although uso officials did not admit this publicly, servicemen had sex with prostitutes and other women if those
women were available, no matter the effort the uso put forth to entice them
into chaperoned clubs hosted by good girls. The uso could provide all of the
wholesome activities it wanted, but as long as some women were available for
sex, some servicemen would engage in it and perhaps contract and spread vd.

2.3. Back of West Adams Los Angeles Area USO identification card
(courtesy of Marilyn Hale)

★ ★ ★

Since one of the USO's primary tasks was to provide "wholesome" recreation for servicemen, it needed, at most, to handpick its hostesses and, at least, to give the public and the military the idea that it was subjecting hostesses to a rigorous set of standards. Local USO clubs made a point of telling the public and the media that they rigidly screened each potential hostess to prevent the suspicion that young women associating with servicemen in USO clubs were anything less than chaste and respectable. A newspaper article about Betty Ward, secretary of the Miami USO, specified that it was Ward's job to "keep in mind and on paper a list of reputable young women . . . who [were] available for parties and dances for service men and officers." Ward required written consent from parents that their daughters could participate and used her own judgment when accepting hostesses.[31] As this example demonstrates, the stringency of the application and interview process varied according to the canteen, the size of the city, and the need for hostesses. In many canteens, the selection process appeared demanding on paper, and some women, such as Anne Luckow, experienced setbacks in the process. The application process itself may have been enough to put off some women who did not want to take the time or energy to prove their good character to USO staff.

Many of the women who served as hostesses did not emphasize the significance of the selection process to their overall hostessing experience. It is logical that they would only remember the process if it posed obstacles for

2.4. Betty Ward, director of the Miami USO
(Betty Ward Collection in possession of Ward O'Connell)

★ ★ ★

them or their friends. Phyllis Mayfield's girlfriend, who worked with her at the Commerce Trust Company Bank in Kansas City, Kansas, encouraged her to join the USO GSO. The only step Phyllis took to become a member was to "talk to the people who were in charge of the USO, the women. . . . They didn't give any kind of a test or anything like that." Phyllis concluded, "I think if you were recommended by someone who was already in there and [the senior hostesses] liked what they saw or they liked your behavior, you were in."[32] Marian Richardson, a hostess in Washington, D.C., and later in Omaha, Nebraska, did not believe "people that didn't want to behave ever came to the USO."[33] The USO's image and reputation preceded it and usually attracted only girls who would meet USO standards of propriety. As shall be discussed in detail in Chapter 4, a positive sexual reputation was paramount to many single young women because that reputation was necessary to secure a spot on the marriage market.

Popular imagery of USO hostesses supported the organization's somewhat stuffy image when it came to good behavior, race, and respectability. Norman Rockwell's widely distributed 1942 *Saturday Evening Post* cover illustration,

"Willie Gillis at the USO," exemplifies the media's propensity to portray white hostesses as the norm; it also highlights the feminine and sexual characteristics at the core of women's USO service. Rockwell's image depicts a dopey Gillis overwhelmed by the feminine attention of a senior and junior hostess; all three characters are white. On one hand, the junior hostess, wearing a red dress, can be distinguished by her open-lipped smile, the revealing curve of her breast, and her inviting posture. By clothing the junior hostess in red, Rockwell emphasized her sexual, vivacious nature. On the other hand, pursed lips, arms held close to her chest, and a critical gaze identified the woman in the demure green dress as a senior hostess to *Post* readers. Rockwell marked each woman's class status by dressing her in exclusive garb including hats and perfect black high-heeled shoes. The senior hostess on Gillis's right attempts to feed him some hors d'oeuvres, while the younger, blushing hostess on his left offers him a plate of sweets. Gillis appears baffled at the number of tasty morsels coming his way as well as at the close proximity of women eager to satiate his palate. Gillis's eyes bulge as he chews one of several doughnuts and cookies selected from a plate on his lap and nervously spills his coffee and spoon.[34] In her review of *Saturday Evening Post* fiction, scholar Maureen Honey persuasively argues that "racist bias . . . permeated white-controlled media and resulted in a race-distorted picture of women on the production front." In advertisements, fiction, and general media, newspaper and magazine coverage underrepresented the actual number of women of color who were war workers.[35] As with the depictions of women war workers, popular representations such as Rockwell's ignored women of color who volunteered for the USO, preferring to make white, overtly feminine women the models for USO hostesses.

The USO's racialized selection processes reinforced Rockwell's depiction of hostesses as Caucasian, while black hostesses challenged the pervasive image of junior hostesses as white women and fought racism both inside USO clubs and on their outskirts. For example, the Philadelphia SDC was unwilling to include African American women as junior hostesses until 1945. This canteen welcomed black servicemen at the same time that it excluded black women, thus tacitly implying that black women were unable to meet white women's standards of femininity and respectability. In 1945, the Philadelphia SDC added two black hostesses to both evening shifts to entertain the small number of black servicemen who visited the canteen. The staff wanted to prevent interracial dancing that offended some junior hostess captains and

2.5. "Willie Gillis at the USO," by Norman Rockwell, in *Saturday Evening Post*,
7 September 1942 (Printed by permission of the Norman Rockwell Family Agency.
Copyright © 1942 Norman Rockwell Family Entities.)

★ ★ ★

servicemen.[36] The Baltimore *Afro-American News* publicized the inclusion of
thirty women in the SDC ranks, and Clara Irvin of the Red Cross commented,
"We must always stress the need to keep colored girls of good character by the
side of our boys when they are off duty, but we will not participate in any
project where there is compulsory segregation."[37] Irvin recognized the importance of the USO project and the black community's desire to provide
entertainment for black servicemen. She embraced black hostesses' participation in the SDC as an integrated club. Barbara Stix, Philadelphia resident and
former hostess at the SDC in New York City, wrote to the SDC to tell the

staff that she was "gratified to find that the Philadelphia Canteen had finally adopted the policy of complete non-discrimination that has long been a fundamental policy of the New York Canteen."[38] The Philadelphia sDC did not provide black dance partners for African American servicemen until the war was nearly at an end, because in its view the South Broad Street uso was the primary club in Philadelphia that African American soldiers, sailors, and hostesses should visit. Volunteers and staff at the Philadelphia sDC were reluctant to challenge social norms that condemned interracial dancing, which sometimes occurred between black men and white women in the absence of black hostesses, or to include black women who wanted to serve their country as hostesses in the popular club. Their decision exemplifies the conservative and contradictory nature of the uso and betrays the organization's desire to avoid racial conflict at any cost.[39]

Though many local uso clubs were not interested in racially diversifying their pool of hostesses, some clubs welcomed nonwhite women when they needed them to entertain servicemen of color. For example, the Nyack, New York, uso club held an impromptu party for Nisei soldiers on their way overseas. The uso sent out an "SOS" for Japanese American women to serve as junior hostesses at the party, and 112 New York City residents complied.[40] In the context of internment and rabid anti-Japanese sentiment, the national uso officially avoided employing Japanese Americans. If the uso could not find anyone else to fill the vacancy, then it would allow "persons of Japanese descent" to work in clubs but not have any contact with soldiers.[41] Once Japanese American men became soldiers, however, the uso did its part to entertain them without prejudice and without racial mixing. Women of Japanese descent danced with white servicemen in Hawaiian uso clubs throughout the war.[42] The uso met the needs of male soldiers and sailors first and included diverse groups of women when they could help the organization achieve this goal.

The national uso organization made every effort to be inclusive with regard to race when it came to selecting junior hostesses, but it reduced its ability to be a real force for social and racial change when it ultimately left the decision to integrate clubs to local forces.[43] This decision was similar to federal management of racial issues regarding military segregation, for example, that observed customary racial hierarchies. uso clubs in Boston chose white hostesses for all clubs serving white soldiers. The Ruggles Street uso Center was the main club in Boston that served black servicemen, so it was where most black junior hostesses volunteered. A majority of the USO Boston Soldiers and Sailors Committee (BSSC) believed that since so few black soldiers visited clubs other than the Ruggles Street Center, it was not necessary to include black women as hostesses in other clubs. The Ruggles Street USO was not as nice as those for white servicemen; "it [was] an old building, poorly located, and not too well furnished."[44] In the interest of racial equality, Ray Guild, president of the Coordinating Council of Colored Clubs for National Defense, member of the USO-Inc., began an effort that lasted several months to have the Boston Buddies Bay State Club located on the Boston Commons register black hostesses. Guild and several others on the BSSC threatened to resign if the committee refused to meet their demand. At the same time, forty white senior hostesses and sixty white junior hostesses signed a petition opposing the admittance of black hostesses to the Buddies Club.[45] After months of committee meetings, threats, and press coverage, the BSSC opened the Buddies Club to black junior hostesses.

Ray Guild offered several explanations for the BSSC's strong resistance to including black women as hostesses at the Buddies Club. He blamed the "southern" influence of individuals opposed to seeing black men and black women together in public for the controversy.[46] Despite Guild's charge that a "southern" viewpoint fueled this controversy, this incident brought to the surface a northern racism that was usually subtle and difficult to pinpoint. While southern states legalized and enforced segregation in public places, northerners most often segregated restaurants and dance halls by custom.[47] The Buddies Club operated out of doors in a historical and prestigious section of Boston. The white community was willing to tolerate, and even welcomed, African American soldiers in uniform at the Buddies Club, but it opposed the fraternization of African American men and women in a white-dominated space. While some black men and women in Boston wanted to use the war to tear down boundaries of customary segregation, the white-dominated BSSC was more interested in preserving the racial status quo.[48] The Boston Buddies Club incident sullied the national USO's effort to provide recreation to all servicemen and revealed the deep cracks in a policy that sanctioned integration in writing but did nothing to support it in practice. With its discriminatory policies, the USO protected a racialized idea of beauty and whiteness on the home front.

African American women played a pivotal role in opening the Buddies Club to young black hostesses. According to Guild, several prominent black women met with three representatives of the white hostesses who threatened to leave the Buddies Club in protest. In Guild's view, "These same colored ladies gave the white [*sic*] hell and I mean it. The whites began to see the light."[49] Guild did not elaborate on this comment, and this leaves the reader to wonder exactly what these female organizers said to their white counterparts. These women evidently believed that young black women's inclusion as hostesses at the Buddies Club was important enough for them to personally and directly confront the measure's white opponents. African American clubwomen throughout the country had a long history to that point of working with white clubwomen to achieve economic and racial justice.[50] Guild's assessment that these "colored ladies gave the white hell" was perhaps an outgrowth of that shared history. Finally, Guild worked within the structure of the USO to make a place for black women in particular in the Buddies Club. According to him, the situation came to a head when he threatened to resign from a separate "Community Fund Drive" for which he often solicited the highest number of donations. Guild knowingly and successfully threatened the "pocketbooks" of the white community, in a move reminiscent of black activists' Depression-era strategies. Whether they launched "Don't Buy Where You Can't Work" campaigns or advanced black-owned businesses, African American communities throughout the 1930s applied economic pressure on white communities to end racism.[51] Guild's shrewd tactic, combined with the efforts of female African American community leaders, led to the addition of black hostesses at the exclusive Buddies Club.

The ability of African American women to serve their country as USO hostesses and to benefit from the rewards of citizenship implicitly transferred to wartime volunteers was at stake in this controversy. White junior and senior hostesses for the Buddies Club may have understood the conflict as one of territory: they had their clubs, and African American hostesses had their own. They may not have wanted to change, in their view, the standards or image of the Buddies Club, or they may have been openly racist. The rationale for excluding black women is less important than the fact that, in their view, African American women had as much right to serve their country as hostesses in all USO clubs as white women did. In the spirit of the black presses' Double V campaign to gain racial equality at home and victory against the Axis powers abroad, African American women and the black community in Boston refused to allow white women to monopolize the citizenship benefits of hostessing, which was for young women a logical way to support the war effort. By successfully challenging the exclusionary tactics of high-profile canteens like the Buddies Club, black women made public claims to citizenship and forced the USO to expand its definition of womanhood.[52]

As they culled junior hostesses, senior hostesses considered age and marital status along with race and class. The national USO requested that young women who were between the ages of eighteen and thirty volunteer for junior hostess duty and strictly opposed the inclusion of women under age sixteen as hostesses.[53] Local clubs made final decisions regarding age limits. The Philadelphia SDC followed this ruling, but the Montgomery, Alabama, GSO invited girls as young as sixteen to join the group.[54] Several young women resisted the CDHC's minimum age limits. One of the CDHC researchers, Laura Servais, observed that two girls from Concord, not her region of investigation, were fifteen and sixteen years old and had attended a recent CDHC function. Servais noted that one young woman whom the club had presumably rejected because she was shy of the age requirement "would be fully justified in feeling that we were discriminating and being unfair" if she found out that the other two girls were in the group.[55] The club was willing to make exceptions for ·certain seventeen-year-old women who met other club standards. For example, the club rejected Lena Jeanson when she was sixteen years old and admitted her when she turned seventeen. Jeanson had lied about her age, and usually the club did not admit someone who had done so; but in this case, the woman's mother believed that her daughter was the victim of white ethnic prejudice, so the club made an exception. Due to a language barrier, her mother did not grasp that the club initially rejected her daughter because officials at Fort Devens refused admittance to dances to women under age seventeen. The fact that Jeanson's three brothers were in the military added impetus to the CDHC's decision to admit her.[56] This incident illustrates the delicate social balance that clubs negotiated between their selection standards and community expectations.

Most women obeyed the USO's age limit because it did not occur to them to disobey the rules. Some women wanted to join the USO when the war began but waited until they met the minimum age requirement. Bettelee Zahn graduated from high school at seventeen and tried to enlist in the WAVES (Women Accepted for Volunteer Emergency Service), but the navy rejected her because she was too young. When she turned eighteen, she became a USO hostess instead of a Wave.[57] Janis Assaff was only sixteen when she became a hostess in McComb, Mississippi. The club welcomed her at age sixteen, but she did not have any interest in dating servicemen because she was so young. They did not seem to have much interest in her either.[58] The national USO advised clubs to give "careful consideration" to admitting younger women when the government began to admit men as young as eighteen into the service. Presumably, older teenagers could relate to these men better than college women in their twenties. For many women between eighteen and thirty, the USO dance hall was the best, even the only, place in town to meet men their own age because most of their male friends were in the military.

As with age, the USO's inclusion of single as opposed to married hostesses varied throughout the country. The national USO welcomed both single and married women, but clubs like the Baltimore GSO required hostesses to be single.[59] While the majority of hostesses were single, some married hostesses volunteered as juniors. Anne Rodriguez met her future husband while she was a junior hostess in Honolulu, Hawaii. After they married, she volunteered as a senior hostess in California because she did not feel comfortable dancing with servicemen other than her husband.[60] Conversely, after she married a serviceman in 1942, Alene McKnight volunteered as a junior hostess in the Walla Walla, Washington, USO. Servicemen "respected" that she was married and "didn't push [to date her]."[61] While married women were not necessarily "bad" women, they were sexually active and had knowledge of sexual behavior that, ideally, single junior hostesses lacked. USO clubs across the country preferred single junior hostesses and geared their advice manuals and activities to suit their needs and interests.[62] Single hostesses helped to keep the atmosphere inside the USO clubs wholesome and at least publicly chaste. Married women automatically possessed a certain status and maturity, while single junior hostesses might have been more likely to respond to the advice and supervision of senior hostesses who tried to shape them into public examples of ideal womanhood.

The USO organized and marketed its public image around beautiful, feminine, well-mannered junior hostesses. These values emanated from the men and women holding middle-class mores in charge of local clubs who attempted to maintain a gendered order in which gracious women comforted needy men. The Fayetteville, North Carolina, Salvation Army club advertised in an anecdote that it greeted servicemen with "our prettiest hostesses, dressed in their loveliest."[63] This theme was also present as members of the junior hostess GSO at the Hattiesburg, Mississippi, USO club organized themselves into several different groups, including the Lazy Daisies, the Pinafore Prissies, and the Military Maids. Each of these names highlighted club members' femininity. The Pinafore Prissies chose their name from the "crisp pinafores" that they wore to entertain servicemen on Monday nights at the club, while the Military Maids contributed to the decoration of the club on carnival-style "game nights," given that "it add[ed] quite a bit to the games to have an attractive girl beside each one."[64] In its regional reports, the Hattiesburg club noted that these "Steeple Chase" game nights became more and more popular with servicemen due to the fun games, or perhaps the "Lazy Daisies [were] drawing the crowds."[65] These senior hostesses were proud of their sweet juniors and pleased when they drew male soldiers and sailors from the seamy streets into their decent USO club. Junior hostesses also presented servicemen with a virtuous feminine distraction in the Midwest. According to the history of Cincinnati USO clubs, one serviceman wrote to his family that "in his opinion there were more pretty girls to be found per cubic foot on the dance floors and in the lounge of the [USO] Fenwick Club than anywhere else he had been."[66] In its efforts to earn tributes such as this, the USO fashioned an image of its hostesses in opposition to more revolutionary women on the wartime scene.

The USO portrayed female soldiers and sailors as unfeminine counterpoints to its own womanly junior hostesses. Historian Leisa Meyer argues that the Women's Army Corps (WAC) attempted to present female soldiers as feminine, middle-class women to assure a skeptical public that soldiering would not strip women of their femininity. The WAC encouraged its members to exercise their femininity by decorating their barracks, while all navy Waves had access to beauty shops.[67] Neither of these factors impressed upon USO SDCs that servicewomen were appropriate companions to entertain servicemen. The director of the American Theatre Wing SDC in Washington, D.C., explicitly stated that "service women [were] not desired at the SDC." She went on to say that USO staff provided "Wacs, Waves, Spars and Marinettes" tours of the canteen and then required them to leave. While inside the canteen, senior hostesses forbade servicewomen to "sit at the tables or to sit on the balcony, dance, or partake of food."[68] The director's rationale for this practice was that "the club was set up to offer men of the service an opportunity to enjoy themselves free from all military restrictions and atmosphere. Women in the armed forces [lent] further military appearance and action to the club while civilian hostesses [gave] a feminine touch to the project."[69] Apparently the other active servicemen in the club, whom the sdc required to be in uniform, did not remind men that they were, indeed, in the military. In the view of the sdc, servicewomen were not real women. They could not take male soldiers' and sailors' minds off their military status by granting comfort and basic physical contact to men like pastel-clad junior hostesses could. This, in the end, was the primary goal of most uso clubs.

One wac lieutenant recognized that women in uniform contradicted traditional notions of femininity and attempted to change their appearance in an effort to earn them admittance to the sdc. She requested that servicewomen be allowed to register as junior hostesses at the sdc in Philadelphia if they visited the canteen wearing civilian clothes. According to the lieutenant, "many of the younger ones would like very much to be allowed to come to the canteen as junior hostesses." In the interest of providing recreation for female soldiers, the Women's Committee of the sdc agreed to admit Wacs in that capacity. The Personnel Committee of the sdc intervened, however, and overrode the recommendation of the Women's Committee. Since members of the wac refused to participate in the ordinary interview process for hostesses and could not commit to filling a weekly shift, the sdc barred them from serving as hostesses.[70] The sdc was unwilling to compromise its rigid and selective process to offer recreation to women of the armed services, while it went out of its way to provide the best entertainment, food, and, in its view, companionship to servicemen.

The sdcs were the most exciting uso clubs in the country. Broadway and film stars as well as the most famous big bands performed on their stages, and local restaurants donated delicious and abundant food for the guests to eat.[71] All members of the military wanted to visit sdcs, and the clubs usually were so crowded that doormen turned away servicemen.[72] Private First Class Warren Weinstock identified the sdcs as "outstanding" and "special, but uso's all around the country were great."[73] By excluding women from the sdcs, the uso was depriving them of more than the chance to listen to canned music in a church basement. It deprived them of a thrilling and sometimes unforgettable evening of entertainment. Marilyn Hale, a junior hostess turned Wave, recalled that servicewomen she knew resented this treatment. Many Wacs and Waves believed they were serving their country in the same way as servicemen, so the sdc should have treated them with respect and affection. Significantly, the Cleveland sdc made a positive impression on Hale because volunteers there always warmly admitted servicewomen and invited them to participate in all activities.[74] In most USO SDCs, however, the presence of servicewomen in uniform subverted the USO's desire to decorate its club with more feminine-looking women for the pleasure of servicemen. In turn, the most popular USO clubs in the country routinely denied servicewomen admittance, and in doing so bred the women's general distrust in the organization.

While many SDCs enforced harsh anti-WAC policies, most USO clubs simply spent so much time focusing on servicemen that they lost sight of the interests of servicewomen. Francis Keppel, secretary of the Joint Army and Navy Committee on Welfare and Recreation, said in 1942 that female staff members of the USO "have been incapable of giving consideration to any but the needs of the men in the service." Keppel went on to say to the audience at the Washington, D.C., USO club that the organization needed to put more effort and resources into servicewomen's recreation.[75] As late in the war as 1944, servicewomen as a whole felt that USO clubs sponsored programs to suit men's interests, not women's, and this discouraged them from visiting USO clubs.[76] USO clubs "teemed with servicemen,"[77] who likely were there to dance and spend time with junior hostesses. This created a date-party atmosphere that excluded servicewomen who did not attend the dances with male dates. Pearl Case Blough, director of USO Services for Women and Girls, concluded that local clubs in fact did not want to exclude servicewomen but succeeded in doing so when they did not try to make the women feel welcome as women. She emphasized in multiple reports and published articles that the USO organization embraced servicewomen and that local clubs ought to do more in practice to make them feel comfortable.[78] Despite Blough's attempt, servicewomen "felt they were not welcome in uniform" in USO clubs.[79] Like USO policies on race, the national USO advertised an inclusive policy toward female soldiers and sailors, but local clubs applied those policies in sometimes exclusionary ways.[80] In the view of the USO, hostessing instead of joining the military was the most appropriate way for young women to serve their country and to express their citizenship obligations.[81]

USO rhetoric emphasized the femininity of Wacs and Waves and their prewar identities as ordinary women to persuade senior hostesses and staff to include them in USO activities. Colonel Martha Hamon of the Salvation Army contended that female soldiers were "tomorrow's homemakers," so they deserved special attention from the USO.[82] The WAC also touted servicewomen's femininity, and one officer requested that the USO "help preserve those feminine qualities we want women to keep." Blough argued that servicewomen wanted to spend leisure time in feminine surroundings after living in the army's "masculine atmosphere" day after day.[83] Major Helen G. O'Neill, assistant director of the marines, suggested that the USO clubs furnish services like "beauty parlors" so that servicewomen might "satisfy their personal pride in appearance."[84] Some women wanted to socialize with men; others, with fellow Wacs. Mostly they wanted to have a public place in which to spend free time. Blough advised clubs that the USO could do much to facilitate public recognition of servicewomen in general by treating them with the same warmth with which they treated servicemen. After all, "service women [were] only the civilian girls we [knew] before the war in different clothes. . . . They want to enjoy . . . the things normal girls in civilian life want to enjoy."[85] In other words, servicewomen were not a threat to common definitions of femininity because in reality they were the same virtuous women they had always been. The public, however, had a difficult time understanding the new category of "female soldier,"[86] and USO clubs in particular remained a site of contestation between junior hostesses who embodied customary femininity and servicewomen who challenged it.

Even women who possessed the most desirable qualities of a junior hostess required training to polish their feminine attributes, so local USO clubs emphasized "charm" lessons for junior hostesses. Senior hostesses and USO leaders believed they were improving young women by teaching them how to present their bodies to men. Charm lessons covered physical hygiene, makeup, and weight management to create a standard of beauty for all USO hostesses to attain. The national USO distributed its rules for junior hostesses along with charm information to all USO clubs.[87] This practice made it clear to local clubs that junior hostesses representing the USO should be both obedient and well groomed. The USO in Phoebus, Virginia, supported national USO standards by holding a "charm school" prior to each dance "so that the hostesses [would] present the ultimate in charm, poise, personality, how to wear their hair and how to play games well." In this club, as in many others, the USO expected junior hostesses simultaneously to look flawless and act as entertaining game partners. The USO went to great lengths to deliver expert training to its hostesses. For example, "a Hollywood casting director gave the USO girls practical ideas on clothes and charm and beauty" in San Diego, California.[88] Some young women appreciated this free charm school training, since this was a common and popular course at the time. Hostesses in Lebanon, Missouri,

2.6. The original caption reads, "After the Ball Is Over. . . . This candid-camera shot of an unidentified USO junior hostess is a tribute to all junior hostesses who faithfully and unselfishly served USO in the past, serve it now and will continue through 1947. Tired and foot-sore as she is after having danced through a long evening, she can rest happy in the knowledge that her gracious hostess-ship is in large part responsible for the success of USO, and for the spirit and courage of the men in the Armed Forces of the United States." USO, New York, New York, Lot 13110 (F) [P&P] (Photograph from NAACP Records, Library of Congress. Thanks go to The National Association for the Advancement of Colored People for authorizing the use of this work.)

★ ★ ★

augmented their training by instigating a trip to the library to learn more about charm.[89] While they performed as USO agents to entertain servicemen, women extracted their own benefits from the organization's emphasis on their physical comportment.

African American women who embraced the concept of the beautiful hostess also exploited it in their own antiracism campaigns for feminine and sexual respectability. In addition to the South Broad Street USO in Philadelphia, African American women worked in USO clubs in Oakland, California; Fayetteville, North Carolina; and numerous other cities throughout the country.[90] The USO for black servicemen in Wilmington, North Carolina, chose "key girls" from a "cross section" of the black population to "keep the soldiers in that 'at home mood.'"[91] Girls from notable black families helped the USO reproduce a homelike atmosphere in its clubs to remind men of their families' moral influences. When the commanding officer of the 348 Aviation Squadron at Charleston Air Base requested that Mrs. Shields of the USO-YWCA in Charleston send hostesses to a party at the Shaw Center for black servicemen, she refused to comply because her clubs' "hostess standards and agreements would not allow them to mix girls on whom they had passed with the girls from the Shaw Center who were not on the USO approved list." The number of USO junior hostesses in this club was low because the club "screened [the girls] carefully."[92] For decades black women had taken seriously issues of sexual and feminine respectability. Beginning in the 1890s, middle-class black women combated white racist stereotypes about their supposed hypersexuality by focusing on their physical appearance and their public behavior. According to historian Maxine Leeds Craig, "Grooming was a weapon in the battle to defeat racist depictions of blacks."[93] Black women carried the association between race, respectability, and bodily appearance into USO clubs. For example, African American women in Waukegan, Illinois, celebrated seventeen young women who excelled in their USO charm lessons at a Valentine's "Graduation Prom."[94] In these instances black women were not simply adopting the practices of white USO clubs; rather, they were relying on their own "politics of respectability" that associated black women with beauty and reserve, as opposed to work, drudgery, and immorality.[95]

Chinese American women embraced the "self-improvement" aspects of the USO, particularly the charm schools. The Chinese Young Women's Society, in Oakland, California, recruited instructors from the Pacific Gas and Electric "homemakers division" to lead female members in USO-type charm classes. Founder Dorothy Eng hoped that classes in "style and dress and hygiene" would acquaint Chinese American women with American culture. Although the USO welcomed Chinese and Chinese American servicemen in its clubs, Eng feared that the USO would reject them as a result of anti-Asian sentiment. She created the Chinese Young Women's Society to entertain servicemen in lieu of a USO club. According to Eng, this was a preemptive measure, because although the USO might have opened its doors to Chinese American servicemen, the men did not want to risk the humiliation of being turned away by the USO.[96] Eng's story revealed both the need for recreational outlets for all servicemen and minority women's genuine interest in USO-style charm classes.

Chinese American women adapted the ideals of the uso to meet their own needs of cultural integration and wartime recreation, just as African American women used the uso to advance their citizenship goals.

Through uso charm schools and advice manuals, senior hostesses hoped to reshape the physical bodies of junior hostesses into those of ideal beauties attractive to men. In doing so, the uso reinforced the leading idea that a woman's proper role was not that of war worker or soldier but of wife. The *Madison Hostess Units Manual* gave hostesses a detailed account of how posture contributed to their "natural attractiveness" and emphasized that "tummies, keeping them flat banishes that curve-in backline and that spare tire around your waist that adds years to your appearance."[97] The Philadelphia sDc forbade junior hostesses from eating food served in the canteen, because members of the community provided the snacks for male soldiers and sailors to eat. To reinforce this rule, the junior hostesses' manual added, "It is better for your figure anyway" to skip the snacks.[98] The implication was clear. The sDc staff preferred junior hostesses to be both charitable and trim. The uso's concern with hostesses' weight was somewhat contrary to prevailing ideas about female dieting. Dieting was not popular among adult women in the Great Depression and World War II due to food shortages and wartime pinups that "glamorized the voluptuous, large-breasted woman." Historian Joan Jacobs Brumberg, however, also locates the beginning of a trend in women's magazines to direct "subdebs" to diet.[99] uso manuals reflected this trend and revealed that senior hostesses, the manuals' authors, considered a woman's shape and size influential in her ability to please men.

Several uso clubs commented on the most personal aspects of women's physical appearance to ensure hostessing standards of proper hygiene. Local clubs elaborated on suggestions from the national uso that junior hostess training courses ought to "stress the importance of personal cleanliness."[100] For example, junior captains at the uso club operated by the Jewish Welfare Board in Philadelphia emphasized that hostesses should "keep themselves neat and clean, being especially careful to guard against 'B.O.'"[101] Similarly, in its sessions on "cosmetics and clothes" the Salvation Army instructed hostesses in "personal daintiness."[102] The Madison, Wisconsin, clubs advised hostesses to "avoid cheap perfumes, especially if they [were] cover ups. A good deodorant, used regularly, an effective hair remover, lots of soap and water and a mouthwash used thrice daily, or at least once [were] essentials."[103] uso manuals reflected the kind of advice advertisements and articles in women's magazines had been giving to women about good grooming for decades. Attention to grooming was a key component of the "middle class feminine ideal."[104] Hostesses needed to smell good, since their job required them to be physically close to men in Salvation Army clubs while talking and playing games or while dancing with them in other clubs. Older women in the community who served as senior hostesses used the opportunity of the war to teach young women how to present their bodies to men in public.

In addition to weight and basic hygiene habits, face makeup played a central role in maintaining women's femininity during the war. The USO emphasized its importance to junior hostesses. The federal government chose not to ration makeup because it was connected with women's morale and the presentation of their feminine bodies to men. By 1941, makeup had become "an assertion of American national identity" with which women were unwilling to part.[105] *Hints for Hostesses* advised women to "use make-up skillfully. Give it special attention — blend it — make clean-cut lines with lipstick and eyebrow pencil, then forget it except in powder room."[106] The *Madison Hostess Units Manual* instructed women to "add makeup as a means of adding to your natural beauty, and not as a mask," then went on to tell hostesses how to apply rouge, lipstick, powder, eye shadow, and nail polish.[107] The "victory girls," who the public believed wore too much makeup,[108] either did not receive or adhere to the advice the USO gave to their "good girl" counterparts. Literary scholar Page Dougherty Delano posits that society and the media portrayed cosmetics and lipstick in particular as both constraining and liberating for women. She aptly delineates between the "sexually evocative woman" and the "sexually independent one" who were both necessary actors during the war.[109] Historian Kathy Peiss argues that makeup was a way to distinguish between them.[110] Makeup application was also one of myriad ways whereby women deliberately or accidentally blurred that demarcation. Given the significance of image and reputation to the USO, young women, and their families, it was dangerous for a hostess to experiment with a scarlet shade of lipstick or another coat of rouge. If authorities mistook her for a "bad girl," they likely would call her sexual reputation and class status into question.

In the 1940s, many women recognized that their appearances mattered to men, and in some cases, they did not mind tailoring those appearances to fit contemporary expectations. The USO's *Hints for Hostesses* told women to "arrange hair becomingly and in a style that remains in place all evening" for club dances.[111] Nancy Brown, who fulfilled her junior hostess duty on Thursday evenings and Sunday afternoons throughout the war at the Hollywood Canteen, found it difficult to satisfy the latter part of this suggestion. According to Nancy, the "coiffure [during the war] was long in back; you had long hair you roll[ed] the top up so you could sort of wrap it along the ears and across the front, and then long and curly down between your shoulder blades, and you could put little flowers up here, little bows." She "had never been happy about [her] hair. . . . And other girls' hair always seemed to be so perfect and [hers] always seemed to be falling down." To remedy this, Nancy frequently visited the ladies' powder room throughout the evening to check her hair. Nancy spent time preparing for USO dances by styling her hair because "all women were sex objects back then." In Nancy's view, "to get a compliment when walking down the street, [like] 'hey, nice legs' was something that 'made your day.'"[112] While Nancy enjoyed receiving praise from men in this fashion, another hostess, Dot Goldstein, resented the "dirty old man" who worked in her department as a supervisor at Wells Fargo Bank in San Francisco because he leered at women's bare legs below their skirts as they took shorthand.[113] These examples illustrate that although junior hostesses like Nancy sometimes welcomed the connection between their appearance and men's interest in them, others such as Dot did not condone it when it emphasized gendered discrepancies of power.

The USO enforced a dress code for junior hostesses that encouraged the male gaze. The Baltimore GSO manual accentuated junior hostesses' "femininity" and beauty and encouraged them to wear attractive clothing because "every bright girl knows that she dresses to please men. Today, more than ever, she must be aware of this little feminine fact. If she doesn't dress up in this present work, she is surely letting the men down." The GSO added meaning to its dress code by combining it with a reminder to young women that servicemen's morale, and their ability ultimately to win the war, depended on whether or not junior hostesses accessorized with a "fresh flower" or a "colored handkerchief."[114] This emphasis on femininity emanated from a prevailing culture of beauty that included Hollywood pinups who adorned the lockers and barracks of men in uniform. Conscious of its hostesses' pocketbooks, the GSO contended that "it doesn't matter how much you spend, but it does matter how feminine you look."[115] Thus, the USO counted on junior hostesses to dress in attractive fashions to distract men from their homesickness and war-inspired fear.

While these organizations encouraged "short full skirts, and bright sloppy

2.7. Two junior hostesses and a sailor sharing a soda (Records of the Boston YWCA,
The Schlesinger Library, Radcliffe Institute, Harvard University)

★ ★ ★

joe sweaters" for junior hostesses, they did not specify a dress code for senior
volunteers.[116] The Montgomery, Alabama, USO for white servicemen con-
curred with national USO standards when it ruled that "girls [could not] enter
building with slacks on."[117] Servicemen in both Boston, Massachusetts, and
Hattiesburg, Mississippi, appreciated it when junior hostesses dressed in formal gowns for special USO dances.[118] When she requested a group of hostesses
from the CDHC attend a dance at the Ayer USO near Boston, Sarah Mongeon,
program assistant for the USO, noted that the dance was a formal one and "girls

not in evening clothes [could not] go on the dance floor."[119] From the turn of the century, elite American debutantes presented themselves at formal balls. These events continued throughout the Great Depression but declined during the war when wealthy young women instead organized debutante balls masked as charity balls to give the appearance of a "democratic affair."[120] Formal USO dances gave the typically middling and middle-class women who attended them the chance to play debutantes for an evening.

To complete their feminine attire, women needed to cover their legs with stockings or leg makeup. Helen Gosnell, a hostess in Miami, Florida, contended that during the war, "it wasn't necessary to enforce a dress code. Hostesses never came to the USO in anything but dresses, or skirts and blouses, and they wore dress shoes and hose."[121] USO hostesses went to great lengths to dress respectably, especially when it came to covering their legs. The government placed an embargo on silk from Japan and rationed nylon to make it readily available for military use.[122] As a result, women had a difficult time purchasing stockings. Sylvia Assyia, a hostess at the Music Box Canteen in New York City, was fortunate because she worked for a law firm in the same building as a store that sold stockings: "I would run down at 11:00 before the lunch hour so I could get the stockings before the crowds came."[123] In Kansas City, Kansas, Phyllis Mayfield did not share Sylvia's experience.

> Oh half the time you didn't have any [stockings], in the summertime especially you'd put makeup on your legs. They had liquid makeup which is something like the foundation we wear now, only it seems to me it was much thicker, and you could get it in various shades, but you just put it on your hands and rub[bed] it all over your legs, all the way up past your skirt line. You had to be careful in the summertime, because if you got real warm and perspired it would run and it would look awful and you'd get it all over your clothes, but it was better than going bare-legged. No one ever went bare-legged then. [The leg makeup] was awful.

Phyllis applied layers of sticky, uncomfortable cream to her legs because all the other hostesses did.[124] It did not occur to them or to women like Helen Gosnell to attend a dance in public without properly covering their legs. The decision to hunt for stockings or apply leg makeup exemplifies the significance of the appearance of feminine respectability to junior hostesses and the USO. In certain regions of the country, every detail of a woman's physical presentation of herself, including her bare or covered legs, indicated whether or not she was from a respectable social class and was a "good girl."[125]

Clothing sometimes determined how men treated hostesses and what kind of sexual behavior they expected from them. The Baltimore GSO specified that girls wear colors that they preferred, as long as those colors simultaneously "cheer[ed] the boys." Khaki, blue, and gray were "out," while pink and white were "most appealing." Hostesses needed to be cautious, however, and not stray too far to one end of the color spectrum. For example, "unrelieved red [was] not a good color to wear."[126] Hostess Alice Roby's experience wearing bright colors explains one possible rationale for this recommendation. After volunteering in the Memphis, Tennessee, USO club for several months, Alice went through a period when servicemen repeatedly "propositioned" her for sex. She could not understand why this was happening because she was not sexually active and believed she had a positive reputation. She asked one of her servicemen friends why men suddenly seemed to expect her to have sex with them. He said, "It's very simple, you are wearing very seductive clothes." She had been wearing "sharp looking clothes" that were "close fitting, [and] bright." From that point on, Alice "quit wearing those kind of clothes and [the propositions] stopped," but she made sure that her outfits did not become "dowdy."[127] This story demonstrates the delicate balance hostesses negotiated when they dressed for the USO — sexy, but not sluttish. USO hostesses had to behave like good girls and dress like them, too.

When it enforced its strict dress code, the USO sent subtle messages to hostesses that it was suspicious of the femininity of women who worked for pay. For example, the staff at the Philadelphia SDC did not make wardrobe decisions easy for junior hostesses when they told them, since "this is your date with the boys," do not wear suits or sweaters because neither is "pretty."[128] This rule explicitly told women that while inside the canteen, they were there to please a crowd of servicemen and must groom and present themselves appealingly. As female soldiers believed, USO clubs were sites where junior hostesses presented themselves as pseudo-dates for male soldiers and sailors. The USO's condemnation of suits on women implied that women who worked for pay were not ideal feminine hostesses. Some women opposed this canteen's definition of appropriate feminine dress by resisting its rigid dress code. Hostess Marjorie Simson wore a suit to the Philadelphia SDC one evening, and the women in charge promptly asked her to leave because she was not dressed appropriately. Simson challenged the dress code in a letter to Mrs. Upton Favorite, president of the SDC, in which she stated that "many of the girls have objected to the regulation concerning dress. . . . Most of us build our spring wardrobes on blouses and suits, which we have found to be . . . acceptable elsewhere." Simson agreed that it was necessary for the canteen to enforce certain rules; but this one rigidly demarcated her appearance to an impractical degree, and she believed that "what we [wore] . . . should not [have been] more important than what we [did]." Simson overestimated an organization where appearances mattered more than actions. Simson resigned from the SDC, and the Philadelphia organization continued to implement its overtly feminine dress code.[129] Other women challenged the conventions of USO dress codes by wearing "very short, wide dresses" and "sweaters" to dances at the USO Labor Plaza in Philadelphia. Members of the Hostess Committee agreed to reprimand hostesses for disobeying the dress code.[130] In this USO club, as in most others, senior volunteers watched juniors to make sure that, if nothing else, they dressed like respectable young women who hid their work identities behind more glamorous, yet traditional, appearances.

The San Francisco SDC took a more flexible approach to its dress code, and to its view of women working in paid labor, when it allowed hostesses to wear suits. Eighteen-year-old hostess Dot Goldstein interchanged dresses, skirts, and suits in her canteen wardrobe. For Dot, wearing suits to the canteen was a practical choice because she did not change her work outfit before she went to the canteen. To save the time it took her to go home to Daly City, eat dinner with her family, and wash the dishes, she stayed in the city on Thursday nights after working a full day as a typist and stenographer. Dot joined one of her girlfriends for dinner, where she enjoyed a meal for under $3.00 at a local Chinese Restaurant and then went to the SDC, where they began their shift at 7:00 P.M. Furthermore, Goldstein's father was a traveling clothing salesman and made suits for his daughter that she loved to wear.[131] Clothes were important to women like Marjorie Simson and Dot Goldstein, and they took pride in their appearance. These modern women did not want to trade their work identity for that of a hostess. Instead, they wanted to combine the two. They allowed the USO to dictate their dress, hair, and makeup to a point, but they resisted total conformity to rules they believed were impractical.

USO-sponsored beauty contests from Boston to Virginia emphasized junior hostesses' physical appearance while highlighting their honorable qualities.

The *uso Bulletin* praised the organizations' ability to bring in the "loveliest girls in the nation" to entertain the country's men in uniform. Many junior hostesses followed the advice of motherly senior hostesses to dress in handsome clothing and to participate in on-site beauty contests to make the uso a place where "beauty reign[ed]."[132] The uso told hostesses in fine print that it did not choose them "because of [their] bright eyes or curly hair, but because [they had] something of value in [their] own person."[133] Nevertheless, local uso clubs' emphasis on beauty and "loveliness" far outweighed any reassuring statements that the organization enrolled women for only their personality and not their physical appearance. Hostesses, both junior and senior, made choices within uso spaces that upheld dominant gender norms that placed women's physical appearance, not their organizational or interpersonal skills, on display.

The army, and in this case the uso, purposefully surrounded male soldiers with images of "beautiful" women both to encourage "heterosexual desire" and to motivate men to fight for "American womanhood." Scholar Robert Westbrook posits that wartime pinups of "girls next door" tended to represent to male soldiers all things American and worthy of protection. He goes on to say that American women participated in this construction when they sent alluring photographs of themselves to husbands and boyfriends.[134] Muriel Ross, a volunteer hostess at the Music Box Canteen in New York City, sent three-by-five professional photographs of herself to five different soldiers and sailors with whom she was corresponding. Saks Fifth Avenue styled her hair for the photo session, and she took pride in a compliment from a random soldier who passed her in the Number One Fifth Avenue Bar. When he saw her he exclaimed, "You look like Helen Hayes!" Muriel sent the five servicemen copies of her picture because she was proud of the quality of the photo, and her letters gave the men something positive to anticipate.[135] Westbrook identifies the phenomenon in which Muriel participated, but his analysis of it does not locate sources of women's agency in this process. Women embraced this particular image of themselves as physically beautiful and wholesome because it was empowering. By defining themselves as beautiful and behaving in a patriotic fashion, women who frequented uso clubs found security and a clear sense of purpose during a time of tremendous emotional upheaval. At the same time, they sought some control over the meanings of beauty.

Historian Maryann Lovelace's analysis of the SDC in Philadelphia rightly contends that the title of "Stage Door Canteen Pin-Up" girl was one that "sexually objectified" hostesses, but the meanings of beauty and sexuality within the context of the USO were more complicated than this.[136] The USO linked beauty, sexuality, and virtue, and many USO hostesses supported and celebrated these linkages. As a twenty-eight-year-old woman, Muriel volunteered at the Music Box because she wanted to expand her social life and help out in the war effort. Corresponding with servicemen and sharing a glamorous photograph of herself with them made her feel like she was doing something tangible to lift their spirits.[137] She found satisfaction in the way she presented herself and felt as though she was having some effect, however small, on the daily lives of soldiers and sailors by sharing her picture with them.

African American women also sent their pictures to servicemen, and some made a conscious connection between race and beauty while doing so. Master Sergeant Theodore R. Senior and Sergeant Edgar B. Anderson wrote to the National Association for the Advancement of Colored People (NAACP) in 1944 requesting that it collect and send to them pinups of African American women. They hoped this would lift the spirits of African American troops in the Pacific who wanted "beautiful photos of our own women . . . that we can pinup and admire, instead of having the beauties of every race but our own as PIN-UPS." Senior and Anderson asserted, "Since we have the most beautiful women on the globe, why not then be surrounded by them while reminiscing over the ones we left behind?" The NAACP complied and asked "all persons who wish to relieve the loneliness of this combat regiment" to submit pictures. Ozell E. Bryant, who was a USO hostess in the Kansas City, Kansas, canteen as well as a radio assembler in a factory, complied. Along with her photograph she included her address because she wanted to exchange letters with Senior and Anderson.[138] Historian Joanne Meyerowitz's study of "cheesecake" pinups from the late 1940s contends that some African American women supported *Ebony*'s publication of seminude black women because they opposed "American racist and classist standards of beauty." Images of white women covered magazines like *Life* and *Esquire*, so in their view, it was fitting that pictures of beautiful black women also appear in periodicals.[139] Rather than have "beautiful" white women stand in for all women, Bryant, Senior and Anderson, and the NAACP, like female *Ebony* readers, took measures to create a new beauty icon. Bryant represented the USO as a beautiful black woman. This challenged both pervasive beauty norms and the USO's projected image of whiteness.

THE USO ATTEMPTED to construct a demure wartime womanhood rooted in the physical appearance of middle-class white women. Selection committees steeped in middle-class cultural values relied on the presumption that sexual respectability accompanied this class status and put forth this version of womanhood as the one worth protecting and preserving. While USO volunteers wanted women like Doretta Cloyed, Nancy Brown, and Bettelee Zahn to be its representative beauties, women of color challenged the USO's implied claim that white women best embodied American beauty norms. Female soldiers contested the USO's narrow vision of appropriate wartime service for women while at the same time trying to gain access to USO services. Although these women demonstrated that wartime beauty and femininity were not static categories, the USO remained a bastion for idealized American womanhood and femininity.

★ ★ ★ ★ ★ ★ ★ **3** ★ ★ ★ ★ ★ ★ ★

Wartime Socializing

Geraldine Stansbery wrote to the mayor of Philadelphia in May 1943 to ask
him if she could be a hostess at the new USO Labor Plaza. She had applied to
volunteer at several USO clubs earlier in the war, but they quickly filled their
hostess positions before receiving her application. Stansbery's description of
herself could have been that of any typical junior hostess: "I am nineteen years
of age, 5′3″, and weigh 102 lbs. I am a stenographer at the Philadelphia Saving
Fund Society. I neither smoke nor indulge in intoxicating drinks." Stansbery
promised to give the USO her "character references" and told the mayor,
"Don't think me a 'prig,' I like to jitterbug and straight dance, or make merry
chatter with lonely people." She implored the mayor not to "consider me too
forward or over anxious, but my only brother is in the service and so are all my
boy friend acquaintances. I want to do my bit to keep up the morale of other
fellows, as I hope other girls are doing for friends in the Service who I know."[1]
Her letter captured some of the contradictions inherent in the USO's expectations of thousands of hostesses. Stansbery was both fun-loving and a good girl.
She would entertain men with smiles and dancing, not with overt sexuality.
Still, she made a point to mention her height and weight. She recognized that
a feminine appearance was important to the USO's image and mission. She also
acknowledged her role as a morale-builder for servicemen.

In hindsight, many women described their hostessing experiences as both
pleasurable and patriotic. Analysis of their actions shows that their desire for
entertainment and socializing often was the motivating force behind their
volunteerism. The war presented women with myriad volunteer options,
from rolling bandages to leading air raid drills to collecting scrap metal.[2] USO
service was unique among these options because it put young civilian women
into direct physical and emotional contact with servicemen in a social setting.
War, fear, and the possibility of dying set the backdrop for their conversations
and elevated them from casual interactions to intimacy. The federal government and the military depended on junior hostesses to lift men's morale

through activities and conversation that both distracted them from the tedium of military life and shored up their masculinity. The government did not allocate much financial support to accomplish this immense task because it expected a civilian core of volunteer hostesses to lift servicemen's morale out of a sense of patriotism. Junior hostesses, as the beneficiaries of men's military service, concurrently owed temporary attention to men and symbolized the stakes of war. Yet these young women resisted the USO's constant demands on their time, chose to socialize with one another sometimes to the annoyance of senior hostesses, and cultivated a women's culture through organizations such as the YMCA's Girls Service Organization (GSO).

UPON REFLECTION, former hostesses assessed their desire to volunteer for the USO in patriotic terms, but a yearning to socialize with other young people induced them to enter clubs and canteens in the first place. Junior hostesses who grew into teenagers during the Great Depression understood that hard financial times limited the number of "marriageable men" available to them. When the war began, a new kind of deprivation occurred as young neighborhood men left their communities to complete military service.[3] Marjorie Hawkins, who attended college in Manhattan, Kansas, recalled that volunteering for the USO "seemed a way to help the war effort. Later, when the college men went into the service, it was recreation for us females too!"[4] Marjorie enjoyed hostessing because it was patriotic and fulfilled her desire to spend time with young men who would otherwise have been unavailable to her during the war. Irene Szuhay expressed a similar desire to spend time with male soldiers and sailors, as she asked rhetorically, "What young girl didn't enjoy meeting servicemen?"[5] Barbara Byko supported her mother financially and was responsible for housecleaning and cooking. Her mother did not want her to volunteer at the USO, but Barbara's aunt convinced her sister that Barbara needed a social outlet. Eighteen-year-old Barbara relished attending USO dances in Linden, New Jersey, because she could socialize with men there and forget about her responsibilities.[6]

USO service had the ability to nurture skills in young women that would be useful to them outside the club or canteen. For example, etiquette in dance halls before the war called on boys to ask girls to dance, but in USO clubs it was the responsibility of hostesses to ask servicemen to dance if they were not already on the dance floor. This practice in the Boston, Massachusetts, Stage Door Canteen (SDC) enabled Ann Gushue to overcome "her shyness."[7] USO manuals reflected Ann's experience and encouraged juniors to become more outgoing and self-confident. The USO's fictional account of "Marilyn Mousie" counseled, "She was awfully bashful, and longed to go into a huddle with some other girls. But instead she made herself walk up to a corporal and say 'Isn't it a lovely evening?' and after that it was."[8] This parable instructed women to make an effort to communicate with men, because this would bring them happiness. This was a logical lesson for women whose parents and society expected them to marry.[9] Through hostessing, young women could cultivate the social skills they needed to achieve that goal.

Junior hostesses also volunteered for the USO because the organization's spaces were both safe and respectable. For Mildred Reca, the USO's "no alcohol" policy was one of the rules that made the Philadelphia USO an attractive place for her to socialize with men: "There was no alcohol allowed, so the servicemen that came to these places were respectful."[10] In 1941, the USO made opposition to alcohol one of its basic tenets, and this policy reduced altercations within the clubs and created a safer, more respectable environment for hostesses, senior and junior alike.[11] The lack of alcohol might have accounted for the popular belief that most of the servicemen who visited the clubs were "very well behaved."[12] Marjorie Hawkins agreed with the rules of the Kansas City, Kansas, USO club, especially the "no alcohol rule." According to Marjorie, "cooperation seemed universal" inside the USO.[13] The lack of alcohol contributed to the USO's wholesome character and appealed to volunteers who supported a middle-class notion that public drinking was suspect and déclassé.[14] In keeping with blue-collar traditions, Anne Luckow, a hostess from a working-class background in Rockford, Illinois, did not object to USO prohibitions against alcohol. She and her hostess friends, however, relaxed after their Saturday night stints at the USO by drinking cold beers at the Jade Room, a local upscale hotel. They also served spaghetti and beer to servicemen at the Verdi Club (an Italian club) on Sunday afternoons. Significantly, managers at both the Verdi Club and the Jade Room required the young women who patronized their establishments to be members of the USO.[15] USO respectability had currency in Rockford, Illinois, and allowed Anne and her friends admittance to other highly regarded clubs that happened to serve alcohol. Anne used her connections to the USO to extend her social life, thus extracting a benefit perhaps unforeseen by the USO.

Other junior hostesses thwarted club rules to fulfill their own individual desires for social activity. To accentuate the notion that the USO recruited hostesses to serve men and not themselves, most clubs instructed women to avoid socializing with one another and focus instead on entertaining servicemen. Juniors, however, did not always follow USO rules. The Philadelphia SDC ruled that it was "absolutely forbidden for hostesses to congregate in groups! This [was] a war job for the purpose of entertaining the boys and not one another."[16] In fact, the behavior of hostesses revealed that they did not always consider hostessing "work"; rather, they viewed time at the canteen as an opportunity to relax and socialize with other women. Keeping junior hostesses quiet during the entertainment at this canteen was the responsibility of senior hostesses and junior hostess captains. Based on the number of times this issue came up in Women's Committee meetings, juniors continued to chat with one another and with servicemen while singers were performing.[17] Junior hostesses who socialized with other hostesses were also a problem at the Jewish Welfare Board USO in Philadelphia, where the club did not permit juniors to "congregate in groups at any time — while sitting or standing."[18] Staff at the SDC wanted junior hostesses to be respectful of entertainers who donated their time and talents to the club. The SDC and the Jewish Welfare Board hoped that women would foster morale and a sense of identity among themselves, but not while they were on duty. Junior hostesses spent time at the SDC, instead, to solidify friendships and wile away perhaps otherwise stressful or boring wartime evenings.

Most junior hostesses showed a strong commitment to the USO's wholesome brand of entertainment by attending clubs on a regular basis, yet some resisted senior hostesses' desire to control their schedules and their free time. This resistance proved that young women's personal autonomy was more important to them than their commitment to the USO. Membership in the GSO in Hattiesburg, Mississippi, jumped from 2 in 1941 to 2,875 in 1942 and reached its peak of 6,345 in 1943.[19] Senior hostesses monitored sizable numbers of juniors and reprimanded those who were tardy or repeatedly missed their shifts. The Philadelphia SDC sent warning letters to hostesses who missed one, and then two, shifts.[20] If a hostess missed three or more shifts, she received the following curt letter from Mrs. Van Horn Ely Jr., vice chairman of junior hostesses:

> As you have been absent so often without letting the office know beforehand, I am wondering if you are ill or for some other reason find it impossible to continue your work at the Stage Door Canteen. Will you

kindly fill out the form below and return to us in the enclosed self-addressed envelope. Also, please enclose your pass, if you are resigning. If we do not hear from you within a week, we will assume that you are no longer able to serve, and will drop you from our lists.

Even as she ended the letter with the "hope" that the junior hostess in question would "soon be back with us," it is evident from Mrs. Ely's somewhat snide tone that she was disgusted with junior hostesses who did not take their USO work seriously.[21] For their part, junior hostesses who did not attend USO events demonstrated their ability to turn down the USO's constant demands on their time. The USO Labor Plaza relied on female members of Philadelphia's crafts unions as well as members' female relatives to fill junior hostess ranks. Carolyn Mullin, director of hostesses, wrote an open letter to Labor Plaza hostesses asking them to attend their assigned shifts and not cancel due to mysterious sunburns, poison ivy, or toothaches. Tardiness was also a problem at the Labor Plaza, where servicemen often arrived at 6:00 P.M. and junior hostesses were not yet there to greet them.[22] Senior hostesses and Labor Plaza staff kept written accounts of specific problems related to junior hostesses to give to union business agents in the event that the Labor Plaza removed them from the roster.[23] All of this supervision exemplified the serious side of hostessing. Junior hostesses made a promise to servicemen and to the state. Those who agreed to socialize with servicemen had to attend the USO faithfully, because theirs was a war job. At the same time, junior hostesses who skipped their shift for whatever reason sent a clear message to the USO that this war service was not the most important or perhaps enjoyable part of their lives.

When hostesses found a fair substitute for the social life that the USO afforded them, such as a new fiancé or boyfriend, they often quit volunteering. A government report titled "Recreation for Women in War Areas" determined that junior hostesses were "overworked," because their numbers were dwindling due to engagements and marriages.[24] One hostess in Concord, Massachusetts, resigned from the Concord Dance Hostess Committee (CDHC) because her "extension work" did not provide enough free time for her to volunteer, and she wanted to spend time with her new fiancé. She complimented the CDHC for recruiting "so many fine young women" to dance with servicemen like her two brothers in the navy, but she could no longer serve.[25] Audrey Armstrong valued her volunteer work at the Burbank, California, USO club, but her "hometown sweetheart" did not approve of it. When he returned on leave from the service, they got married, and he asked her to quit the USO. He did not want her "to dance with strange men." Audrey complied with his request and "did not miss hostessing" because she socialized with her married friends instead.[26] Warren Weinstock did not object when his fiancée, Dot Goldstein, continued her volunteer service with the USO in San Francisco. Dot, however, stopped hostessing because men paid more attention to her when she was wearing her engagement ring. In her opinion, men "probably thought [she] had experience." These two examples denoted the sexual undercurrents present in USO dance halls. Private Woods did not want to share his wife, Audrey, with hundreds of other servicemen even if it was only for a brief dance. Seaman First Class Weinstock knew that Dot was true to him because she was "a committed type person,"[27] but she did not want to contend with advances from servicemen who, she believed, assumed she had sexual experience just because she planned to marry. USO hostessing was exceptional among wartime volunteer work. The act of dancing in many cases was casual and simple, but in some instances it was filled with tension. This tension caused some women to forgo dancing with male soldiers and sailors and begin cheering them from the sidelines, somewhat to the disappointment of senior hostesses and even the federal government.

The U.S. military and government relied on the physical and personal connections that hostesses made with servicemen on the USO dance floor because those connections contributed to servicemen's positive morale. The state placed a high value on the importance of morale when it came to the conclusion that servicemen's confidence, courage, and sense of purpose affected their abilities to do their jobs.[28] Federal security administrator Paul McNutt characterized morale as "the concern with the individual as an individual, with his spiritual life, his attitudes and appreciations, his relations with his fellows, his easy adjustment to military life, [and] maintenance of personal ideals of conduct."[29] According to McNutt, to keep servicemen's morale high, an organization such as the USO ought to focus on servicemen on a person-by-person basis, rather than as a collective unit. Once a man had a sense of self-respect, he would be better able to coexist with his peers and carry out his duties as a soldier.

Connections USO volunteers fostered between themselves and home affirmed the self-worth and humanity of servicemen. While commending the African American USO–National Catholic Community Services (NCCS) club in Fayetteville, North Carolina, Major General James M. Gavin, commander of the 82nd Airborne Division, concluded that the military taught the service-man skills, but "he [was] not a soldier until what he [took] on the inside [was] a belief in himself that [could] only come from his association he finds in his home and with the fine and faithful people of the USO."[30] Advocates of the USO made great claims to its importance, suggesting that it was the USO that made men true soldiers. In this case, soldiering was more than mastering the tech-niques of war. The USO understood true soldiers as embodying and following an elevated, virtuous calling. A sure sense of self and a connection to humanity made noble soldiers, and it was this quality that would make it possible for hypermasculinized servicemen to return to their homes after the war.

Wholesome recreation inside and outside army camps was extremely im-portant to the military, considering venereal disease (VD) rates and the imprac-ticalities and dangers associated with hordes of bored servicemen filling local communities on weekends.[31] John D. Rockefeller Jr., chairman of the USO National Campaign, argued that to maintain morale the USO needed to offer "a wholesome atmosphere, the companionship of fine women and girls, recre-ations that [were] normal influences that [would] keep [servicemen] clean, and worthy."[32] In this case, Rockefeller couched VD prevention in morale-building terms. The military and the government needed young women to maintain servicemen's health and "worth" through emotional work. To be worthy of a postwar world that included normative heterosexuality and procreation within families, vast numbers of servicemen could not return from military service with their bodies tainted by VD.

The military articulated this serious purpose, while USO member agencies placed the burden, or privilege, of fulfilling that purpose in the hands of junior hostesses. Navy commander John L. Reynolds challenged the USO: "Your USO buildings and your USO activities must be made so attractive to the men that they will choose those buildings in preference to some of the other commer-cial entertainment of various sorts which might be more or less thrust under their noses."[33] Junior hostesses personally represented those USO buildings and activities. Young women at the Salvation Army Donut Center in Cincin-nati "knew that if they succeeded in providing a pleasant evening of whole-some entertainment for the men in uniform at the Donut Center, the men would be apt to visit other USO centers in other towns in the future rather than seek out less wholesome places." It was up to these women to be "friendly, courteous, and considerate at all times" so that male soldiers would not think they were aloof and choose bars and brothels over the USO as a result of their conduct.[34] The USO and the military put junior hostesses on the front lines of their auxiliary war to keep men free of VD and immorality. The stakes were high for junior hostesses because men's health and fitness for service were on the line.

Some junior hostesses described their own war work as having patriotic value, but they believed servicemen were sacrificing more than they were for the war effort. Hostess Nancy Brown characterized men's visits to the Hollywood Canteen as "high quality therapy." Volunteers enjoyed providing that therapy because "everyone was aware that these poor young guys did not want to be where they were, they wanted to be home doing what they had been doing, but they were going to go and win the war, and everyone who could not do that wanted them to know how . . . thankful" civilians were. Nancy's comments betray the seriousness of wartime. The young men with whom she socialized at the USO might fight in combat and become injured or lose their lives. Nancy determined that she and her junior hostess peers were unable to take up arms as male soldiers and sailors did, thus supporting the contemporary military policy and accepted notion that men, not women, engaged in mortal combat. By dancing with servicemen, Nancy implicitly praised their courage and their manhood. Whatever enjoyment Nancy took from her USO service waned as the war continued. Toward the end of the war the "high of [volunteering] wore off." She "loved the dancing, loved asking Marlene Dietrich for another plate of sandwiches." According to Nancy, hostessing "was fun, but it was also connected to the tragedy of war. Even at that tender age I was intelligent enough to be aware of that. I wasn't there partying. . . . It was a service."[35] Though Nancy was not paid, for her, hostessing within this emotional context was indeed a war job. Similar to Nancy, Bettelee Zahn, who volunteered at the San Francisco USO, "wasn't in it for any popularity; none of us were really. It didn't matter how many persons you danced with; you wanted to make sure they were having a good time." She volunteered on a weekly basis because she believed parents were pleased that their sons were spending time in a "nice place" like the USO.[36] These women did their best to help male soldiers and sailors "forget where they had been and where they were going."[37] Nancy and Bettelee identified their volunteer work as pleasurable and as beneficial to servicemen. They revealed how the underlying gravity of wartime was ever-present in their service, and this strengthened their devotion to the USO.

Other hostesses, and even historians, suspected that socializing with servicemen under the guise of patriotism was not in itself a significant contribution to the war effort. The USO in Cincinnati speculated that some junior hostesses believed "what we were doing didn't add up to much in comparison to the sacrifices others were making, but it helped us to think that this was even a small way to make it a little easier for the fellows who were doing the toughest jobs."[38] Historian D'Ann Campbell also argues that women's wartime volunteerism raised civilian morale but "had little impact on the winning of the war."[39] Hostess Doretta Cloyed did not believe that dancing with servicemen was overly important: "It really wasn't a tremendous help to the war effort compared to the people who [were] working double shifts, drilling, and making defense weapons."[40] In one sense, Doretta was right. Dancing with servicemen in Washington, D.C., was not as tangibly significant to the war effort as producing munitions. Junior hostesses were not at risk for the sort of suffering that millions throughout the war-torn world underwent, and their involvement in the war was not on the same scale as that of men in the military or of women and men who worked in dangerous defense production jobs. Yet Doretta's description of her own gendered labor as insignificant is worth exploring, especially when coupled with a similar rebuff by female veterans. Veterans of the Women's Army Corps compared their wartime contributions to those of male soldiers and then dismissed them as less significant. When it came time to claim GI Bill benefits, a large number of female veterans chose to forgo that compensation and no longer associate themselves with the military. Many believed that employers would penalize them for perpetuating a connection to the military when the public perception of a veteran worthy of government benefits was that of a man. One Navy Nurse Corps veteran said, "We had enormous pride in having served . . . but somehow many of the women didn't place their contributions on an equal level with men."[41] Ultimately, for women like Doretta and female veterans who chose not to claim GI Bill benefits, it was not the nature of their work that caused them to undervalue it but, rather, the fact that the work was being performed by women instead of men. Furthermore, this work took place in the context of a war that emphasized proper gender roles as well as the notion that men were protectors and women the protected.

The USO lauded women's central role in maintaining male morale, even as it contributed to the dominant notion that women's work was not as important as men's. In March 1942, national USO campaign chairman Prescott S. Bush named Elizabeth Luce Moore the chairman of the USO's National Women's

Committee. Moore acknowledged the importance of women's contributions to the USO by saying that "women's place in the USO effort cannot be too greatly emphasized." She went on to outline women's specific obligation to the USO and the war endeavor. Moore declared that Americans "should not ignore the need for preservation of the national spirit. That is women's biggest duty now, to prove in every way that we are united behind our fighting men."[42] In this depiction of women's work, women themselves provided the support necessary for men to do the fighting—an important position, to be sure, but a secondary position nonetheless. Stella Moore, director of the Philadelphia SDC, described hostessing as "high morale building as evidenced by the very change of expressions on the boys' faces from depression and downheartedness when entering the Canteen to smiles and hopefulness as they [left]."[43] Perhaps Moore used this positive picture of the effects of hostessing on servicemen's morale to justify her position and the role of her canteen in the war effort. The amount of time and rhetoric that military and federal government officials dedicated to servicemen's off-duty activities, however, tended to support Stella Moore's theory that morale work was important, but it contradicts Doretta's assumption and Campbell's conclusion.

The attitude and sociability of junior hostesses were central to the USO's ability successfully to lift the morale of servicemen and to compete with brothels and bars for their patronage. According to a USO survey of soldiers' expectations of USO clubs, soldiers disliked hostesses who were "indifferent, formal, disinterested, impersonal and condescending."[44] Junior hostesses had to seem polite and perky to maintain the USO's appealing image. Carolyn Mullin, director of hostesses for the USO Labor Plaza in Philadelphia, worried that hostesses did not always warmly welcome servicemen. Mullin cautioned hostesses that "one cool, 'no, I don't care to dance,' [did] more damage to the whole spirit of the place than a million 'I'd love to[s].' "[45] Junior hostesses had to be friendly to all servicemen at all times to win the competition with potentially dangerous women for servicemen's attention.

The military learned during World War I that cultivating positive morale among servicemen was essential to building an effective army. As a result, the Army and Navy Special Services Division hired and paid hostesses during World War II to coordinate recreational activities for soldiers and sailors in Army Service Clubs and Navy Ship's Service Clubs in camps. Approximately 350 senior, junior, and canteen hostesses, 3 per camp, worked with morale officers and with community volunteers. These paid hostesses coordinated the camp dances to which the USO and other civilian organizations sent busloads of hostesses. Some community leaders worried about the safety and reputations of paid army hostesses. The Reverend M. R. Hamsher wrote to the joint army and navy boards and committees to find out whether or not the government was encouraging the "conscription of young women employees of the federal government."[46] This was similar to public fears about the so-called conscription of women into an army corps presumably to meet servicemen's sexual needs.[47] Frederick Osborn, chairman of the Joint Army and Navy Committee on Welfare and Recreation (JANCWR), assured Hamsher that the military was not conscripting women. The women were paid civilian employees who worked in camps alongside 10,000 men.[48] Young civilian women volunteered for the heavily chaperoned USO, while army hostesses had the daunting task of working in close proximity to thousands of servicemen at posts that were understaffed and assumed to be unchaperoned. This lack of surveillance put the sexual reputations of paid army hostesses at risk.

The government considered servicemen's recreation to be a central part of their military training, but it did not allocate more funds to hire extra hostesses to work inside camp or to hire new ones outside camp. The creation of the USO reduced the government's need to pay for recreation in towns because the USO organized women to meet men's recreational needs while they were off duty. The military repeatedly stressed the importance of alternatives to brothels and bars for servicemen, so the Federal Security Administration constructed buildings to lease to the USO as a place to present that entertainment.[49] It did not go so far, however, as to pay those many women who did the entertaining. This choice glamorized hostessing by making it a voluntary and therefore self-sacrificing form of war service at the same time that it took hostessing for granted and essentially devalued it.

Recognizing the importance of morale work to the proper functioning of the army, the USO attempted to elevate hostessing from voluntary service to war job. USO propaganda likened junior hostesses' morale work in the USO to military service. One Chicago USO club informed new hostesses that when they joined the USO, they also joined the army, navy, coast guard, and marines: "You're in there in a mighty important capacity too — that of making the club a gay, friendly and gracious place that the boys in uniform will remember with pleasure."[50] Memories of the USO had the potential to sustain men emotionally while they were on duty. Stella Moore credited her Philadelphia junior hostesses with being "faithful" to the USO and minimizing their absences "because they consider[ed] this a war job."[51] Senior volunteers in Hattiesburg, Mississippi, were pleased when their junior hostesses began "to realize the responsibility which [was] being placed upon their shoulders" to entertain servicemen.[52] The Madison, Wisconsin, Hostess Clubs emphasized that hostessing was "a JOB — but it [was] not a chore."[53] Instructions such as these reminded women to take their USO work seriously yet to see each contact with individual servicemen as emotionally fulfilling and not as an impersonal task.

The military and the USO included masculinity and humanity as components of morale. So the USO embedded in each of its activities the goal of fellowship and gendered that fellowship to instill feelings of comfort, security, and manliness in servicemen. The Hostess Training Institute of Madison, Wisconsin, printed the following poem in its program that summarized the attitude of the ideal junior hostess toward her work:

> You're the girl behind the man behind the gun. You can give our soldier
>   boys a lot of fun.
> If you just forget yourself. Put your ego on the shelf. And make sure the
>   hostess' job's well done.
> If I'm going to be a hostess, I'll be the best I know. I'll look my best, act
>   my best and go when I say I'll go.
> I'll be proud to be a hostess, and honored as can be, because I know that
>   little things can mean so much to me.[54]

For a hostess, putting her "ego on the shelf" sometimes included hiding her skills or intelligence. For example, hostess Helen Scheidel once beat a soldier at a game of checkers at Mayor Kelley's Servicemen's Center in Chicago: "I beat him and he got mad." The angry soldier accused Helen: "You must have been cheating!" Helen decided not to win any more games after that incident because she was "supposed to entertain the boys, not get a fat head."[55] This male soldier could not believe that a young woman defeated him at a game of checkers. When he accused her of cheating, Helen was annoyed but remembered that her primary job was to make him feel good about himself. Her choice to squash her own competitive impulses reinforced his masculinity and her supportive "feminine" position. Army chaplain Lieutenant Russell Becktell instructed hostess groups that "the boys' don't like brazen girls — they like them friendly and modest in games. Don't try to teach them too many new things — do the things they know."[56] Becktell articulated a well-established view of prewar gender roles that made women responsible for preserving male egos.[57] According to him, servicemen preferred to play games at which they excelled so that they did not have to risk their masculinity by losing to women. USO hostesses who followed Becktell's suggestion helped to keep in place a false gender dichotomy that reinforced traditional notions of male intellectual prowess.

USO hostessing and maintaining morale was gendered emotional work because, as the USO understood, while hostesses inhabited USO spaces they would remind soldiers of their hometown "girl" or wife. For example, the USO persuaded juniors to "just pinch hit for that hometown girl a service man [was] honing for."[58] The organization asked girls to listen to boys talk about the "girl back home" and "not try to compete with her."[59] USO staff and senior volunteers wanted juniors to help servicemen perpetuate connections to women at home, not break them because of their visits to the USO club. A 1943 USO *Information Sheet* article contradicts most USO expectations of juniors by saying that hostesses "must not be expected to act as substitute for mother, wife or sweetheart."[60] This denied the reality of pretty junior hostesses who fit the profile of ideal sweethearts and wives while inside canteen walls by dressing in attractive fashions and attentively listening to men's stories. Effective junior hostesses juggled USO advice with the reality of their position at the USO as servicemen's pseudo-companions. In doing so, they also put aside their identities to become the mutable "every woman" that bands of servicemen needed at particular times.

Economically successful films such as *Stage Door Canteen* perpetuated the romantic notion that GI's could find love in USO clubs and that junior hostesses were willing and eager to be whomever soldiers wanted them to be.[61] In the film's loose plot, three GI's on leave in New York City visit the famous Stage Door Canteen and meet three young hostesses who serve as their companions for several days. In a subplot, virginal "California" yearns for his first kiss from a "nice girl," and junior hostess Jean accommodates his wishes by acting as "his girl" while he is within the confines of the canteen. When the canteen lights go down during a dance, Jean coaxes California to "pick his moment" and kiss her. Cal becomes nervous and fails to meet his goal that evening. When he returns to Jean the next night, he is determined to take "his moment" on the dance floor, but another soldier cuts in and whirls away with Jean. Cal quickly asserts his manhood by reclaiming Jean as his dance partner and then confidently kisses her. Given the flirtatious foreplay leading up to the kiss, the palpable feeling of climax when Cal finally kisses Jean, and the distinct pleasure he feels at shedding his "virgin" status, it is evident that this kiss was a metaphoric representation for sex. In this Hollywood version of hostessing, young women were eager to fulfill innocent soldiers' requests for a "first kiss." Indeed, Jean went so far as to refashion herself to fit California's image of the ideal girl. For example, when he asked her age, she told him to "name it," and he replied that it was "important" that she be eighteen. Jean laughed at the compliment but did not give her correct age. She allowed California to use her to fulfill his "first-kiss" fantasy and simultaneously to gain his manhood before the army sent him to the battlefront.[62] While hostesses often danced only once or twice with the same serviceman, by remaining pleasant and pretty they had the potential temporarily to fulfill servicemen's fantasies, and those fantasies promised to lift their morale.

The USO trained junior hostesses to entertain men through a variety of wholesome activities, thus shoring up conventional gender roles by placing men's comfort ahead of women's. The Hattiesburg, Mississippi, USO club instructed GSO members to "make a conscious effort to entertain the servicemen in whatever small activity they might express an interest."[63] While under the tutelage of senior hostesses, junior hostesses were responsible for serving food, decorating the canteens, engaging soldiers in non-war-related chit-chat, and "partnering" with male soldiers in multiple activities including dances, Ping-Pong, and card games.[64] The YWCA taught young women how to hostess. Required dance and card-playing classes ensured that "hostesses [were] ready to take an active part in all the recreation that [was] planned."[65] The "Salute to Miss Jones" USO advice manual included the fictional account of "Priscilla Potts" to demonstrate to juniors that their job was to participate in any wholesome activity that a serviceman chose, despite hostesses' immediate interests. Priscilla "was dying to dance, but got stuck with a guy from Kansas, who had a passion for ping-pong. So she played ping-pong, and ping-pong, and ping-pong. He was very happy."[66] If a hostess made a serviceman happy, then she had done her job, and this, not meeting her own interests, theoretically provided her with satisfaction. Catering to servicemen was how she met her obligations to the wartime state. Behaving selflessly in an unquestioning manner, moreover, did not threaten the existing gender order.

In addition to being beautiful, well-dressed, and attentive, junior hostesses

3.1. Ping-Pong at the Miami USO
(Betty Ward Collection in possession of Ward O'Connell)

★ ★ ★

were expected to fascinate men with their personalities. The Salvation Army manual recommended that USO clubs include Margery Wilson's 1934 volume *Charm* in junior hostess training programs. Wilson matched the advice given in hostess manuals when she posited that one could cultivate self-esteem by casting off "affectations of any sort or description."[67] The USO hoped that young women who volunteered for service possessed the qualities that made an ideal hostess, mainly that "she [was] just naturally charming, interesting, and wholesome."[68] While the USO endorsed lessons in charm and behavior,

3.2. More Ping-Pong at the Miami USO
(Betty Ward Collection in possession of Ward O'Connell)

★ ★ ★

some local clubs set out criteria that were both contradictory and demanding. *Hints for Hostesses* offered the following description of the personality of the consummate hostess:

> Eyes that laugh and sparkle; spontaneous, witty come-back; a happy disposition; an interested but not curious manner; a relaxed yet alert attitude; a sense of humor; an air of comradeship and understanding; a friendly manner; optimistic outlook; a willingness to work; the ability to put yourself in the background; you can be strictly yourself — no extra flourishes — no playing up — no exaggerated enthusiasm. In other words, a good scout, a nice person to meet, a better person to know and remember.[69]

To seem this sincere and natural, the fictive junior hostess had to perform subtle emotional gymnastics. Her presentation to servicemen included "an interested but not curious manner" so that she could make him believe she found his stories appealing but was not probing or gossipy. She tried to soothe him with her "relaxed manner" but was animated enough so as not to bore him. A hostess juggled both being at the center of a male soldier's attention and a willingness to fade into "the background" when he was ready to move to another conversation partner. On balance, she behaved like an amiable pal whose attractive image a serviceman could carry with him after he left the uso.

As part of their unpaid labor, junior hostesses went to great lengths to maintain a constant level of optimism inside uso clubs. Given the frightening wartime context, this was not always easy. Like their senior counterparts, junior hostesses put on a "happy face" to raise the morale of male soldiers, despite their own war-related concerns or losses.[70] According to prescriptive literature, a volunteer hostess "learn[ed] to leave out of her line of talk all her own personal discouragements, not to talk about them." They "learn[ed] in fact, how to forget them and let them slide away into oblivion."[71] As with married volunteers who missed their husbands, the uso designed junior hostessing to help single women forget their problems by dancing them away with endless groups of soldiers. It is plausible that volunteer work did exactly that, but it is also evident that the uso and the government expected women to shelve their own fears and concerns to focus on the troubles of male soldiers, because the government wanted them to defuse men's fears and their moral reservations about war. The Baltimore gso advised junior hostesses, dressed in their finest dresses or skirts, to "forget about what you have on your back and concentrate on being as interesting and friendly as possible."[72] The uso expected junior hostesses to be "good listeners" so they could meet the needs of servicemen who were "wound-up for the evening."[73] According to the ywca, "The really skillful junior hostess will discover [servicemen's] wants, and make them hers."[74] The best hostesses carried out an "ego-boosting" project for the military by distracting soldiers from their military duties and their uncertain futures.

It took junior hostesses more patience and energy successfully to complete this project than either the uso or its bulk of hostesses often were willing to discuss or articulate. After all, for women to complain about such work, which was at its core pleasurable, would have shown disrespect to servicemen who were relinquishing so many of their liberties while the great majority of American women resided safely at home. This understood but rarely articulated sentiment made Philadelphia sdc junior hostess captain Margaret Halsey's comments even more startling. She used the negative encounters she had with various servicemen to teach her junior hostess peers that bad manners were not in themselves racialized. She reminded junior hostesses that white servicemen could be as insolent and disrespectful as black servicemen: "You meet plenty of white servicemen whose conduct fails to enthrall. Few outsiders realize, but all of us know, that being a Junior Hostess and entertaining unselected strangers for three-and-a-half-hours is difficult at best." She asked hostesses to make their own experiences in the canteen more pleasant by being as kind to black servicemen as they were to white soldiers and sailors.[75] In the midst of war, Halsey pinpointed the difficulties that went along with building the morale of an unkempt "unselected" army of strange men.

It was not just junior hostesses but white servicemen, the military, and the uso that levied numerous slights and outright injustices against African American servicemen. As a result, they suffered from instances of low morale in greater numbers than white servicemen. Lack of government funding for African American servicemen's recreation, in particular, hindered the development of positive morale among black troops. For example, in Washington, D.C., 400 black soldiers shared one dayroom, one Ping-Pong table, and a radio at Fort Meade.[76] The National Urban League's Southern Regional division reported that the Poydras St. uso club in New Orleans was "inadequate to handle the present load" of black troops moving in and out of the train station.[77] The division concluded that African American soldiers needed recreational outlets more than their white counterparts, because black soldiers battled racism and segregation on a daily basis.[78] Racial discrimination was felt by most African Americans in the nation.

For its part, the military publicly claimed that it wanted to station African American troops in communities that were favorable to their presence, had adequate recreational facilities for them, and already had a sufficiently large black population. The army found it difficult to meet these criteria, or chose not to meet them, and located most training camps for all servicemen in the south. Citizens from Wyoming to Texas to Mississippi complained to their U.S. representatives when the army stationed black troops, or what they considered to be too many black troops, in their towns. Southerners vehemently opposed the presence of northern black troops in their communities. The uso, along with the Red Cross and community organizations, attempted to fill the wide gaps in recreation for black servicemen.[79] According to William Y. Bell, associate regional executive of the National Urban League's Southern Regional division, black troops needed the "uso's therapeutic services." If black soldiers had access to the uso, they sometimes "arrive[d] at the

USO club . . . upset by their experiences in getting there," because white taxicab and bus drivers often refused to transport them from camp to town. This anger created "psychologically negative prospects for any sort of program participation" at the club.[80] Since the black community in the South contained only a small middle class, the recreation available to black servicemen there was limited to "sub-standard pool halls and theatres."[81] Servicemen's negative experiences with poorly staffed and sparse USO facilities led to low morale and to the belief that their government did not value them as soldiers, sailors, or citizens.

For their part, African American activists refused to allow the USO to disregard the needs of black troops. The National Association for the Advancement of Colored People (NAACP) pushed the USO to provide services for black troops, and by November 1942 the USO operated forty-one clubs for black servicemen. The Office of Community War Services argued that through the USO it offered "more recreation facilities per man" for black troops than for white servicemen, and that it valued "the morale of Negro troops."[82] The NAACP expressly opposed any USO club that "by express statement or intent, spread the ugly pattern of racial discrimination or segregation."[83] The NAACP opposed the opening of a USO club for African American servicemen operated by black volunteers in Newark, New Jersey, because the club would essentially be segregated. The main USO facility on Commerce Street hosted an average of 17,000 servicemen, only 30 of whom were black, even though 1,000 black servicemen worked in the area. Apparently, African American troops did not "feel welcome . . . at Commerce Street." In this instance, the national USO responded to the NAACP by writing that it did not support segregation but acknowledged that separate facilities amounted to de facto segregation. It was important to the USO and the black community in Newark, however, that the USO provide African American soldiers and sailors with services in a new club, rather than continue to let them go unserved.[84] African American citizens themselves were fearful of promoting segregation, yet they were caught between white clubs and hostesses inhospitable to blacks and the total absence of services for black troops. They reluctantly staffed segregated clubs rather than neglect their troops.

Decades after the war, white hostess Bettelee Zahn recalled some of her own difficulties in interacting with America's fighting men as a junior hostess at the San Francisco USO. She believed that the parents of some of the men who came to the club did not teach them to treat women "with great respect."

She and other junior hostesses had the following experiences with servicemen and senior hostesses.

> We found it a little uncomfortable when [servicemen] were not as nice as we thought they should be. I [did] not like them if they [gave me] a swat on the rear-end . . . or if their hand [came] too far around to the front [of my body]. There were some things we just didn't want to have to put up with, [so] after the music was over we could say thank you and say we had to go check in. We would just not be available to dance with them again. [Chaperones] would say we had to help behind tables, but they never confronted [the servicemen] with anything, because the whole idea was for them to have fun, but we felt protected. I thought that was a nice way to do [it]. Some of [the servicemen] would have been crushed if they had been confronted.[85]

Zahn's experiences signified the general atmosphere inside USO clubs. Senior hostesses prevented disorder and protected juniors from unwanted sexual advances from servicemen. Servicemen, in contrast, gained access to junior hostesses' bodies even when their wandering hands offended the women. The women's acceptance of this behavior made it possible for male soldiers and sailors to move on to the next hostess, if they chose, and repeat the same offensive behavior. In sum, both juniors and seniors safeguarded the feelings and masculinity of servicemen who might have been "crushed" if someone questioned their rude conduct. In doing so, junior hostesses sacrificed their own comfort because it would have been unpatriotic and selfish to shame a serviceman.

Junior hostesses' conversations with servicemen both about innocuous topics and about men's heart-rending concerns illustrated men's vulnerabilities during wartime and the emotional depths of junior hostesses' interactions with them. Donna Smith easily conversed with servicemen about hometowns, families, and hobbies at the Kansas City, Missouri, USO, and Betty TePoorten covered the same material with visiting soldiers and sailors in Asbury Park, New Jersey.[86] In more serious interactions than Donna's and Betty's, some hostesses buoyed servicemen who had "fear[s] [about] going overseas."[87] Alene Gwinn talked with servicemen about their families at the Walla Walla, Washington, USO and felt the weight of her responsibilities and of the wartime climate when she talked with reflective servicemen. "So many were so very young, right out of high school. [They discussed] what hopes they had for the future, if we would even have one; what they planned, college, jobs, return to farms, everything. You were the last person lots of them would see. They wanted to tell you their fears, hopes, and dreams."[88] Alene legitimated servicemen's "hopes and dreams" simply by listening to them. Sharing aloud one's plans for the future helped to make them more real, more attainable. For men who might leave the security of the United States for the European or Pacific theater, these conversations were especially significant. They reaffirmed soldiers' and sailors' humanity, reminded them that their current situation was temporary, and assured them that they would someday be home with their families. Gender was a key factor in these scenarios. Some servicemen felt more comfortable admitting their fears to junior hostesses, who were basically anonymous and closer to their own age than senior hostesses. By talking to women whom they likely would never see again as opposed to their male supervisors or peers, they preserved their pride and masculinity.

To protect the men in their care, hostesses avoided gossip and discussions of military details while they talked with servicemen. U.S. propaganda posters announced to all Americans that "loose lips might sink ships" and fostered the suspicion that spies could be anywhere, including in USO dance halls. In her analysis of wartime representations of women, Susan Gubar reveals that British, American, and Finnish posters condemned women for spreading sensitive military details and serving as spies.[89] When women conversed with servicemen, the USO did not want them to discuss details about their own personal lives, such as where they lived or the men's travels and assignments.[90] The USO held women and men accountable for their discussions in clubs but placed the burden on junior hostesses for shifting conversations from sensitive material to less dangerous territory. The Philadelphia SDC cautioned women not to "let him endanger his own life and that of others by allowing him to tell you the name of his ship, when he [was] leaving, and where he [was] going."[91] By using these particular terms, the SDC raised the stakes for hostesses. A hostess harmed a soldier or sailor and put those around him in danger if *she* could not prevent *him* from discussing war-related details. The belief that the United States harbored military saboteurs during the war was pervasive. Nancy Brown underwent a security clearance check to hostess at the Hollywood Canteen because the USO "had to make sure that [she was] not going to open [her] mouth to some innocent-looking sailor from Ohio who was really a German spy."[92] The seriousness of war substantiated government and USO concerns about security. In this case, the USO's tendency to privilege men's

3.3. Junior hostesses and soldiers playing games at a Boston area USO club (Records of the Concord Dance Hostess Committee, courtesy of Concord Free Public Library)

★ ★ ★

desires and needs over women's perpetuated the idea that women were at best irresponsible and at worst treasonous. For their part, many junior hostesses counteracted stereotypes that women were frivolous gossips by limiting their conversations with servicemen to men's private lives and general anxieties.

Not every USO club or affiliate disregarded hostesses' needs while privileging men's. The NCCS and the YWCA considered hostesses' wartime problems important and attempted to guide women through difficult times. The NCCS implored its volunteers to see hostesses not as "commodities" but as "young Americans who [were] offering to serve their country and their community through the USO." The NCCS encouraged USO organizers to listen to suggestions from the Junior Hostess Council and to include them in program planning.[93] Peggy Jane Peebler, a social services employee for the Phoenix USO-YWCA, focused on the needs of young women during the war. She, along with the YWCA, believed that the war affected them as much as it did men, just in different ways. She offered training courses in "personal hygiene" for

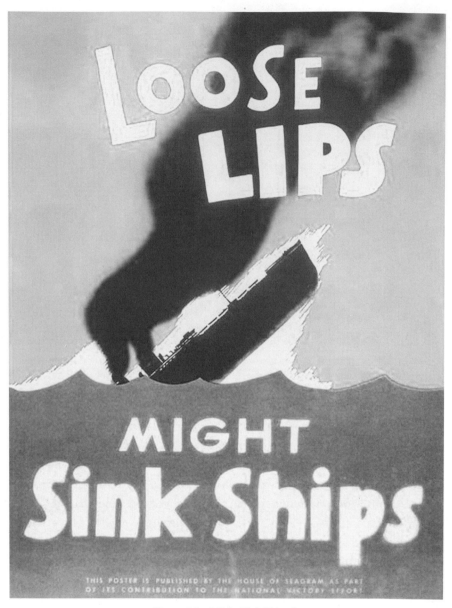

3.4. "Loose Lips Might Sink Ships," 1942
(courtesy of National Archives, ARC identifier 513543)

★ ★ ★

hostesses and encouraged them to take advantage of the USO as a respectable place to meet young men.[94] Along with the usual USO course in social etiquette, the NCCS trained junior hostesses to deal with the mental stress of wartime.[95] Other organizations, such as the Jewish Welfare Board in Philadelphia, instructed junior hostesses through charm classes, "with emphasis on civic, religious and social obligation." The club contended that its hostesses expanded themselves by socializing with "a great variety of Uncle Sam's soldiers, Jew and non-Jew, from all parts of the country."[96] Local USO clubs provided junior hostesses with more training than they did seniors. The Salvation Army recommended that junior hostesses participate in a twenty-four-hour training course over a period of two weeks, while the YWCA led the planning of hostess training courses in the Cambridge area.[97] These training courses were more than charm lessons. By learning about current events and civic projects, junior hostesses in these organizations broadened their minds as well as perfected their bodies. They were also able to find within USO clubs and USO work a respite from the rigor of wartime anxiety.

Unfortunately for junior hostesses who sometimes had to deal with servicemen in real emotional or physical pain, the USO, on balance, geared its training sessions toward teaching ladylike behavior. USO rules instructed hostesses in great detail how to behave like "ladies" so as to maintain a positive reputation for the USO,[98] but many hostesses believed they conducted themselves appropriately on a regular basis, so they did not find it hard to do so within clubs. For example, Donna Hendrickson stayed "on [her] best behavior" as a hostess at the Kansas City, Missouri, USO club.[99] Despite these hostesses' point of view, USO rules identified improper behavior, such as smoking, gum chewing, and drinking.[100] The Philadelphia SDC told hostesses not to chew gum "because it [made one] most unattractive."[101] National standards for junior hostesses specified that clubs should never allow junior hostesses to smoke on the dance floor, but "if the mores of the community [did] not oppose it" the club ought to allow smoking in designated areas.[102] The CDHC director pleaded with her junior volunteers to "be lady like in the powder room. . . . Leave it just as neatly as you found it or neater. I cannot overemphasize this; we will be judged by this as much as by our conduct with the men."[103] The reputation of the CDHC was in the balance even when junior hostesses used the bathroom. The USO cautioned women to behave appropriately because the USO was not a "private party"; rather, it was a "very public affair," and "how you get along here will reflect glory (or otherwise) not only on you, but on the agency that sent you here and on the name and fame of the whole USO."[104] For junior hostesses, USO dances were not simply a time to relax and socialize with young men. This type of war work involved some social and personal risk, because hostessing put young women's very abilities to be proper women on display for their communities and hundreds of male strangers.

Junior hostesses likely found basic psychological or social service training more effective than charm lessons in dealing with a variety of male problems and personalities. The national USO suggested that psychologists train junior hostesses to be especially sensitive to the emotional and physical limitations of veterans.[105] At chaperoned visits to convalescent homes in San Diego, California, junior hostesses entertained men by "playing cards, checkers, or dominoes or by telling fortunes."[106] Organizers implored hostesses who visited the Cushing General Hospital in Massachusetts to ignore the men's medical conditions and ask them to dance. They did not, however, have to "tolerate ungentlemanly remarks or actions" because the men were ill. The USO valued respectability and proper conduct on the road, not only inside its clubs. Hostesses needed to remember that they visited Cushing General "not so much for [their] own pleasure as to give pleasure to these men who are trying to adjust themselves to normal living conditions."[107] USO hostesses who visited veterans' hospitals encountered men and women with horrific injuries. This type of volunteer work brought women into contact with men who had served in battle and would not be attending dances in USO clubs. To prevent one's "heart from becom[ing] involved," event organizers encouraged hostesses to mingle with all of the men, rather than focusing on one or two.[108] With advice such as this, USO organizations recognized the emotional cost of morale work for women but still did not go far enough to train junior hostesses to cope with the effects of this work on their own psyches.

Dolly Monaco, who volunteered as a hostess and a dance performer at the USO on Lakeshore Drive in Chicago, Illinois, rebuked the USO for not preparing her adequately to handle the sight of severe burn victims in a Battle Creek, Michigan, hospital. She was shocked when she walked into the hospital ward and saw veterans with "no ears, no nose, just a slit for the eyes, a little slit for the mouth." Dolly was horrified, so "when [she] saw them [she] cried and . . . ran off." She felt terrible about her actions, so she returned to the ward, apologized to the men, and performed a dance number with the other hostesses. Volunteer work in veterans' hospitals required sensitivity and a certain amount of compassion. Unlike the majority of hostesses who limited their service to dance halls, Dolly continued to visit hospitals and joined USO camp shows and traveled overseas as a paid performer.[109] She found personal satisfaction in her volunteer work, despite the USO's missteps in training her. While the USO did not provide any substantial psychological support for hostesses who interacted with troubled servicemen, some clubs strengthened other skills in women.

Large USO clubs like the SDC in Philadelphia retained junior hostess captains to keep order among hostesses, and this hierarchy helped to foster leadership traits in women. Norma Williams was one of five of these junior co-captains. At twenty-two, she considered herself one of the "older people" at the canteen, since most hostesses were eighteen or nineteen. Captains helped the canteen to run smoothly and made sure that their peers followed the rules. They gained valuable skills in diplomacy as junior hostess captains.[110] Their job came with the responsibility of having to confront their peers when they were "recalcitrant" or "late merely through neglect."[111] Norma rarely had to confront her friends about their dress or behavior, so her position as an overseer did not become a personal problem. The SDC rewarded captains by allowing them to visit the canteen to enjoy its top-notch entertainment at any time, not just during their assigned shift.[112] The junior captains in Baltimore acted as liaisons between junior and senior hostesses to promote a "high morale" within the junior hostess corps.[113] This was a more positive and inclusive approach to organizing young women than that of the Philadelphia SDC, which was interested above all in enforcing its rules. Some USO clubs were as interested in happy hostesses as they were in obedient ones.

As a previous employee of the YWCA, Carolyn Mullin, director of hostesses at the Philadelphia Labor Plaza, learned that young women benefited from leadership training. Sophie Gevov, a member of the Labor Plaza Hostess Committee, believed that members of this committee "should attend the Junior Hostess Council meetings." Mullin strongly disagreed because the senior hostesses would present "too much of an adult attendance and would defeat the purpose of the Junior Hostess Council, which [was] to permit them to express themselves freely" and to encourage hostess morale.[114] The Labor Plaza Junior Hostess Council acted as a club for young women, but the senior hostess committee often made suggestions to them about what to cover in their meetings. For example, junior club members took turns at meetings presenting current events topics to the other members for discussion.[115] Though the senior hostesses at this USO limited the amount of creative autonomy they granted junior hostesses, young women managed to assert themselves as a group in other clubs. The national USO *Information Sheet* reported in 1944 that junior hostesses in San Bernardino, California, began the year by reorganizing their group. They re-registered all hostesses, created a training course, and most importantly, made sure that the San Bernardino USO included at least one of them on each of its committees. The USO staff listened to and implemented some of the junior hostesses' suggestions when it updated its program. As a result, "a real esprit de corps was born among the girls," and their "dubious frowns have turned to inspired smiles." When it reported this story, the national USO reminded readers that "junior hostesses need[ed] morale lifting now and then the same as the boys they entertain[ed]."[116] This sentiment was absent in most USO clubs, despite the national organization's call for USO staff and volunteers to pay more attention to the needs of junior hostesses. Those junior hostesses who took the initiative to make changes in the organization enhanced their own leadership and communication skills in the process.

As Carolyn Mullin's actions illustrated, the YWCA and YMCA did more to cultivate a sense of unity among junior hostesses and to encourage women's leadership and service than did the national USO or other member agencies. Female YMCA volunteers in Waukegan, Illinois, wanted to provide more service for soldiers and sailors, along with dancing, so they created the GSO. Seventy-five GSO clubs around the country had over 20,000 members by 1942. They employed the same selective criteria for their members as the USO did for its hostesses, but their organizational system made them distinct. GSO members wrote their own constitutions, elected officers, and initiated their own rules for conduct.[117] The annually elected chairman presided over monthly GSO meetings, and every member carried an identification card and wore a GSO pin.[118] The Baltimore GSO encouraged its members to share their talents in art, dramatics, dance, and music with servicemen at USO functions.[119] On 3 December 1941, Phyllis Mayfield joined the GSO in Kansas City, Missouri, with one of her girlfriends. They often sang the following song at GSO meetings to inspire unity and patriotism:

The GSO of the USO
Are the girls who are ready for fun,
They sing, they play, they dance the hours away,
After their day's work is done.

No glamour girl is the GSO
She's rather like the girl next door.
Their hearts are true to the red, white, and blue,
They'll be your friends forevermore.[120]

GSO members identified themselves as selfless "girls next door" and not as self-involved "glamour girls." They understood that entertaining servicemen for the USO was a serious war job, but they could enjoy themselves while doing it. These "good girls" wanted to befriend servicemen, not necessarily date them; thus they positioned themselves in opposition to pickup girls. When they created and operated a GSO club separate from the USO, young women focused on their own needs. The GSO performed morale work for "the boys" as it strengthened a women's culture.

USO volunteerism had positive lifelong consequences for outgoing women who used it as a stepping stone to other volunteer projects. Peggy Campbell attended mass regularly at her Catholic church in Birmingham, Alabama, and joined the USO because she was naturally outgoing and "gabby."[121] The USO looked for and fostered these qualities in hostesses. At age seventeen, Aileen Cooperman "expanded her horizons" at the Chicago USO, where hostessing served as her "first introduction to the rest of the world." She met men from all over the country and learned about different groups of people because she socialized with them in the dance hall. Years after the war, after her husband died, Aileen used the skills she acquired as a USO hostess to work professionally as a hostess at the Arizona Biltmore and the Wrigley Mansion in Phoenix, Arizona.[122] For others, the USO set them on a path of lifelong volunteerism. According to Shannon Kelley the USO "prepared [her] for volunteerism in the later years" of her life, and hostess Doris Machado continued a pattern of volunteering for Air Force Family Services after the war.[123] Women like Aileen Cooperman who attended temple regularly and had outgoing personalities naturally gravitated toward USO service because it brought them into contact with women and men from diverse backgrounds.

The USO rewarded junior and senior hostesses for their service with small gifts such as pins and certificates. The national USO encouraged local clubs to give dedicated volunteers award pins for their hours of service. Volunteers purchased their own pins presumably to reduce costs.[124] The USO awarded certificates of service to junior hostess volunteers. Norma Williams earned one of those certificates, and Dot Goldstein took home a "thousand hours"

3.5. USO certificate (courtesy of Margaret and Roger Fredrich)

★ ★ ★

pin for her commitment to the San Francisco SDC.[125] The Boston Soldiers and Sailors Committee recognized the commitment of CDHC members to war service and awarded certificates to them.[126] Junior hostesses also earned praise from servicemen such as those in 370th Fighter Squadron who wrote, "We departed from Massachusetts with regret as the citizens of your locality were very cooperative and did everything in their power to entertain and assist the members of this unit."[127] These tokens of thanks celebrated women's commitment to volunteer work.

Junior hostesses seized an intangible psychological wage or sense of gratification from their service. Beverly Littlejohn took "pride" in her USO service because "dancing with a man who was far away from his home and his girlfriend was the least I could do as a teenager for the war effort."[128] The fact that she derived pleasure from her time on the dance floor did not detract from the benefits hostessing accorded servicemen and the military as a whole. According to Julia Currie, her USO service was important because "it was great for the servicemen; they had a place to go and they met people their own age which . . . they needed."[129] By supplying a site where servicemen socialized with hostesses, the USO brought strangers together, and this amplified the pain created by the realities of war. Bettelee Zahn was keenly aware that San Francisco was a departure point for the servicemen she entertained. She "always felt that [she] could be nice to [servicemen] so that when they left they would always have the memory that their last few days [were] a nice time for them." Bettelee had never met these servicemen before she started dancing with them at the San Francisco USO club, but she wrote to many of them after they went overseas. As a result, hostessing "had many moments [when there were] lots of tears shed by lots of us. Letters would stop coming [or a] mother would write that [her son] had not returned." For Bettelee and her hostess friends, news of servicemen's deaths created a "bare spot in your heart," because "you had seen them smile [and] talked to them."[130] The harshness of war was not lost on these women as they laughed and joked with servicemen. Unlike the volunteers who chose to support the war in a fashion that did not bring them into contact with troops, such as selling war bonds,[131] these young women spent personal moments with soldiers and sailors. Separation and death punctuated the USO's light recreational atmosphere and heightened the significance and meaning of young women's wartime volunteerism.

LIKE MANY YOUNG women on the home front, junior hostesses sought social connections to enliven their daily lives. They volunteered at the USO to spend time with other women and to socialize with servicemen. While USO senior hostesses and the federal government attempted to elevate women's morale-building work inside USO clubs to the level of a war job, women proved through their resistance to constant monitoring of their time and social lives that they valued the USO both for its patriotic purpose and as an amusement. The gendered construction of USO service, in which the military and the organization expected young women's docile behavior to sustain men's masculinity, helped to maintain a conventional gender order. While junior hostesses focused on men's needs, they managed to extract benefits from this morale work for themselves, such as friendships with other women, leadership skills, and a sense of gratification and personal fulfillment. When the USO chose junior hostesses on the basis of their sexual reputations and class status, the organization made it clear that women's morale work, at is core, was sexual.

Nice Girls Didn't, Period
Junior Hostesses and Sexual Service

One evening early in her career as a junior hostess, Audrey Armstrong sneaked out of the USO with a sergeant and accompanied him to the Hollywood Palladium. When her mother, Mildred Armstrong, found out, she was upset and chastised Audrey: "How does it look to have the daughter of the director and a senior hostess sneaking out with a soldier?" Audrey's interpretation of USO rules conflicted with that of her mother and revealed an intergenerational conflict over the sexuality of a respectable young woman in the context of the USO. As director of the Burbank, California, USO, William Armstrong had told his twenty-year-old daughter, "There is a position [at the USO] for you too." Once a week for three years one of Audrey's parents chaperoned her while she danced and talked with servicemen at USO dances. With the exception of the Palladium incident, Audrey followed the rules and did not date servicemen. She valued being "clean" and a "good girl." This reputation was important to her. Besides, she did not want to tarnish her parents' reputations or the USO's image, so she chose not to break the "no-dating" rule again.[1] Audrey's story exemplifies the significance of female sexual respectability to the USO and to junior hostesses. The historiography of women, sexuality, and World War II analyzes women as prostitutes, pickups, soldiers, and pinups. According to observers at the time, the aggressive or self-assured manner in which these groups of women presumably commanded their own sexual agency threatened dominant notions of female sexual respectability. For example, federal, state, and local authorities identified prostitutes as women who exchanged sex with men for money, while the excitement and upheaval of war supposedly induced some young women, or pickups, to have casual sex with servicemen. The USO, along with the middle-class American Social Hygiene Association (ASHA), labeled women who engaged in any form of sexual activity outside marriage as "bad girls." These organizations and the women they identified operated within a sexual spectrum that by necessity also included so-called good girls.

The practice of the state, ASHA, and the USO to form and identify the "girl next door" in opposition to her "bad girl" counterpart was part of a larger societal trend to order human behavior and prescribe power by placing individuals into certain categories. Societies construct norms and deviance at the same time and in opposition to one another. This study investigates the good girl's sexuality, in particular that of USO hostesses, in proximity to several other groups of women whom critics labeled and then attempted to marginalize. Hostesses benefited from the confines of the "good girl" label just as they attempted to subvert them. They also upheld the good girl/bad girl binary with their own dedication to the USO's image of respectability, thereby inadvertently condemning women who did not have access to USO respectability, to state surveillance and criticism.[2] A comparison between various groups of women reveals the active role that so-called virtuous women performed on the home front to classify and protect their own sexual identities.

The army and the navy encouraged a masculine peer culture that depicted women as sexual objects even as they feared the debilitating effects of venereal disease (VD) on servicemen. Statistics from the Social Protection Division of the Office of Community War Services (OCWS) show that the U.S. Army lost 7 million days of service to VD during World War I and could not afford to do the same during World War II.[3] The U.S. military did not have broad access to penicillin until 1944, so it relied on education programs and the control of prostitution to limit men's contact with women who could potentially infect them.[4] Moreover, the legacy of World War I, specifically families' fears that VD and the immorality that they believed plagued military training would corrupt their sons, shaped the government's plan to overcome VD in the 1940s.[5] The military needed chaste, attractive women both to raise servicemen's spirits inside chaperoned clubs and to keep them away from "diseased" women.[6]

The USO recruited reputable, young, usually middle-class women and advertised their pure sexual image because it relied on them to domesticate servicemen and prepare them to return to their homes and to family life. The state's appeal for USO junior hostesses to dance and talk with lonely servicemen was a request for a sexual service. The USO did not expect or want these women to have sex with servicemen. It required hostesses, rather, to use their bodies to tantalize and comfort men with common physical contact. The USO, the military, and the federal government designated this physical contact to be a substitute for sexual intercourse. Any substitute, no matter how wholesome, for that form of sexual activity must also be inherently sexual, otherwise it would not begin to qualify as a viable substitute. Moreover, a young woman's very identity as a junior hostess depended on the status of her sexual reputation, and this in itself made her service to the USO sexual. If socializing with servicemen inside USO clubs had nothing to do with sexuality, then any woman could have done it, not just "good girls." Many parents, along with the USO, placed a high value on women's sexual reputations and did not want USO service to sully their daughters' respectability. By recasting American servicemen who came from diverse economic, regional, and ethnic backgrounds as good neighborhood boys who were away from home serving their country, the USO helped to make sexually respectable young women's contact with them at chaperoned events less threatening. Chaperoning also reflected anxiety regarding the intentions of those so-called good boys. Junior hostesses, at the same time, responded to the USO's appeal for their service out of a sense of patriotism and as a way to meet their own wartime goals of volunteerism and safe sexual expression.

IN CERTAIN CASES, discourses about sexuality work to control men and women, yet counter-discourses simultaneously offer space for resistance to that control. By "naming" or "defining" a problem, reformers and the state can control the population in question.[7] ASHA was a central institution that "named" women who had sex with soldiers as the "problem" at base in VD control during World War II, while the USO constructed its junior hostesses as the "good women" capable of distracting servicemen from the bad. By associating titles, including "prostitute," "amateur," "delinquent," and in the case of the USO, "girl next door," to women's actions or supposed actions, these dominant organizations could manipulate the wartime discourse on female sexuality as well as regulate the behavior of all women.

ASHA worked in tandem with the USO to eliminate prostitution around service camps and to bolster recreational alternatives for servicemen. Predominantly native-born white Americans led ASHA, an influential organization that came into existence during the Progressive era. ASHA spearheaded local, state, and national publicity campaigns to encourage men and women to keep sex within marriage and to preserve the nuclear family in order to eradicate VD.[8] ASHA conducted research and produced statistics about VD and prostitution near military areas for the Social Protection Division of the OCWS in the

1940s. ASHA's activities and the information it gave to the government were not publicized.[9] In 1941, the coordinator of Health, Welfare, and Related Defense Activities requested $50,000 from the USO to pay ASHA for this investigative work.[10] The USO, via John D. Rockefeller Jr., asked the Markle Foundation for a grant to fulfill the ASHA request, but the Markle foundation did not have the funds to spare.[11] Nevertheless, in 1948, Lindsley Kimball concluded that since the USO "financed a large part of the War Service of the American Social Hygiene Association," ASHA should be invited to join in the creation of any new USO-type agency.[12] The connection between ASHA, the federal government, and the USO is significant because it reveals the efforts of all three organizations to exert control over men's and women's sexual choices during the war. The USO's patriotic goal to offer "wholesome" recreation to servicemen makes only tacit connections to VD and, by implication, sexual control. The organization's financial connections to ASHA, however, reveal VD control as a key USO goal.

ASHA's need to control prostitution stemmed from its belief that women's bodies were sites of contagion. According to historian Mary Spongberg, "The idea that women were the source of VD draws on a long tradition of western thought in which women were seen as abnormal, deformed or diseased."[13] During World War I, reformers and the military asserted that 60 to 75 percent of prostitutes had some form of VD.[14] In 1939, ASHA's associate director of legal and protective measures, Bascom Johnson, argued that the licensing of prostitutes to control the spread of VD was ineffective because when women discovered that they were carriers of VD, they relocated and continued in the same occupation.[15] According to ASHA, there could not "possibly be such a thing as a safe prostitute."[16] By linking prostitutes to VD during a time of national crisis, reformers, police, and state and federal governments justified the surveillance of women's bodies.[17]

In the early stages of its anti-VD campaign, ASHA, along with the federal government and local police, located the source of the "problem" in the commercial prostitute. Prostitution is difficult to define, because it could mean "a sexual relationship or a work contract, a private act or public commerce."[18] ASHA took this definition a step further when it said that prostitution was the "indiscriminate *receiving* [their emphasis] as well as the giving of the body for sexual intercourse."[19] This definition included all women and men who engaged in sex outside marriage. As "modern" women in command of their bodies, "prostitutes" spurned the notion that women should remain chaste outside the realm of marriage. During World War II, the state took extra steps to criminalize the sexual activities of this highly visible group of women. The federal government passed the May Act in July 1941 making "vice activities near military institutions a federal offense."[20]

Designed to "supplement" the power of local authorities, the May Act constituted a drastic increase in the power of the federal government to police sex work.[21] Elliot Ness, director of the Social Protection Division, gathered "together police chiefs, mayors and city managers to do their part in the campaign against prostitution." "Their part" included the arrest, compulsory pelvic examination, and mandatory treatment of women infected with VD.[22] Although the Social Protection Division superseded the powers of local governments by officially invoking the May Act only twice, its corollary power was much greater. It prodded local authorities to crack down on sex for hire,[23] thus limiting the access of "prostitutes" to public space and curtailing their sexual and economic autonomy.

After securing extensive legal measures to repress "commercial" prostitution with the May Act, the military and ASHA expanded their attack on the VD "problem," and their assault on women's sexual freedom, when they identified "promiscuous" girls as the greatest threat to the health of male soldiers. The army and the navy, along with ASHA, turned their energies toward the elimination of "amateur" prostitutes, also referred to as "victory girls," "khaki-wackies," "chippies," "pickups," and "clandestine prostitutes." The military warned soldiers against these women, who "look[ed] so nice" yet almost certainly harbored VD.[24] According to historian Allan Brandt, "A federal committee noted . . . she is more dangerous to the community than a mad dog. Rabies can be recognized. Gonorrhea and syphilis ordinarily cannot."[25] Furthermore, an ASHA editorial contended that "clandestine prostitutes' . . . activities may definitely be classed as sabotage [as they kept] servicemen and industrial workers out of the ranks."[26] By constructing the "promiscuous" girl as a threat to "manpower," ASHA and the federal government brought her under the rubric of prostitute. These institutions manipulated a powerful wartime discourse that included loaded terms such as "sabotage" and "treason" to further construct women's sexual activity outside the marital sphere as "immoral."[27] When deployed, this discourse limited women's mobility, yet it did not eliminate their resistance to an unequal sexual-economic system that allowed men greater sexual liberty than women.

Like ASHA, USO member agencies such as the YMCA and the Salvation Army wanted to confine sex to marriage and to control what they perceived to be easily corruptible young men and women. For example, the National Catholic Community Service (NCCS) instructed servicemen that sexual intercourse outside marriage was a mortal sin. USO volunteers searched for sexually respectable women to serve as junior hostesses because they believed that young men had "some need, whether [they] recognize[d] it or not, for the companionship of good women." The NCCS maintained that men policed their own behavior and morals when in the presence of good women, arguing that such "women [had] a refining influence on [men]."[28] According to historian Nancy Bristow, this sentiment was also prevalent during World War I when reformers who provided recreation for servicemen through the Commission on Training Camp Activities argued that women were men's "moral guardians."[29] In 1943, the Salvation Army proudly proclaimed that men who visited their clubs were "clean cut Americans, the sort who attend[ed] church or the [Salvation] Army back home, did little or no devil-raising, the boys who now gravitate naturally to the wholesome environment of our USO clubs."[30] This portrait of USO clientele confirms that the organization believed good girls attracted and helped to preserve the morality of good boys. Members of ASHA held the opinion that "to uphold the morale of our armed forces, servicemen must be allowed to meet girls from time to time." This *Journal of Social Hygiene* article went on to say that it did not condone or encourage "illicit sex relations" during these morale-enhancing encounters.[31] In an article titled "Building Morale in the U.S. Army and Navy," the armed services posited that athletics, church picnics, and civilian socials were the keys to a "healthy" army. To sustain "the best of our young manhood," it was necessary to find pure women who would do the essential ego-boosting work for the armed forces yet who would say "no" to sex.[32] These women stood both in proximity and in contrast to so-called bad girls identified as prostitutes and pickups.

The USO fashioned itself as the chief source of wholesome sexual companionship for servicemen in the United States. Charles Taft, assistant coordinator of health and welfare at the OCWS, argued that servicemen "want[ed] social contacts with attractive girls and older people like their parents at home," and they could find these at local USO clubs operated by YMCAS and YWCAS.[33] Army morale officers divided soldiers into three groups when they addressed the problem of VD in 1941. They concluded that 15 percent of all soldiers would have nonmarital sex despite the consequences, 15 percent would never have nonmarital sex, and the "majority of 70% [would] expose themselves only under special circumstances, and usually not at all when more wholesome feminine companionship [was] available. For them, a major element of disease control [was] the provision of such wholesome and normal feminine contact through organized recreational opportunity."[34] The function of the "good girl," the junior hostess, was a sexual one. She was supposed to use her beauty and charm to entice male soldiers and sailors away from brothels and into policed USO spaces. There, a man could get close enough to a hostess to smell her perfume or her hair while he held her in his arms on the dance floor. The act of dancing itself required physical contact between partners, whether it was a slow waltz or a fast jitterbug. Junior hostesses committed their bodies, not just their conversational skills and time, to the USO and ultimately to the state.

The military publicly agreed with the USO's and ASHA's moral stance on nonmarital sex but was chiefly concerned with the health of its servicemen. It launched and maintained an aggressive sex-education program that warned soldiers about the risks of having indiscriminate sex with women, while it staffed chemical prophylaxis stations on army posts, naval bases, and in immediate civilian areas in the event that servicemen did not heed these warnings.[35] A "Navy Venereal Disease Contact Investigation" revealed that within a three-month period in 1944, 16,216 white and 7,204 black sailors in the United States had sexual contacts, and 14.1 percent of white sailors and 10.7 percent of black sailors contracted VD as a result. According to the study, sailors overwhelmingly named "pickups" as the women with whom they had sex.[36] A larger army survey revealed that only 25 percent of servicemen overseas abstained from sex, leaving the other 75 percent to spread and contract VD.[37] In the words of one captain in the medical corps of the U.S. Navy, "Armies and navies use men . . . of the very essence of masculinity. . . . [They] are sexually aggressive. . . . They must be if they are going to be good soldiers and sailors. . . . We can only hope to control and educate."[38] In this explicit connection between manhood, sex, and fighting, the navy outlined its plan to control male sexuality without subverting it.

The central role that heterosexual activity and imagery played in the production of servicemen's attitudes toward women during the war cannot be overstated. According to historian John Costello, the connections between combat, sex, and death were unmistakable in U.S. servicemen's behavior overseas. The military and GI's themselves saturated army and navy life with sexually suggestive music, films, and of course, pinups.[39] *Yank*, an army publication, issued seminude photographs of stars like Rita Hayworth and other actresses in bathing suits.[40] *Yank* printed one cartoon of harried male designers attempting to create a bathing suit amid wartime shortages of fabric by "using as little material as possible . . . and still covering the places that have to be covered." The accompanying drawing shows a designer measuring a buxom, curvy woman wearing a skimpy, two-piece swimsuit.[41] On the same page, one cartoon depicts a woman in her underwear who has just lost her dress to a fast jitterbug with a soldier, and another depicts five women in a row, each with a shorter dress, in response to investigations that American women were opting for less formal, knee-length dresses at dances. The cartoon speculates what would happen if dresses became "more informal as the war [went] on."[42] The army publishers of *Yank* laced their issues with sexually suggestive photos and cartoons of scantily clad women to entertain and distract GI's from boredom just as the USO hoped to do with more subtle imagery.

Cartoons and pinups printed in *Yank* appear to be fairly harmless, albeit sexist, attempts at humor and consolation. Indeed, servicemen's contacts with women were often limited to encounters with emotionally distant prostitutes and inanimate pinup girls. Historian Robert Westbrook acknowledges the sexualized aspect of pinups of female film stars but contends that pinups mainly were wholesome in nature. To servicemen, pinups represented their female relatives at home.[43] Not everyone agreed with this characterization. For example, in 1943 Postmaster General Frank C. Walker launched a campaign to prevent *Esquire* from using the mails.[44] *Esquire* was popular among servicemen because it contained Alberto Vargas's illustrations of provocative pinup girls. As a battle between Walker and *Esquire* raged in the courts, the media expected average American women to respond to men's perceptions of pinups by embodying the sexy yet pure "girl next door" image.[45] USO hostesses and other young women sent posed photos of themselves to their boyfriends in the military, adding support to Westbrook's contention that women participated in the manifestation of themselves as objects worthy of men's desire and protection.[46] The Philadelphia Stage Door Canteen (SDC) supported this practice by holding a "pinup girl" contest and then distributed 25,000 postcards of the winner's photo to servicemen in area hospitals and at the SDC.[47] The USO had already screened these hostesses and deemed them appropriate companions for servicemen and representatives of American womanhood. As a result, the USO could reproduce and distribute the winner's image without regret because the screening process had proven that her sexuality was of the wholesome sort. Despite the wholesome image of pinups, it is necessary to refocus on their sexualized side, because it is dangerous to examine pinup girls separate from the military's view on sexuality.

The totality of servicemen's sexual influences informed the multiple ways in which the military understood and used both virtual and real women. The larger military culture of female objectification and misogyny played a role in this process. In a sharp analysis of this culture, Susan Gubar asserts that Allied literature and propaganda portrayed women as deceitful wives, contaminated prostitutes, and little else.[48] For example, a U.S. War Department pamphlet advised servicemen to avoid "prostitutes, Pick-Ups, Push-Overs and Easy Women." The pamphlet cautioned, "You are badly mistaken if you think you can tell whether or not a girl has a VD by her looks or her clothes or by listening to her story. You can't." Furthermore, servicemen needed to be wary of women who feigned love and simply wanted to marry them in order to collect "a nice fat Government Allotment check."[49] By characterizing these wartime women as diseased, money-grubbing whores, the War Department assumed servicemen were likely dupes who must suspect all women's motives and actions.

In its efforts to preclude homosexual activity, the military tacitly allowed soldiers to have sex with certain classes of foreign women as well as with women who appeared sexually available on the home front.[50] Whiteness and identification with middle-class status acted as markers for respectable womanhood in the view of the military, just as they did for the USO. According to historians David Farber and Beth Bailey, male soldiers and sailors stationed in Hawaii waited in exceptionally long lines to spend a few minutes having sex with female prostitutes. As a transition point, Hawaii hosted young men who were often on their way to or from the battlefront.[51] Their use of prostitutes for sex was a symptom of both their heightened sense of mortality and the heterosexually aggressive military culture to which they belonged.[52] For example, Private First Class Robert Williams was eighteen when the government drafted him in 1943, and he never left the mainland throughout his wartime service. He "got VD from a local girl," however, while he was stationed in Tennessee. In his view the army "almost expected" that men would get it. The military placed Williams "on restriction" for another case of VD he contracted in Alabama, but his peers never stigmatized him for his illness or sexual behavior.[53] The pervasive sexual double standard that allowed men to have sex with women outside marriage but condemned women for the same behavior made it possible for Williams to shrug off his bouts of VD. Having sex with "local girls" was simply a part of this man's routine that united him with his fellow soldiers. This military culture attempted to solidify a good girl/bad girl dichotomy.

The military chose to control its VD problem by condemning the women with whom men like Williams had sex. Officers encouraged men to report women who might have given them VD, and then local police sought out and sometimes detained those women for VD examinations.[54] A sex education pamphlet for soldiers warns, "It's best to GIVE her Name!" regardless of her social status. The "girl who infects" the soldier might be a "barfly who is interested in you just for your money" or a "nice girl, a bit too promiscuous perhaps, and from a respectable family."[55] Advice such as this drew all women, even "nice girls," into a net of suspicion regarding their sexual character[56] and necessitated the USO's concerted effort to strengthen its hostesses' reputations. In any case, a soldier would "be doing her and society a great favor in having the Health Department advise and treat her, without jeopardizing her socia [sic] position."[57] This pamphlet reinforced the importance of containing VD but masks the damage that a visit or a phone call from the health department could do to a young woman's reputation if news of such contact spread to family or friends.

The military wanted servicemen to report any woman who gave them VD, but the police acted on class assumptions about sexual respectability when they looked for and arrested supposedly infected women. Women in danger of being labeled "pickups" were usually those who visited bars, walked near army posts after dark, or simply occupied public space unescorted by a man.[58] Historian Marilyn Hegarty argues that certain occupations open to working-class women were "marked employment." For example, police required some waitresses to carry their health cards, which proved that they did not have a VD.[59] Health departments distributed cards that listed the carrier's name, "age, address, place of employment and hours of work." Police kept copies of health cards and used them to locate women "named as contact sources of VD."[60] The repercussions were fierce for women who authorities believed passed VD to servicemen, and consequences could include arrest, physical examination, and "quarantine."[61] These practices underscored the importance of men's health and supported the fallacy that VD only moved from women to men.

As "good girls," USO hostesses were to perform virtuous sexual services in a public, chaperoned setting. A hostess's ability to provide these services to her country depended in part on her own physicality and sexual reputation. The military and the USO expected her to use her feminine body to entertain a serviceman but never to use that same body to have sexual intercourse with him. According to the USO, a junior hostess's main goal was to "render the important service of giving our soldiers a happy, healthy bit of recreation during their off duty hours."[62] Junior hostesses accomplished this by dancing, playing board games, and chatting with soldiers and sailors under senior hostesses' supervision. USO volunteers believed it was possible for women to lift the spirits of servicemen and this would strengthen their ability to fight for their country in battle. When it came to the contributions of junior hostesses, this morale work was a tame form of sex work. By volunteering for the USO, junior hostesses became public women because they completed their war work outside their homes. The USO monitored their services to make a clear distinction between hostesses, pickups, and prostitutes, the other public women with whom servicemen associated.

Women in the United States wrestled with cultural assumptions about sexual behavior and respectability decades before World War II, but these issues were particularly weighty for middle-class women.[63] In the first half of the twentieth century the Victorian belief that women were "sexless" and devoid of passion was giving way to an ideal that held that even "good" women could enjoy sex within marriage. This modern sexual discourse increased women's power within marriage to enjoy sex for pleasure, not just reproductive purposes, at the same time that it cast suspicion on all single women's sexual behavior.[64] In the 1910s and 1920s, advice columnists encouraged middle-class parents to allow their daughters to spend time with boys to encourage heterosexuality. It was necessary, nevertheless, for parents to keep a close eye on their daughters so that they did not go too far in expressing their sexual desires.[65]

Columnists and experts accepted the idea that women enjoyed sexual pleasure, but mainstream society condemned any woman who crossed the line from necking and petting with "steadies" to having sexual intercourse with men whom they were not going to marry.[66] This contradiction was a pervasive aspect of the wartime sexual order. For example, a New Jersey Health Department pamphlet outlined the emotional costs of nonmarital sex for women. They included "a loss of self-respect, a sense of guilt and shame, the breaking off of friendships with persons of higher standards, the sorrow of parents, and the sordid gossip of scandal mongers."[67] The USO made every effort to reign in the chaos by creating a "good girl" whom authorities and observers could distinguish from overly sexual "victory girls." The former performed a patriotic sexual service inside USO clubs, while the latter engaged in the false patriotic act of having sex with servicemen and potentially infecting them with VD.

The Concord Dance Hostess Committee (CDHC) was unique in that young women managed it, but the junior hostesses in charge usually relied on the same class- and race-based notions of sexual respectability that senior hostesses used in other clubs when selecting juniors. The CDHC supplied hostesses to dance with servicemen at USO clubs throughout the Boston area. The organization maintained a "high standard of conduct" and characterized its dances as "good clean fun." In a speech to potential donors a CDHC representative maintained, "The girls have been most cooperative in upholding our standards and good name." The club's director, Miss Julie Anne Foote, enlisted the help of two older, married women outside the organization to investigate the "age and character" of potential members. Club members labeled these women "guardians of our morals" and added, "It is to them that we report the case of any girl who misbehaves while attending functions sponsored by the committee."[68] In one instance one of these ladies, Laura P. Servais of West Concord, asked several community members about a young woman who hoped to join the CDHC. Servais reported to the director, "In each instance [I] got the same answer. Therefore I do not feel that I can recommend her — certainly not without reservations, and I think we do not want to have that responsibility."[69] Servais was discreet in her letter and did not specify exactly what information she received about the young woman that made her an inappropriate candidate for the Concord club. The club tried to recruit members from a variety of social and economic backgrounds. In other letters, investigators warmly endorsed other young women for membership. For example, Eleanor Greenman recommended two young teachers from West Acton to the Concord Club. She attested that they were "fine teachers" who worked for her husband.[70] With the emphasis that the CDHC placed upon its "popularity," it is possible that it excluded the young woman Servais investigated because she had a sexual reputation that threatened the public image of the CDHC. This story illustrates that a discourse of reputations existed and affected women's social and service opportunities.

Laura Servais understood the importance of her role as a CDHC investigator of young women's backgrounds. Upon completing another investigation, she reluctantly recommended an eighteen-year-old woman to the club. Servais did "not turn this name in with as much enthusiasm that she [would] be an addition to the group as I could wish." Once again Servais did not specify the source of her displeasure with the candidate. What is significant in this letter is the seriousness with which Servais approached her task. For instance, she admitted that "if [the candidate] abides by the rules, I suppose that is all we can ask, and we must be absolutely fair with each one."[71] Servais decided to give this young woman a chance to prove herself as a CDHC member rather than to exclude her based on inadequate evidence. Her decision to be "fair" to all applicants reveals that the CDHC did not want to exclude women haphazardly, but it took care to maintain its positive reputation. In the end, the CDHC's reliance on a politics of reputation made fairness elusive.

According to the USO, junior hostesses should not use service clubs as places to hunt for dates and marriage partners, yet servicemen ought to satisfy their need for female companionship within the confines of USO spaces. For instance, the *Hints for Hostesses* pamphlet instructed junior hostesses to "be a *substitute* for [soldiers' and sailors'] *friends* at *home*, not a 'female wolf'" [emphasis in original].[72] Apparently VD conditions outside the clubs were hostile enough for the military and the USO to risk unleashing the "female wolf" on innocent servicemen. In the case of the USO, gendered contradictions about women abound. Women had the capacity to be both refining influences and predators against whom wary soldiers should guard themselves. Respectable junior hostesses, nevertheless, helped to create a tame heterosexual environment inside USO clubs. For men, this had the potential somewhat to normalize military life by exposing them to female companionship that reminded them of their civilian life.

To ensure the virtuous atmosphere of the canteen and to protect its young volunteers, clubs developed rules for junior hostesses. In many cases, the rules did not allow women to date soldiers.[73] Significantly, it was the responsibility of the junior hostess to say "no" politely to men who pursued her for dates or who asked for her phone number despite their knowledge of the rules. The USO placed the responsibility for curtailing such contact on the women in question and assumed that men would listen to the women. This approach excused men from any accountability for pursuing hostesses sexually when it was against club rules. For example, the national USO discouraged junior hostesses from dating male soldiers and advised them to "understand this, and make it easy for the boys."[74] At a meeting about local servicemen's recreational needs, Lieutenant Russell Becktell, chaplain in Bedford, Massachusetts, argued, "A soldier won't go any further than a girl permits."[75] This point of view reinforced the notion that all wartime sex was consensual and that women were responsible for men's sexual behavior. The USO had a habit of treating soldiers and sailors like children in need of motherly guidance. From its point of view, the USO expected junior hostesses to uphold the morals of the canteen by giving the boys an obligatory spin around the dance floor and then gently dousing their hopes when they asked for something extra. In a clear example of the connections between USO service and sexuality, the Phila-delphia SDC hosted a game of spin the bottle between servicemen and host-esses at the same time that it did not allow young women to leave the premises with servicemen.[76] The USO sent its hostesses mixed messages to tempt ser-vicemen with their sexuality but to behave like sisters.

The appearance more than the actuality of female sexual respectability was paramount to the status of local USO clubs as "wholesome" environments for servicemen. Clubs that did not explicitly forbid junior hostesses from dating clearly prohibited them from leaving club premises with male soldiers and sailors. The Baltimore YMCA reminded its Volunteer Hostess Club members on numerous occasions to "return to [their homes] immediately after each dance."[77] The Shirley, Massachusetts, club went so far as to note on hostesses' membership cards, which they carried with them at all times, that hostesses should never use the exit at the back of the building. This rule specified, "The cement walk and stairs in front of the building is as far as you are permitted to go" during a dance.[78]

The USO asked junior hostesses to make servicemen feel good by providing feminine companionship, but they were not supposed to make them feel too good by providing explicit sexual contact. Rules regarding junior hostesses in Massachusetts reminded the young women to dance with any soldier who asked and stipulated that "girls may not dance together or participate in activities unless with Service men." The rules asked junior hostesses to pre-serve the innocence of their interactions with servicemen by specifying that "no side-line petting" was allowed. The club argued that "it [was] out of place and [made] others feel uncomfortable."[79] In this case, the USO assumed that the girls they carefully selected and chaperoned were also sexually willing and, in some cases, even sexually aggressive. This assumption fits, given the sur-rounding sexual climate in which child-rearing manuals advised parents to allow their daughters to pursue heterosexual relationships.[80] USO volunteers were aware that junior hostesses had probably experimented sexually with the opposite sex before they volunteered for USO service, but it was presumed that they had not engaged in intercourse, because respectable members of the community had vouched for their honorable reputations.

USO volunteers knew that men tempted junior hostesses to date them, but the organization established penalties for breaking the no-dating rule, including dismissal from the USO. A Chicago USO club reminded hostesses that "slipping out on a private date [meant] slipping out of the USO forever." Junior hostesses ought to "leave the club in a group with [their] chaperone. (and she won't be wearing sailor pants!)." According to USO advice, the fictional "Sallie Smyth" successfully resisted the lure of the uniform when she refused the request of "a handsome thing with wings [who] whispered in her ear, 'Let's sneak out of this mob and go some place cozy and quiet.'" Sallie was "'awfully sorry.' (and *was* too)."[81] This cautionary tale reveals that the USO understood the dilemma women faced when attractive men in uniform asked for their intimate attention, but many clubs forbade dating in order to maintain the USO's image of sexual respectability. Some servicemen were persistent in their desire to spend private moments with junior hostesses. As a "twenty-one year old, lonesome for company," Private First Class John S. Kelly Sr. and his friends asked junior hostesses for dates because "we were normal males. . . . That's what we were born for." Hostesses declined Kelly's requests by saying, "I won't be back here [at the USO] if I date." Senior hostesses made sure that servicemen "did not take girls into a corner or take them out" of the building.[82] The USO fought a losing battle that it was not entirely devoted to winning, to prevent men and women from dating on their own time.

Senior hostesses tried diligently to keep track of junior hostesses during dances, but they simply could not monitor their behavior after dances. Hostess Alice Roby believed that the USO did not ban dating simply to restrict her freedom. She interpreted the rules as "protection . . . because then we could use that as an excuse . . . if we didn't want to go out, but if we wanted to go out there were always ways to get out." Her definition of protection was different from that of the USO, which wanted to prevent her private encounters with male soldiers, not allow her to select the men with whom she would have them. Alice often made plans to meet men outside the USO club after dances.[83] She recalled, "Most of the young men were quite satisfied to have an evening of fun of various kinds so we did not have to bother about STD's."[84] She added, "I am sure that some of the girls may have had some problems [with the men], but I was always very particular with who I went out with." For

Alice, the USO's image of sexual respectability was not a constraint, and neither were the rules that helped to support that image. She used the club to meet and spend time with servicemen whom she perceived to be "gentlemen."[85] Alice and others like her did not flout the rules of the club by leaving with servicemen, and as a group, USO hostesses did not gain a reputation for loose sexual behavior. Junior hostesses' choices to date servicemen indicate that their actual behavior with men was more important to them than strict conformity to USO rules. The rules, whether or not junior hostesses obeyed them, acted as a type of shield of respectability for the organization and its young volunteers.

Junior hostesses actively participated in upholding the reputation of USO clubs. The public nature of the USO provided a context in which young women policed one another's activities more so than in typical dating situations. Audrey Armstrong remembered a particularly "bad situation" when she and the other Burbank junior hostesses noticed that one girl left the USO club on several occasions with different servicemen. This young woman was "engaged to a local boy" who was overseas, and his location "made things even worse." It was apparent to Audrey that the young woman was sexually unfaithful to her fiancé while he was defending his country. Audrey and her friends approved when senior hostesses, led by Audrey's mother, ejected the hostess from the USO club.[86] This action helped to preserve the reputation of all Burbank hostesses and made it clear to them that neither dallying with servicemen nor cheating on them was suitable behavior for junior hostesses.

The USO manufactured and monitored a wholesome environment. This environment, in effect, provided junior hostesses with a degree of safety and freedom to make dates with servicemen. Hostesses could expect those servicemen to behave on dates and not pressure them to have sex. In some towns it was an open secret that hostesses dated servicemen at the same time that they refrained from leaving USO clubs with them. The USO attracted "mannerly and gentlemanly" men, according to hostess Rosemary Anderson, and she felt comfortable dating them outside the USO.[87] Servicemen were aware that USO hostesses were probably not going to have sex with them on a date. For example, Private First Class Robert Williams attended a USO dance at the Gunner Hotel while stationed in San Antonio, Texas. He recalled that "mothers [were] stationed at the elevators to keep girls inside." Williams and his friends thought that this USO dance, like most others, was "too restricted." He declared, "Most men were mavericks so they went to 'The Cave' to meet local girls."[88] These men did not want chaperones to limit their contact with women, so they went to bars, exactly where the USO and the military hoped they would not go. Servicemen had a range of entertainment options and could tailor their behavior to fit differing norms and needs. Their choices enforced the notion that some women were available for sex and others were not.

Those few senior hostesses who openly encouraged juniors to date servicemen usually hand-selected women with a high social status and fostered a club culture that resembled that of an elite sorority. This is not to say that junior hostesses enjoyed a sisterly bond with one another; rather, prominent community members bestowed the "honor" of club membership upon them. Vera Ruth Prentiss was the director of the Montgomery, Alabama, Girls Service Organization (GSO) that supplied junior hostesses for USO and army post dances. In devising the rules for the club, Prentiss specified that senior hostesses could make introductions between juniors and soldiers, and "they can make on [sic] dates with permission of the hostess."[89] When asked in an article written for the public "how one person . . . control[led] the action of everybody on that dance floor," Prentiss responded, "That's easy . . . I just pick my girls." Prentiss selected members of the GSO based on her personal interactions with them and her knowledge of their backgrounds. She introduced them to servicemen after "the boy [was] O.K.d."[90] In this southern club, Prentiss and senior hostesses acted as matchmakers for certain white soldiers and white hostesses. The white Hattiesburg, Mississippi, club also sanctioned dating. The club's August 1942 narrative report included a mock letter from a soldier named "Sam" to his "Mom." According to Sam, "If I'm lucky enough to meet one of those GSO girls I've heard so much about, I may even enjoy a free date next week. . . . They tell me they have a date dance here every Sat. night." The Hattiesburg USO acted as a vehicle for servicemen to meet hostesses and serve as their dates outside as well as inside the club. Sam reassured Mom that "these people are *very* particular about the kind of girls who are at their affairs," lest she be worried that he was meeting the "wrong" kind of girl at the USO.[91] For these hostesses, an established image of sexual respectability opened the door for them to date servicemen with community support, not reprisal.

Many working-class and poor women outside the USO circle did not share in the security that an image of sexual respectability could afford. Organizations such as ASHA located the source of promiscuity in the occupations open to working-class and poor women. According to the Children's Aid Society of

Buffalo, New York, young girls who worked as "waitresses" or "hostesses in taverns" were likely to become prostitutes.[92] Similarly, the Women's Army Corps (WAC) based its recruiting strategies on the presumption that female sexual respectability corresponded with a middle-class upbringing.[93] When they needed to work, junior hostesses usually filled clerical jobs and could avoid nighttime or stigmatized work as a result. When they did work in the evenings, it was most often in USO clubs as entertainers or paid employees.[94] The unpaid nature of women's USO work inside alcohol-free clubs persuaded men to see junior hostesses as respectable, middle-class volunteers. The USO hoped that its reputation gave all of its hostesses a certain freedom from soldiers' unwanted sexual advances. The USO Bulletin publicized the experience of the "virtuous" junior hostess in a vignette titled, "Yes, It Really Happened": "A weary USO girl going home late after a long day in the Service Department. A seat in the subway, four U.S. sailors eyeing her prettiness, trying to catch her eye, making wisecracks, — the girl too tired to pay much attention. Suddenly a sailor spies on her coat the linked letters of a pin — USO. 'Holy Moses, guys, don't get her she works for the USO!' "[95] These sailors observed this woman's lack of male companionship in public at night to judge her sexual character. They then refrained from making a pass at her because she was affiliated with the USO. The outcome of the story would have been different with a barmaid or a textile worker in the subway seat instead of a likely middle-class junior hostess. This story demonstrates how the USO constructed, enforced, and relied on a clear division between good and bad girls.

The unique arrangement of the outdoor USO Labor Plaza in Philadelphia challenged the USO and authorities to make material distinctions between good and bad girls on a nightly basis. Unlike the SDC in Philadelphia, the Labor Plaza operated in a neighborhood unaffectionately dubbed the "Barbary Coast." This area contained bars and brothels and attracted both young female runaways and male soldiers and sailors.[96] The Labor Plaza was different from typical USO clubs in that it allowed servicemen to bring nonhostess dates into the Plaza with them. The confusion that resulted from this policy was exactly what the USO and its volunteers worked so hard to avoid in the majority of clubs. According to police reports, young women who were not approved USO hostesses congregated outside the Labor Plaza every night hoping to meet unaccompanied servicemen who would bring them inside the Plaza to enjoy its "bright lights and music." USO volunteers and police opposed this practice, because they did not want women who were strangers to the USO and to the men to gain entrance to the club and then to seek out additional male companions once inside its boundaries. Between July and October 1943, female police officers questioned 1,499 women who were lingering outside the Labor Plaza without a male companion. They escorted 20 of these women to City Hall for interrogations but did not arrest any of them.[97] Norma Carson, supervisor of policewomen, hoped her staff could limit female juvenile delinquency and the spread of VD to servicemen by identifying suspicious young women and instructing them to leave the Plaza district.[98] The fact that Carson and her crew questioned all women who did not wear a USO badge or who were not on the arm of a soldier from the moment they arrived in the Barbary Coast neighborhood indicates that ultimately it was not always possible for the USO or police to identify women and control them based on their appearance or affiliation with men. At the same time, however, Carson's tactics underscored how women's official connections to the USO could protect them from the state's doubts and intrusions regarding their sexual and social conduct.

Senior hostesses chaperoned contact between male soldiers and junior hostesses to ensure that both were upholding the standards of USO clubs and to assuage concerned parents' fears about threats to their daughters' safety and sexual reputations. Prior to 1920, heterosexual "courtship" took place in the parlor of a young girl's home, within close proximity to alert mothers. The emergence in the 1920s of a new "national culture," which included "dating," moved courtship out of the home and into the public domain.[99] The reformers who operated War Camp Community Service dances for troops during World War I chaperoned those dances to foster middle-class dance styles and to limit more sensual working-class styles of dance.[100] It is evident that during World War II the USO relied on the practice of parlor-style courtship when it stationed senior hostesses throughout public USO clubs to monitor physical contact between servicemen and junior hostesses. Servicemen's distance from home warranted this practice. In San Diego USO clubs, for example, "senior hostesses kept a close eye on the girls" to ensure their proper conduct and their security. Thus, "due to the influence of senior hostesses . . . discipline problems" were virtually nonexistent in San Diego USO clubs.[101] Although junior hostesses and male GI's technically were not dating inside the clubs, senior hostesses subjected them to regulations that inhibited sexual contact by limiting their privacy. This action was due, in part, to the fact that middle-class parents had previously taken great care in sequestering their daughters from working-class men, but the USO's need to entertain a "democratic" military disturbed this practice. In the early twentieth century, for example, mothers served as gatekeepers to their daughters' social lives by commanding the "calling system" that required a man to present himself to both the girl and her mother before they would welcome his advances.[102] By circumscribing private contact with male soldiers during World War II, senior hostesses curtailed but did not eliminate the possibility for junior hostesses to damage their reputations or offend their parents by dating across class, community, religious, and ethnic lines.

Junior hostesses' parents, on the whole, supported the USO and believed that the presence of chaperones guaranteed a safe atmosphere for their daughters. Peggy Campbell's father refused to give his daughter permission to join the WAC because he did not approve of the "environment" that Peggy would be in as a Wac. He believed that "hanky-panky" took place between servicemen and female soldiers. He enthusiastically, nonetheless, approved of her attendance at weekly USO dances in Birmingham, Alabama.[103] Historian Leisa Meyer contends that the WAC created a new category of "military woman" that competed with archetypal "bad" women such as prostitutes and camp followers whom the public associated with a standing army. Furthermore, the public and the military bureaucracy perceived the addition of a "feminine" element to the military as a challenge to its established "masculine" structure and, ultimately, to male power.[104] Junior USO hostesses, on the other hand, fit neatly into a preestablished gender framework that constructed women as the objects of male protection. Even as senior hostesses protected junior hostesses and policed their contact with servicemen in a family setting, servicemen who left their own homes to serve in the military became the ultimate protectors of these women and the home front at large. Churches, schools, and employers cautioned young girls, moreover, to confine their contact with male soldiers to "properly organized channels" such as the USO to deflect suspicious glances and rumors about their sexual behavior.[105] When young women heeded this advice and volunteered for the USO, they placed themselves in a male purview yet did not tarnish their reputations. It is probable, moreover, that they enhanced their position as "good" marriageable girls, because their choice to volunteer was at once patriotic and suitably "feminine."

The USO marketed and benefited from junior hostesses' wholesome sexual image, but hostesses were partners, not pawns, in this endeavor. They

4.1. Betty Ward's original caption for this photo was "Wholesome Kids" at the Miami uso
(Betty Ward Collection in possession of Ward O'Connell)

★ ★ ★

supported middle-class notions of sexual respectability because a positive reputation was valuable to them. As historian Beth Bailey has argued, in the
1940s a white, middle-class woman's sexual reputation was her currency, her
ticket to marriage, children, and a stable life.[106] Audrey Armstrong grew up
alongside other future hostesses in Burbank and shared their values, believing
"we were all nice girls."[107] "Nice girls" did not have sex outside marriage.
Aileen Cooperman, a Chicago hostess, never considered having sex before
she got married because she did not want to disrespect her father's values.[108]
Alice Roby engaged in plenty of "necking" with boys whom she met at the uso
in Memphis, Tennessee, but always stopped short of having sex with them.
According to Alice, "nice girls didn't, period."[109] Toni Chapman lied about
her age to volunteer for the San Rafael, California, uso. She was only sixteen
at the time. Toni "thought it would be exciting to meet and dance with what
seemed to [her] to be men as compared to high school boys." She enjoyed
"kissing and hugging" particular servicemen while waiting for her bus, but
"like most girls then, [she] was terrified of becoming pregnant," so she did not
have sex with any of them.[110] Toni used the uso to meet men and engage in a

type of safe sexual expressiveness. She took advantage of the USO's obsession with appearances. Club rules camouflaged her sexual conduct with servicemen and helped her keep her sexual reputation intact.

Not all women who attended USO functions had flawless reputations, and the USO's standing in the community did not shield all hostesses from criticism. Marilyn Hegarty argues that conflicting messages from the media about healthy sexual service and prostitution put all women in danger of crossing the line from sexual respectability to "promiscuity."[111] The existence of chaperones and the vigilance with which the USO policed its hostesses, however, made accusations of sexual impropriety less of an issue for young women affiliated with the USO than for those who were not. These precautions, however, did not persuade everyone that junior hostesses' contact with servicemen was always respectable. The USO/YWCA in Phoenix, Arizona, employed Peggy Jane Peebler to organize activities for servicemen and to train and manage junior hostesses. The YWCA's goal was to meet the needs of young women who volunteered as hostesses. Peggy Jane approved of young women's need to socialize with boys and recognized that the war limited their opportunities to do so. She took offense when a local minister insinuated that her junior hostesses were "loose" sexually. She believed that the young women were all of good caliber, and it angered her whenever someone tried to cast "aspersions" on the girls. Peggy Jane declared that she "was not born yesterday" and knew that girls would date servicemen, and she did not condemn them for doing so. According to her, the USO provided a safe, respectable place for girls to meet servicemen.[112]

On rare occasions white and African American male soldiers and sailors named the USO as the site where they met women who later transmitted VD to them through a sexual encounter. These instances were few in comparison with the number of times men identified the most popular sites, such as bars and private homes. For example, a USO report reveals that in Norfolk, Virginia, at one point during the war 10 percent of infected white and 20 percent of infected African American servicemen claimed to have contracted VD from women whom they met at a USO club.[113] In various Social Protection Division reports, servicemen listed white USO dances as sites of VD encounters. One might wonder why such a negligible number of VD cases connected with the USO would be worth addressing. It is impossible to discern whether or not the servicemen were telling the truth about their sexual encounters or whether the women they were with were official USO hostesses. That said, it is not appropriate to discount reports such as these simply because the USO screened its hostesses and declared them to be a respectable lot. Junior hostesses were not saints, and some of them may indeed have had sex with servicemen outside marriage. Most importantly, these cases prove that junior hostesses were in as much danger as any other woman during the war of contracting VD from a fling with a serviceman. Sexual respectability was usually the primary concern for these women. When one added pregnancy and disease into the mix, hostesses' lives became just as complicated as those of "pickups."

For the USO's part, senior volunteers attempted to inform women about the dangers of catching VD from male soldiers and sailors. In 1943, Mrs. Maurice Moore advised senior hostesses to "tactfully and casually" tell junior hostesses that VD rates were increasing and they should listen to the radio to learn more.[114] Despite its great attempts to create an image of sexual respectability for its hostesses, the USO bureaucracy accepted that at least some of those young women were sexually involved or could become so with servicemen. In a rare candid moment, one hostess manual from the Fort Dix Community Service in Pointville, New Jersey, warned junior hostesses not to kiss servicemen because one "goodnight kiss" with a "clean" soldier could result in an embarrassing case of syphilis or gonorrhea.

> The risk and often tragic results for the girl are far too great for the momentary fun of kissing a strange soldier goodnight. Any girl who is willing enough and stupid enough to run this risk, knowing its dangers, must also be willing to pay the price of possibly contracting a serious social disease from a soldier she will probably never see again.
>
> Remember . . . the soldier who kisses you goodnight, after an evening's acquaintance, has no doubt kissed dozens of girls before you and will kiss dozens after you. No one blames the soldier. Everyone blames the girl, including the girl herself. *Is it worth it?*[115]

Just as the army warned servicemen to be wary of "clean" girls, this manual instructed its female charges that "clean" servicemen could harbor unseemly diseases. A junior hostess who disobeyed seniors' advice to restrict her contact with male sailors and soldiers to the USO club risked the great humiliation of contracting a social disease that would damage her reputation, not the serviceman's who gave it to her. Moreover, this passage cautioned the junior hostess that no matter what she said or did, the serviceman did not think the girl in question was special; rather, she was one of many with whom he had shared

4.2. "She May Look Clean — But," poster, ca. 1941–45
(courtesy of the National Library of Medicine/National Institutes of Health)

★ ★ ★

his affections. Junior hostesses, for their part, balanced USO rules and advice with their own desire for a pleasurable goodnight kiss.

The issue of VD was more of a problem for African American USO clubs than it was for white clubs. Lester B. Granger of the National Urban League criticized medical studies in the 1930s that measured the VD rates of blacks against those of whites and then concluded that African Americans had higher rates of the diseases. He argued that the studies would be less stereotypical and reveal more about the VD problem as a whole if they instead compared individuals who shared the same "income levels and living conditions."[116] Mixed-class black neighborhoods usually hosted USO clubs for African American servicemen, whereas middle-class sections of town operated USO clubs for white servicemen. This geographical difference likely accounted for the problems African American USO clubs encountered with VD. For example, the USO-YMCA for African American soldiers and sailors in Columbus, Georgia, struggled to keep black women identified as prostitutes out of its club. In a letter to Brigadier General William H. Hobson, E. E. Farley, the director of the USO, requested that the city create a unit of black policemen who could monitor the area around the USO. This was a poor neighborhood, and Farley believed "it would be an extremely dangerous thing to call [white] city policemen to chase colored women around in an area in which there are hundreds of colored soldiers concentrated." Farley opposed the racial implications of this prospect and most likely feared a race riot would ensue if white police attacked black women in the presence of black soldiers. Historian Daniel Kryder's findings substantiate Farley's fears. Kryder argues that white military police "were as likely to cause as to quell disturbances," because they were racist and the military did not provide them with proper instruction. As a result, military police "freely struck and harassed" African American soldiers.[117]

Since he could not call for the police, Farley was in a bind, because he did not want "these bad women" to pass "deadly" diseases to black soldiers. With the adoption of the good girl/bad girl dichotomy in his own language, Farley revealed his acceptance of class-based definitions of norms and deviance. He hoped that a black police officer familiar with the townspeople "could more easily differentiate between the respectable citizens and these undesirable women" than white police officers could.[118] Several black soldiers reported to Farley that the women with whom they had sex told them to keep their addresses confidential and "mention the USO" if authorities questioned them.[119] Whether or not these women fell under the contrived category of "prostitute" or "pickup," their decision to use the USO as a cover to continue meeting soldiers to conduct business or personal matters was a savvy one. The decision illuminates their own understanding of the USO's image of sexual respectability. For his part, Farley was concerned with the reputation of his USO club at the same time that he wanted to protect black servicemen from illness. He criticized the obvious lack of recreational facilities for black soldiers near Fort Benning and pointed out that servicemen gravitated to bars when the local USO could not accommodate their numbers. This was the main issue for Farley. He believed that the number of times servicemen mentioned black or white clubs as sources of VD encounters were negligible and were not "an indication of laxity or carelessness on the part of the USO personnel."[120] Farley probably tried to fill his clubs with pre-selected junior hostesses from the African American community but did not have the volunteer personnel to police the entrance and exits of his building at all times.

Most women could not rid themselves of vd if they caught it, and many single women found it difficult to acquire contraceptives during the war years. These factors dissuaded many women, but not all, from having premarital sex.[121] The numbers of white middle-class women who became pregnant outside marriage noticeably increased during World War II. For social workers in maternity homes, this was a marked change from their usual working-class and poor clientele.[122] Some junior hostesses found it difficult to control their sexual desires. Former hostess Toni Chapman recalled her limited knowledge about sex and pregnancy during the war years: "I wasn't even exactly sure how one became pregnant but I knew it had something to do with unmentionable parts of the body, which must be invisible at all times. I went to Catholic schools for the eight years of elementary school and I knew one wasn't even supposed to have a body. But curiosity and hormones put up a good fight."[123] In this passage, Toni cynically recounts the limited knowledge of reproduction that the Catholic Church imparted to her. She also resents the sense of discomfort and unease with which the church taught her to view her own body and its sexual function. Lack of knowledge about the body did not eliminate Toni's desire for sexual intimacy; instead, it promoted "curiosity" that could have led to a dangerous outcome had Toni not chosen to control her own sexual impulses.

Like Toni, former hostess Aileen Cooperman avoided sex before marriage. While she was living in a boardinghouse near the University of Illinois in Champaign, one young woman's experience with unwed pregnancy made a vivid impression on Aileen.

> I lived on the third floor, we had three floors, and there was this one girl from New York who, when we met, was very nice. We didn't think anything of it, but she always wore huge sweaters with a big letter on, a fraternity letter, and we didn't pay attention to it. She said she had her boyfriend, you know so, "OK." Well I think about two months into the semester on a Saturday night I was home, because my future husband was back in Chicago. He would come down every other weekend. This girl was in the room next door to me and I heard a lot of commotion in her room. The door was locked. I knocked on the door and I said, "What's

wrong, can I help you?" "No no, I'm fine go away, go away." OK, so I didn't pay attention.

There was a community bathroom, but only one commode in the bathroom. We had three sinks, and one commode and one tub, and one shower. So, we sort of made arrangements as to when we would go in and get ready. Well I went down, I guess to go to the bathroom and I see a commode full of blood. Well, I ran down and told the housemother. I said, "Something's wrong, somebody is ill and I don't know who it is!" So she ran up to see and we couldn't flush it. And she said, "Is she [the woman from New York] home?" I don't know whether she suspected or knew. And I said, "Yes, I heard some commotion, but she told me everything's OK." So we went back upstairs and knocked on the door and she did open the door 'cause she was laying in a pool of blood. Naturally we called the doctor and the ambulance. She had cut her own cord and flushed, tried to flush the baby down the commode. So when I saw that, I mean, I wouldn't go near a guy, except to dance with him, you know, it, it was too scary.

According to Aileen, after the ambulance took the woman to the hospital, she never returned to the house "and we never saw her again and we [didn't] even know what happened to her." (The University of Illinois expelled the young woman and the man who fathered her baby.) Aileen surmised, "That was a very traumatic experience for me and it certainly let me know that I should not get into trouble."[124] The consequences for women having sex with a man before marriage in the 1940s were at times severe and life changing. Gruesome stories such as this one, the desire to please one's parents by remaining a virgin until marriage, and personal or educational goals made many junior hostesses stay away from premarital intercourse.

Junior hostesses actively created and upheld their own sexually respectable images as they guarded against pregnancy and disease. Furthermore, these women used the USO to fulfill personal wartime agendas that included pleasure and volunteerism. They understood and negotiated the unclear territory between female promiscuity and respectability that authorities and the media created. Alice Roby used the USO to advance her social life and believed that as long as she and her date stayed "above the neck" during petting sessions, she was not breaking any sexual taboos. Alice did not engage in any behavior that she or her friends construed as "wild."[125] Most hostesses respected the authority of senior hostesses and embraced the idea that female chaperones brought decorum to the clubs. When she was a hostess in Miami, Florida, Helen Gosnell did not witness any "dissension among those attending the dances" and believed that "if there had been unacceptable behavior by anyone, hostess or serviceman, they would have been expelled and not allowed to come back. Senior hostesses were always present at the club to supervise the behavior."[126] Helen made a point to safeguard her own reputation by spending time with servicemen in the purview of USO senior hostesses. Historian Marianne Lovelace does not make room for junior hostesses' knowing support for the sexually respectable image of the USO. Lovelace posits that with the approval of the USO, "women accepted the burden of wartime responsibilities but continued to maintain the centrality of domesticity and relationships with men in their lives." With all of the new opportunities swirling around them, from industrial work to military service, most women during World War II chose to place their families ahead of all other commitments.[127] The fact that junior hostesses chose to support the war in a manner that did not break the boundaries of femininity or sexual appropriateness for women does not necessarily lead to the conclusion that the "overwhelming forces of traditional society"[128] rendered them senseless and unable to make their own choices. In fact, junior hostesses attended USO dances week after week because doing so made them happy and helped them to feel as though they were influencing the war effort.[129] Rather than interpret their service in limiting terms, we should widen our scope of analysis to see that junior hostesses completed gendered labor for the USO to gain personal satisfaction and reshaped the definition of the good girl in the process. USO service gave them as well as men a safe place to experiment with sexual behavior. As they accomplished this, they also supplied the wartime state with indispensable sexual services in the form of morale work.

WOMEN LIKE Audrey Armstrong, Alice Roby, and Peggy Campbell responded to the call of the USO. They provided a respite for servicemen and upheld a requisite image of sexual respectability for themselves and the USO in the process. Indeed, junior hostesses' respectability was enhanced by the USO as well as being a prerequisite to their affiliation with it. They tried to please male soldiers and sailors by offering them a form of sexual service. The USO marketed their services as benign, yet they were definitely sexual. They were rooted in the assumption that servicemen needed physical contact with "good" women

— to dance with them, to talk with them, and simply to be in their presence. At the same time, most junior hostesses benefited from the USO's positive image and derived pleasure and satisfaction from their service. Most of the young men from their communities were in the armed forces, and the so-called manly and attractive men on the scene were those in uniform. In a context where the government and the media found sexually promiscuous women suspicious, the USO afforded junior hostesses an opportunity to practice interacting socially and sexually with men without damaging their sexual reputations. Servicemen understood that the USO was a place where they could spend time with "good girls," and for the most part they respected the sexual boundaries hostesses set. Junior hostesses sometimes bent no-dating rules to match their desires to socialize with men, while minding the importance of the appearance of sexual respectability to themselves, their parents, and the USO. Hostesses carried these practices and values with them as they entered USO dance halls to socialize with servicemen.

★ ★ ★ ★ ★ ★ ★ **5** ★ ★ ★ ★ ★ ★ ★

Courtship and Competition in the USO Dance Hall

Hundreds of male soldiers and sailors sporting snappy uniforms and dozens of well-coiffed junior hostesses decorated in bright-colored dresses and lipstick packed uso dance halls on Saturday nights throughout the war. Cigarette smoke and the smell of hot coffee permeated the air while couples jitter-bugged across the dance floor.[1] High-heeled hostesses spun from one man to the next as each serviceman in the long stag line took his turn holding one of the anonymous women in his arms for a slow waltz or fox-trot. The big-band sounds of Glenn Miller and the Tommy Dorsey Orchestra enlivened the room. Servicemen and hostesses happily forgot the war for a little while as they moved to the music.

For some men and women, dancing served as a gateway to dating and romance. Junior hostess Phyllis Mayfield recalled that her favorite part of uso service was dancing with servicemen at Fort Leavenworth, Kansas. After all, "to the young single women the men in uniform were exciting and glamorous, like something from the movies." A soldier's or sailor's uniform provided a man with immediate respectability and made him deserving of compassion in the eyes of junior hostesses. Many women found men wearing those uniforms sexually appealing. Seventeen-year-old Phyllis met Second Lieutenant Larry Baldridge at one of these dances. The b-24 pilot had "blue eyes and blond hair, and a big engaging smile. . . . He had an outgoing personality and was enthusiastic and a lot of fun." Senior hostesses chaperoned uso dances to create a safe environment for junior hostesses and did not allow juniors to leave with servicemen, so Larry and Phyllis skirted club rules to meet privately. The couple started dating one evening after Larry met Phyllis's Girls Service Organization (gso) bus in Kansas City after a dance at the fort. Phyllis went on one or two dates with Larry before the army relocated him to Pampa, Texas, for training. The two wrote letters to each other for the next year, and he visited her when he was on leave. After he completed his training, Larry went to Kansas City and proposed to Phyllis. They moved to Springfield, Massachusetts, where Larry had just been stationed, and married at the Westover Field Chapel on 20 November 1943.[2]

USO dances such as the one where Phyllis met Larry supplied a venue for potential courtship between junior hostesses and servicemen, because the act of dancing was a physical one that included a sexual undercurrent. The USO deliberately created a ritualized set of heterosexual courtship practices to attract men and women to its clubs. Lack of available young men for women to meet outside the military and a pervasive culture that encouraged women to marry and raise children further established the foundation for USO romances. The USO complemented and in some cases consumed the social life of junior hostesses and servicemen in the war years. Though dancing in the USO environment led to heterosexual dating, deep conflict infused both of these companionate activities.

It was within dancing and dating that the unavoidable clash between the USO's need to entertain a democratic army and its practice to screen and select reputable junior hostesses occurred. The USO had established itself as a place for men to socialize with so-called respectable women, in an effort to keep servicemen from having improper sexual relationships with less respectable women. The USO, however, abandoned traditional selection practices that had kept objectionable men from socializing with sexually respectable women, because it wanted to welcome all servicemen regardless of class background and personal character into its clubs. The war, moreover, wrenched people from local and familiar contexts, thereby affording men and women the opportunity for new and sometimes disturbing kinds of relationships.[3] Uniforms concealed servicemen's class and regional backgrounds, and the USO dance hall afforded a high degree of anonymity for men moving from one community to another who wanted to bend the truth to attract junior hostesses' attention. These factors, coupled with the USO's persistent effort to create a heterosexual atmosphere in its clubs, inevitably led to both romance and conflict.

USO dances and dance forms such as the jitterbug posed a challenge to the mores and controls of "respectable" society. Dance as a racialized art form threatened the white middle-class control of senior hostesses. The jitterbug, in particular, had African American origins, and the mere performance of the dance in some USO clubs caused great discomfort for senior hostesses who worried how its racial connections might undermine white junior hostesses' sexual respectability. In addition to their racial connotations, dance forms illuminated generational conflict over morality when servicemen and junior hostesses performed them in an overtly sexualized manner.

Interracial dancing, in particular, highlighted the tension between the USO's goals of maintaining a racialized respectability for junior hostesses dependent upon racial segregation of dance halls and its equal handling of servicemen. The USO assumed that middle-class white women were inherently sexually respectable, and it relied on this premise to select hostesses. In black communities, sexual respectability was also associated with class status, but women could claim a higher status than their economic income allowed by holding themselves to "bourgeois standards of respectability and morality."[4] As long as the USO maintained segregation in its clubs, observers could not call the racialized respectability of white women into question. The USO attempted to maintain social order and social respectability along with democracy in a context where the presence of men of different races put democracy and social respectability at odds. In this setting, where the USO created faux dating situations, racism became more transparent. A white junior hostess's refusal to dance with a serviceman of color carried more racial meaning, because that dance was actually more than a turn around the dance floor. For the USO, dancing represented a heterosexual coupling, and in the case of interracial dancing, this sparked fears of miscegenation and gossip.

Junior hostesses sought heterosexual companionship and pleasure at USO dances within a wartime atmosphere that was at once anxious and exhilarating. They met men of various economic and social backgrounds at these dances and responded first to their uniforms and later to their upbringings. This was not a problem for couples like Phyllis Mayfield and Larry Baldridge but proved to be a significant obstacle to the long-term relationships of other couples.

DANCES PLAYED A central role in the youth culture of the first decades of the twentieth century, offering young singles public spots to socialize with members of the opposite sex.[5] The dance "craze" began prior to World War I, and later, college students made dancing to jazz and ragtime music the most common pastime on campus. College officials and dance chaperones viewed new dance forms such as the shimmy as morally suspect. Rather than condemn dancing as a whole, they attacked certain dance moves, thus forcing students to rein in their bodily movements to keep the administration at bay. Ultimately youth determined the character of the dance craze by "self-chaperoning" other students' behavior on the dance floor. The dances they engaged in avoided the "indecent" but privileged what students perceived to be risqué pleasurable moves over staid ones.[6] By 1941, the contentious relationship between respectability and dance had not disappeared. Senior hostesses attempted to shape young peoples' dance tastes by constructing so-called wholesome contact between servicemen and junior hostesses inside uso spaces, but they could not avert conflicts that arose between servicemen and juniors of different backgrounds.

uso clubs opened their dances to all servicemen, with the exception of some segregated clubs, because the organization wanted to prevent as many servicemen as possible from visiting bars and brothels. A traditional class-based screening process, therefore, did not apply to these events. This democratic treatment presented a quandary to middle-class senior hostesses because they could not prevent servicemen from diverse class and ethnic backgrounds from socializing with and perhaps dating junior hostesses, most of whom came from the middle class. Prior to the war, middle-class and elite hosts managed admittance to dances through invitations, social connections, or requirements that participants belong to more exclusive groups, such as fraternities and sororities.[7] Since this was not the case with the uso, servicemen, under cover of their uniform, were not clearly situated in regard to background or character. This anonymity, along with the sexually charged intimacy of dancing, caused great concern among senior hostesses. Junior hostesses' interactions with these servicemen were potentially intimate and more dangerous than dates made prior to the war because community and family networks could not reduce the chances and repercussions of "inappropriate" pairings. This danger remained an underlying tension for the organization as it offered a chaperoned dance space for young people.

Volunteer organizations such as the uso, along with the media, harnessed the popularity of big-band dancing in the 1940s by equating it with patriotic service. Servicemen on maneuvers in North Carolina attended dances sponsored by the Legion Auxiliary where Mrs. Leon Schlosberg chaperoned. Schlosberg asserted "that it [was] the duty of the young women to . . . show their patriotism by cooperating with us in making these dances a success."[8] While women presumably enjoyed themselves at the dances, it was their obligation, not only their choice, to entertain servicemen by dancing with them. Mrs. Maurice T. Moore, head of the National Women's Committee of the uso, announced, "Dancing [was] certainly tops as a uso activity. Without a doubt it [was] the most popular with the boys. They [couldn't] get enough of it."[9] uso clubs adopted creative themes to embellish their dances and make the evening more pleasant for participants. For example, senior hostesses at the Hattiesburg, Mississippi, uso club for white servicemen infused regional culture into one of its dances by distributing baskets "filled with snow white Dixie cotton sprinkled with red, white, and blue stars" to all of the junior hostesses in attendance.[10] Servicemen and hostesses who attended "Star Lit" dances on the ymca Roof Garden in Baltimore received coveted formal invitations to these special events.[11] Junior hostesses who flooded uso dance halls did their patriotic duty and indulged their desire to ballroom dance and jitterbug with servicemen.

Dancing was exhilarating and exciting, an intensely physical act that the media and military believed lifted the spirits of soldiers, sailors, and civilians alike. The Physical Fitness Division of the Office of Civilian Defense launched a Dance for Defense program to help male and female civilians alleviate the tensions generated by wartime. The organization Dancing Masters of America worked with the army and navy to teach soldiers and sailors "ballroom and square dancing."[12] Writers for *American Dancer* affirmed the benefits of "dancing parties in attractive halls with sweet, pretty dancing partners" for "our boys," arguing that the war would not displace dancing as "the mainstay of social intercourse."[13] This contention implied that ballroom dances were the correct venues for a heterosocial dating culture. *American Dancer* described a serviceman's experience with social dancing: "Though he may be a serial number to the Army he can and does express his personality on the dance floor. Even if he hasn't any conversation he can hum the words of the dance tune into his partner's ear and press her hand a little. This gives him a sense of power." The author seems to be referring to the power that comes from expressing one's identity, but implicit in this observation was the sexual intimacy of dance that made it possible for a man to "whisper in his partner's ear" and "press her hand a little." Moreover, this columnist confirmed the underlying sexual energy of uso dances when he asserted that "dancing also provid[ed] one of the soldier's few opportunities for falling pleasantly into the society of the fair sex."[14] For servicemen, "dancing [was] a refreshing flashback to the more gracious way of living which the soldier [was] fighting to preserve."[15] Holding a woman in his arms and swaying to music represented

5.1. Dancing at the Miami USO (Betty Ward Collection in possession of Ward O'Connell)

★ ★ ★

that "gracious way of living." Sexual and gendered subtleties infused inter-actions between hostesses and servicemen within the medium of dance.

Due in part to the sexual implications and physically liberating qualities of dance, men and women in some religious institutions did not share in the wide-spread enthusiasm for the form throughout the country. The USO's own Salvation Army club opposed dancing and offered servicemen card games and religious uplift in its USO clubs as an alternative.[16] Furthermore, some churches, particularly in the South, believed that dancing was sinful. This belief affected the Hattiesburg, Mississippi, USO's ability to retain junior hostesses. In 1946, the Methodist and Baptist churches in the Hattiesburg region led a spiritual revival that had "a very decided effect on the youth and adults" of the area. For example, junior hostesses who joined the "local Youth-for-Christ movement" decided to "give up dancing" and resigned from the USO-GSO, which was still operating at this time. The USO placed this female religious fervor in the context of the immediate postwar period, contending that those with increasing "religious obligations" were "making every effort to build a better post-war community for the men who are returning from military life." Despite this religious movement, the Hattiesburg USO continued to host dances for area servicemen.[17] The USO seemed reluctant to confront the young women and remind them of their patriotic obligations to entertain servicemen. With the war at an end, the Hattiesburg club likely believed it could lose a number of hostesses and still have enough dance partners for the decreasing number of military visitors to its club. Fortunately for the USO, an organization that depended on dances to draw servicemen to its clubs, the form retained its popularity throughout the war despite the objections of a minority of hostesses.

Senior hostesses often relied on "mixers" such as the "Paul Jones" to get USO dances started and to acquaint servicemen with local hostesses. The Baltimore YMCA Volunteer Hostess Club relied on its junior hostesses to show soldiers "from Pittsburgh and points north" how to begin this originally southern dance.[18] In New Jersey, hostesses also had to show some soldiers how to do the Paul Jones. Basically, to perform the dance, hostesses formed a circle facing servicemen, who formed an outer circle facing the women. Hostesses walked to the left, and men walked to their right. When the leader blew a whistle, the couples facing each other began to dance. The process was repeated as the music continued.[19] These types of mixers defused the sexual potential of dancing to some degree, because they relied on the constant rotation of partners.

Square dancing was popular in USO clubs "from Maine to California." Those who did not know how to promenade and do-si-do watched as others modeled the dances for them. By early evening most servicemen were swinging their partners on the dance floor.[20] The square dance "caller" made it possible for people who had never square-danced before to feel comfortable performing the sometimes complicated dances.[21] Former USO-YWCA employee Peggy Jane Peebler described how junior hostesses who dressed in western attire and square-danced organized the "Swinging Spurs" dance group. The Swinging Spurs earned praise for the Phoenix USO-YWCA because the upbeat square dancers lifted the morale of servicemen and made them "excited to dance."[22] Square dances and the Paul Jones eased the tension between men and women who had likely never before met, and they added to the relaxation and welcome feeling USO clubs tried to cultivate for servicemen.

Big-band music was the foundation of 1940s-style ballroom dancing, and it set the tone for the evening's USO entertainment. Many of the big-band leaders who gained fame in the 1930s rode that popularity into the war era. Popular bandleader and soldier Glenn Miller died in a plane crash early in the

5.2. Square dancing and the Paul Jones at the Miami USO
(Betty Ward Collection in possession of Ward O'Connell)

★ ★ ★

war, but hostesses and servicemen continued to dance to recordings and covers of "In the Mood" and "Moonlight Serenade." Duke Ellington, Harry James, and Tommy Dorsey also commanded large followings of military and civilian fans.[23] Popular songs such as Dinah Shore's "A Boy in Khaki, a Girl in Lace"; "There'll Never Be Another You," by Sammy Kaye and Joan Merrill; and the Benny Goodman Sextet's "On the Sunny Side of the Street" accompanied dancers in USO clubs.[24] Nearly every community and military base had its own local band that played these tunes. Sometimes All Girl Orchestras provided the music for those dances.[25] Junior hostesses asserted their own prerogatives in San Diego by selecting USO dances on the basis of the notoriety and reputation of the big bands scheduled to perform and by rejecting venues that offered "canned" music instead of live bands.[26] This was a testament to the popularity of live bands and to the ability of junior hostesses to favor their personal pleasure over their so-called patriotic duty.

Couples dancing waltzes and fox-trots to big-band music filled USO dance floors. A stage performer created the fox-trot, which included a "fast but simple trotting step," in 1913. According to historians of dance expert Arthur

5.3. Anne Rodriguez dancing with a sailor at the USO in Honolulu, Hawaii, 1942
(courtesy of Anne and John Church)

★ ★ ★

Murray, this dance was "so typically American in its rhythm that it pushed all the other dances into the background."[27] Pleasure dancers found it easier to learn the fox-trot than the waltz, and they enjoyed the dance's "improvisational nature."[28] Nevertheless, wartime couples also enjoyed the waltz, perhaps one of the world's most enduring partner dances. The waltz required a man to wrap his arm around his female partner's waist and draw her to him as they "revolved around each other and around the dance floor." In the Victorian era, many critics described this new dance floor intimacy as risqué.[29] According to historian Lewis Erenberg, social etiquette at elite balls required participants to dance with multiple partners, and this reduced the chance that one couple would become too close through repeated waltzes.[30] By the beginning of the twentieth century, most dancers viewed the waltz as somewhat stuffy.[31] Throughout the 1940s, junior hostesses and servicemen made the waltz commonplace at USO clubs.

The less-respectable and racialized but much-loved jitterbug punctuated USO parties usually filled with waltzes and fox-trots. This dance was often the highlight of the evening for hostesses and servicemen. Jitterbugging emerged in the 1930s as a form of swing dance in which partners performed "fast kicking steps . . . in a bouncy upright fashion."[32] Dayton, Ohio, hostess Irene Szuhay "loved" to dance but preferred the jitterbug to all other styles. One evening, "everybody clear[ed] the floor leaving my partner and I jitterbugging all by ourselves. He was great!"[33] Dance historians debate whether or not the Lindy Hop, developed in 1928 by African American dancer George "Shorty" Snowden in New York City, and the jitterbug are the same dance. Most agree that they have the same origins but that "white swing enthusiasts" called "jitterbugs" added steps to the Lindy Hop to make it the Collegiate/Shag. In any case, the jitterbug had its roots in African American dance forms and interracial dance halls, such as the Savoy Ballroom, in New York City.[34] Unlike the waltz and the fox-trot, the jitterbug relied on "solo improvisation" that kept the dance fresh and invigorating and made it similar to jazz as an art form. Dance historian Ian Driver contends that jitterbugging had a "raw appeal" and "became not so much a dance as a state of mind."[35] As part of an organization grounded in conformity and convention, some USO clubs frowned on the jitterbug.

The jitterbug's connection to African American culture and its inherent threat to white women's racialized respectability led some white USO clubs to ban it. In the 1930s, midwestern dance halls forbade jitterbugging because

5.4. Jitterbugging at the Miami USO (Betty Ward Collection in possession of Ward O'Connell)

★ ★ ★

residents characterized "white jitterbugs" as wild and self-indulgent.[36] A few years later, USO clubs outside the Midwest, such as the Fort Dix Community Service in Pointville, New Jersey, also forbade jitterbugging. It limited dancing to "the Fox Trot and Waltz, in fast and slow tempos." This organization coached hostesses on how to handle jitterbugging soldiers: "Many of the soldiers like to Jitter-Bug but after much consideration, it has been decided by the committee in charge to eliminate Jitter-Bug dancing entirely. If a soldier starts to Jitter-Bug with you, tell him it is against the rules. One of the main objections is lack of room. Other objections are obvious."[37] This dance brought to mind both the apparent sense of abandon that critics believed typified African American culture and the "mindless 'mass man' behavior symptomatic of and conducive to totalitarian societies."[38] Southerners in particular feared "white jitterbugs." Director Vera Ruth Prentiss made sure that there was "no 'exhibitionism' or 'too hot' dancing" in the Montgomery, Alabama, USO for white servicemen.[39] Her term "exhibitionism" subtly referred to the connections between African American jitterbugging and "white jitterbugs." She likely feared white hostesses and servicemen who might engage in uncontrollable dancing supposedly connected to African Americans. The USO's concern that certain dances were morally suspect because they had African American origins revealed the implicit connections that the USO made between women's respectability and whiteness. Even without African American servicemen in the room, the idea of white junior hostesses jitterbugging with white soldiers had the potential to compromise white women's respectability, simply because the jitterbug had African American cultural connections.

For some white junior hostesses, senior hostesses' objections to the jitterbug seemed old-fashioned, thus signifying both a generational and a racial conflict over the dance. Reba Muller, a junior hostess who often sang at the Birmingham, Alabama, USO, objected when a "senior member would break up dancing she didn't approve of." According to Reba, "We all thought that was silly—Jitter Bug [was] not dirty dancing."[40] Conversely, at the Dallas, Texas, USO club, junior hostess Beverly Littlejohn "stood on the sidelines in awe when the jitterbugging really got hot."[41] Meanwhile, seventeen-year-old Beverly marveled at the sexual heat some hostesses and servicemen brought to the dance. It was Reba, however, who by not defining jitterbugging as "dirty dancing" signified a generational gap between senior and junior hostesses. Senior hostesses feared the implications of young white women enjoying a sexualized popular culture shared by white and black youth, while Reba did not.[42] These chaperones perceived shared dance styles and interracial dancing as threatening. The former presumably led to the breakdown in morality and middle-class sexual norms among white youth, while the latter had the potential to do that as well as lead to interracial sex.

Senior hostesses monitored the behavior and dance styles of servicemen and junior hostesses to maintain sexual propriety and general order inside the club. As it fielded numerous incoming requests for hostesses to attend dances for servicemen, the Boston Soldiers and Sailors Recreation Committee insisted that hostess clubs also furnish volunteers to chaperone the young women.[43] USO clubs simply expected that young women would attend dances in the company of older women to watch over them. This was in keeping with the dance culture of the 1930s and 1940s that relied on adult chaperones to supervise young men's and women's dancing.[44] Twenty-four hostesses, accompanied by nine chaperones, from the Concord Dance Hostess Committee (CDHC) attended a dance for sixteen servicemen at the Concord Country Club.[45] The small number of servicemen in attendance along with a high number of chaperones suggests that chaperones wanted to attend dances because the events provided social and patriotic evenings for them as well as for junior hostesses. Volunteering for chaperone duty also exemplified women's desires to welcome servicemen to their community. To illustrate, chaperone Ruth Hill resigned her position from the CDHC because she believed hostesses' mothers should supervise young women at the dances. She declared that her "patriotic duty . . . [had] been completed."[46] Hill equated chaperonage both with patriotism and with a mother's historic duty to monitor her daughter's interactions with young men.

Not all women performed this patriotic, motherly task to servicemen's liking. According to *Hints for Hostesses in Service Clubs*, for the senior hostess, " 'being the chaperone' was one of her most pleasant yet difficult duties [because it] call[ed] for an amazing amount of tact and understanding."[47] Navy recreation officers surveyed several hundred sailors in the Ninth Naval District in the Midwest about the USO. According to Lieutenant Commander F. S. Mathewson, district welfare and recreation officer, several sailors presented some "facetious and amusing replies" to the questions. For example, some wanted "less shadowing, supervising, and chaperoning," along with "more goodlooking [*sic*] WACS" and "more and better looking blondes" at USO dances.[48] At the same time, hostess Carol Brooks "didn't feel watched" while she danced in the USO club in Minneapolis, Minnesota.[49] In her experience, female chaperones did not stifle her ability to have a good time. Her definition of a fun evening likely was different from and more innocent than that of men who disdained chaperoning and sought the companionship of "better looking blondes." These men made up the precise group the USO was targeting, and they more than likely were also the same men who were not going to visit the USO on a regular basis. Hovering senior hostesses sent some men whom the USO had hoped to divert from local bars and venereal disease (VD) in that direction.

With regard to dances, senior hostesses' responsibility was to chaperone, and this job disqualified them from dancing with servicemen unless it reinforced their function as substitute mothers. The Philadelphia Stage Door Canteen (SDC) "banned . . . senior hostesses from the dance floor" and only made an exception when a southern serviceman asked a senior hostess to dance with him at Christmastime just as he would have with his "mother on Christmas in his home."[50] In this instance, the canteen overlooked its own rule because the senior hostess in question explicitly maintained her role as mother as she danced with the young serviceman. Across town, volunteers at the African American USO club on South Broad Street encouraged senior hostesses to dance with servicemen so as to help them "break the ice" and join the party but reminded them that they were "not junior hostesses." The South Broad Street USO likened its club to home and reminded older female volunteers that "a hostess always takes the lead in stimulating wholesome participation in her home."[51] The Hostess Committee of the USO Labor Plaza permitted senior hostesses to dance with servicemen after 9:45 in the evening as long as they continued to monitor junior hostesses' behavior. The committee and senior hostesses recognized that some soldiers and sailors wanted to dance with women who were more mature than juniors. The committee reprimanded these women, however, if they spent too much time dancing with servicemen and neglected their chaperone duties.[52] In these Philadelphia USO clubs, as long as senior hostesses behaved as motherly chaperones, the USO tolerated and sometimes welcomed their dancing with servicemen.

As for junior hostesses, they practiced a reversal of etiquette inside USO dance halls by asking men to dance instead of waiting for men to escort them onto the dance floor. USO clubs encouraged junior hostesses to be aggressive when it came to finding dance partners. In doing so, the USO inadvertently empowered junior hostesses to take charge of their own pleasure. The organization acknowledged that asking men to dance might be unusual behavior for them. The Baltimore Volunteer Hostess Club advised hostesses, "It is not necessary to be unbecomingly forward in speaking to those backward ones [servicemen] but, in your capacity as hostesses, no one can take exception if you intelligently try to see that those men get into the dances."[53] Baltimore volunteers eased new hostesses at the club for the first time into this practice by pairing them with servicemen on the dance floor.[54] Young women maintained their supportive feminine roles as they assumed the traditionally masculine task of asking a partner to dance, because they ultimately fulfilled their duties as good hostesses while doing so. Another club instructed hostesses that many servicemen were "surprisingly shy," so the women ought to use "a little humor and a smile" when they asked them to dance.[55] For some hostesses this took a bit of practice. The USO Labor Plaza Hostess Committee noted that junior hostesses "have shown a decided improvement in poise and manner of approaching servicemen."[56] The Labor Plaza discouraged its senior hostesses from pairing servicemen with specific junior hostesses unless special circumstances arose, because the Labor Plaza wanted junior hostesses to assert themselves.[57] Junior hostesses engaged in this reversal of etiquette because they were in familiar territory, whereas the soldiers and sailors were visitors to their club and their town. The practice of women asking men to dance encouraged the women to be bold and to have more self-confidence, but given the large numbers of "stag lines" and the fact that men usually outnumbered women, one should not overinflate the significance of this practice.

Popular memory of the USO in the 1940s brings to mind the flashing skirts of smiling junior hostesses as jitterbugging GI's twirled them across a crowded dance floor. While the dance floors were certainly crowded, some of the "jitterbugging GI's" had two left feet, and by the end of the evening all of the junior hostesses had "aching feet." To begin with, often there were not enough junior hostesses at each dance to accommodate the flood of male soldiers seeking a partner. San Diego clubs attempted to locate approximately one junior hostess "for every three men" but contended with girls' fiancés and steady boyfriends to do it.[58] On balance, the sex ratio at USO dances nationwide was five men to one junior hostess, but numbers of men could be much steeper depending on location.[59] The 300 invited servicemen from Camp Shelby who attended one USO dance in Hattiesburg, Mississippi, began "pleading" for hostesses' attention shortly after 8:30 P.M. when the formal dance began.[60] Elizabeth TePoorten estimated the ratio of servicemen to hostesses at dances in Asbury Park, New Jersey, at three to one.[61] On rare occasions there were not enough servicemen to provide partners for hostesses. One 1942 USO dance in Cincinnati was a flop because the ratio of hostesses to servicemen was three to one. Hostesses did not have very much fun at this dance because there were not enough servicemen to dance with them.[62] USO clubs in the Boston suburbs kept CDHC members dancing every weekend. For example, Barbara Miller, head of the CDHC, turned down the USO's request to send hostesses to a Christmas Eve party, opting instead to have the girls stay with their own families.[63] Lack of male partners was not the norm, so many women continued to volunteer for the USO, because when they danced with Harry, John, and Phil, they fulfilled a required and gendered duty to the war effort to raise soldier morale. Philadelphia SDC junior hostess Marjorie H. Foster summarized her sometimes painful and exhausting commitment to hostessing: "So while I am making the hour's trip that takes me home after the canteen, where I have worn out another pair of shoes for my country, and by [sic] back is aching because a sailor danced pump-handle fashion, my mind is full of the fun and sadness of the evening. I take with me the hope that I have in some small way helped to repay the boys of my generation for the great sacrifices they are making."[64] As Foster indicated, dancing with servicemen was sometimes hard work and physically exhausting, but usually fun. In this case, Foster interpreted dancing with servicemen as payback for their protection.

Some historians argue that the war marked a transition from a system in which women achieved popularity through numerous dates and dance partners to one where "going steady" became a marker of female popularity. They do not, however, completely demonstrate how and why this transition occurred. At the time, people saw the shift from "rating and dating" to "steadies" as due to the desire of young men and women to secure a steady partner, a direct result of the uncertainty of war and the shortage of "marriageable" local men.[65] It was at dances such as those held at the USO, however, where the "rating and dating" system that had defined courtship in the 1920s and 1930s lost its immediate effectiveness. With hundreds of servicemen waiting to dance with a few hostesses, all women became popular. Senior hostesses did not allow juniors to be passive observers and instructed them to ask servicemen to dance. Indeed, Montana hostess Nora O. Robertson confirms that there were "three men to every girl. There was never a wallflower."[66] Furthermore, the scarcity of available men in places other than USO clubs made the USO itself the primary place for "respectable" women to enjoy popularity and male companionship.

USO rules enhanced junior hostesses' popularity at the same time that the organization's image developed the women's wholesome reputations. Across USO clubs, "every hostess [was required to] dance with anyone [who asked her] on the dancing floor."[67] The Philadelphia SDC asked hostesses "not to dance too long with any one man." Since male guests greatly outnumbered junior hostesses, the women needed to "divide [their] favors evenly."[68] These rules granted servicemen physical access to an array of junior hostesses. Hostess Doris Machado was an excellent dancer, and she "did not have a good night" if she ever sat down. For Doris, the Salinas, California, uso club was a "safe" place to go for entertainment and socializing. At nineteen, she was too young to go to the bars and did not want to patronize them, because she did not want to be "picked up."[69] Doris enjoyed dancing with numerous servicemen as long as they treated her with respect and not like a pickup girl. She was fully aware of the uso's reputation, added to it, and benefited from the good girl/bad girl dichotomy that it perpetuated. uso clubs made sure that all male visitors spent some time with reputable junior hostesses. This nearly communal availability of women physically on the dance floor catered to the desires of gi's who wished to spend time with "girls" who reminded them of home. Likewise, the uso effectively intended these comparisons between junior hostesses and "hometown girls" to inspire men to sacrifice their time and their safety to protect the values of "home."[70]

The uso advertised its clubs as places where junior hostesses could dance with servicemen and in fact enjoy the war. For instance, as the uso repeatedly encouraged hostesses to meet men's needs, it also cautioned, "Don't let it be the idea that Junior Hostesses are in for a long, dismal war spent entirely in forgetting themselves and thereby missing all the fun."[71] For young women, the war did not have to be "dismal"; instead, it could be "fun" if they served as hostesses. This statement trivialized the realities of death and emotional pain that, for many people, the war engendered, but it also implied that the war did not negatively affect the lives of all Americans. For the most part, junior hostess Helen Carroll did not pay any attention to the pain of war, because she was too busy having a great time dancing and singing at the Philadelphia uso. The blackouts frightened her; but she did not have any friends or family in the military, so she did not dwell on fear and death.[72] Similarly, junior hostess Alice Roby felt a constant "adrenaline rush" during the war and suffered from an emotional letdown when the conflict ended. She was grateful that the war was over but missed the excitement that it had brought to her life in Memphis, Tennessee.[73] Other women were not always able to remove thoughts of war from their minds, but they attended uso dances because they "loved to dance."[74] As the government had hoped, listening to music and dancing were positive activities that raised civilian spirits and diverted their attention from war deaths.

Just as dance had the potential to bring two bodies together with ease, it also had the capacity to reveal partners' discomfort with each other and with the rhythm and steps of the music. Marjorie Foster, an sdc hostess, recalled,

"It could be as much a tragedy to dance as it could be a pleasure." Foster was a good dancer, but her "jitter-bug [was] unmentionable. [She] knew it . . . pained many G.I. Joe's more than the wounds they may have received on other battlefields."[75] Senior hostesses quizzed one junior hostess in Baltimore who refused to dance with a soldier. He had asked her to dance "one after another, after six times I thought I had done my duty, as he could not dance, just moved his feet around and stepped on me."[76] Despite pressure from senior hostesses, this woman refused to put her body through another arduous and lumbering waltz. Many USO clubs offered dance classes for servicemen where they could partner with a junior hostess, learn basic dance steps, and reduce their clumsiness.[77] Despite the tedium of giving dance lessons to inexperienced soldiers, ten junior hostesses volunteered for the Fort Dix dance "Teaching Corps" every evening that a dance was held. After each junior hostess assisted two servicemen in learning to dance, she walked with them to the main dance hall and found a partner for each man. According to the Social Corps Manual, "This is a service we can and must give." For these volunteers, dancing was serious because it often was the vehicle by which a soldier felt at home and comfortable in the USO club. Some servicemen took advantage of these dance lessons at Fort Dix and elsewhere. African American servicemen taught one another bebop and jitterbug in the "private setting of the camp," because they wanted to appear like accomplished dancers in a "public" USO club. For those men and women who did not learn to dance at home or in an urban setting, public social dancing was a daunting prospect.[78] It was also the primary vehicle for black and white servicemen to meet young women and to enjoy an evening of "wholesome" recreation at the USO. Ultimately, USO dances and dance classes demonstrated proper social etiquette to unsophisticated servicemen.

While trying to raise the social awareness of its democratic army, the USO feared the conflicts that the intermixing of black men and white women, in particular, provoked in its clubs. Senior hostesses in Philadelphia attempted to prevent contact of any kind between white hostesses and black servicemen because such contact might have been offensive to white servicemen. Interracial contact made some junior hostesses feel uncomfortable. If a hostess had a problem with a rude serviceman at the Philadelphia SDC, she reported the incident to her junior captain or senior hostess, but the canteen expected "scrupulous politeness at ALL times to ALL men in uniform."[79] Some junior hostesses ignored this message and refused to dance with some servicemen of color. Members of the Women's Committee of the SDC, in 1943, concluded that staff ought to instruct senior hostesses to tend to black servicemen "and thus relieve the junior hostesses of this responsibility."[80] Personnel at this SDC desperately wanted to treat all servicemen, regardless of race, fairly. At the same time, these senior hostesses revealed their hidden anxiety that integrated canteens would lead to interracial dancing, and that this interracial contact would destabilize white hostesses' claim to a class- and race-based sexual respectability.

Interracial contact was an uncomfortable issue for women in Hawaii as well as on the mainland. African American men stationed in Hawaii did not frequent Hawaiian USO clubs because, according to one black serviceman, "the girls at the USO [didn't] care to dance with Negroes. They have been told we have tails like monkys [sic]." Seventy-three percent of these men believed that Hawaiians acted "worse" toward them than did citizens in the rest of the country. The federal government blamed the lack of a large supportive black Hawaiian population, not white attitudes and behaviors, for such discrimination and discomfort on the part of black servicemen.[81] Early in the war, Hawaiians greeted African American servicemen with respect, but by 1944 when the government conducted this survey, white southern soldiers and sailors had spread the racist rumor that black men had tails. Hawaiian women also fell for the rumor that all black men were inclined to rape women.[82] Lack of knowledge about African Americans and blatant racism, as well as a concern for their reputations, guided hostesses in their choice to either dance with or snub black soldiers and sailors.

While African American dance forms like the jitterbug disturbed volunteers in certain parts of the country, interracial dancing had the ability to incense hostesses and service personnel alike. In January 1945, a white junior hostess at the Philadelphia SDC asked an African American soldier to dance, and he accepted. As they danced, two junior hostess captains reported the couple to an army major who happened to be on the premises. The major told the man that the SDC "was no place for a colored soldier" and he, instead, should patronize the "Negro Canteen." The soldier countered to the major that "he had been fighting overseas for 3 years, and thought he was fighting for democracy." The major again told him to leave, and, infamously, the soldier became "the first serviceman of any race, creed or color . . . asked to leave the Stage Door Canteen." As a result of this incident, the Philadelphia SDC recruited African American hostesses for the first time.[83]

This soldier was not the only one to equate his treatment at the Philadelphia canteen with the failings of American democracy. A white merchant marine brought his Hawaiian friend to the SDC with him. After one white hostess danced with the Hawaiian serviceman, she told him she "never would again" because "of his color." When the white man reported this incident to Mrs. Upton Favorite, director of the canteen, he said, "I hate to think that things like this is what we are fighting for. What makes me feel so bad is when I go to a foreign post I am treeted [*sic*] so nice and a poor fellow like my buddy has to take insults like this one from the girls here."[84] Conversely, despite their "shock [at seeing] all the Negro fellows at the Lovell General Hospital," white hostesses near Boston, Massachusetts, engaged in an evening of "games, dancing, and just conversation" with them.[85] This incident illustrated how young women's socialization as hostesses could promote more democratic behavior on their part. The desire of white hostesses to avoid interracial dancing and the manner in which they rebuffed their potential partners had strongly negative effects on African American servicemen.

The U.S. government feared the reactions of white American men and women to interracial dancing. Segregated from their white colleagues by day, African American servicemen jitterbugged with white British women after hours in England. White working-class women mixed freely on the dance floors with black and white GI's in many clubs. When *Life* magazine published photographs of interracial couples dancing in Britain, the American Bureau of Public Relations censored all future photographs of interracial couples.[86] The role of the military in repressing knowledge about more egalitarian racial mores and practices stemmed from fears that African Americans who experienced such mores overseas might expect equal treatment from American society when they returned home.[87] Scholar Les Back argues that the Nazi Party used the Allies' anxiety toward interracial dancing against them in party propaganda, making "the meaning of jazz itself . . . an emblem of a wider struggle over the opposition between liberal democracy and fascism."[88] For their part, many of America's British allies refused to enforce the U.S. military's request that civilians not associate with or befriend black servicemen. At the same time, white GI's in Britain opposed interracial dancing and sexual intimacy by perpetrating violence against black men. The British government nearly always forbade marriages between Anglo women and black servicemen, citing the illegality of miscegenation in the southern United States as its rationale.[89] In this instance, some Britons were more racially progressive than their leaders.

In the United States, interracial dancing within a uso context that welcomed all servicemen regardless of race and cultivated a heterosexual faux-dating atmosphere made racism transparent. The uso Labor Plaza tried to avoid interracial dancing by advising white junior hostesses kindly to inform African American servicemen who wanted to dance with them that the Plaza "had colored hostesses to dance with the colored servicemen." The Labor Plaza staff Hostess Committee did not believe that they discriminated against servicemen on the basis of race. It issued the following statement, however, on its interracial dancing policy: "It has come to the attention of the Hostess Committee that there has been inter-racial dancing at the Plaza and in view of the remarks and attitude of some of the servicemen present, we feel that this practice has not been to the benefit of the operation of the Plaza."[90] The executive director of the Plaza, William Fulton Kurtz, privileged the rights and opinions of racists when he ruled against interracial dancing: "Solely in the interest of the safety of the thousands of uso-Labor plaza guests, any practice that might arouse antagonisms on the part of prejudiced persons should be discouraged." Servicemen and hostesses who condoned interracial dancing had to forgo it because such dancing might have provoked violence on the part of "prejudiced persons."[91] As was to be expected from the conservative nature of the race policy of the national uso,[92] the organization's desire to integrate local clubs did not extend to interracial dancing, because that would have challenged long-held assumptions that African American men posed a sexual threat to white women's chastity.

A number of white servicemen and hostesses welcomed African American servicemen in their canteens, and some junior hostesses went so far as to chastise their racist peers for their ill treatment of those men. These junior hostesses helped to undermine conventional race relations. One white serviceman wrote a letter in which he praised the Philadelphia sdc for including black hostesses in its ranks: "These colored men were fighting as hard as I was and as far as I was concerned I liked the canteen and a few colored girls didn't bother me." He added that several of his buddies, however, objected to the presence of black women at the sdc.[93] The national uso wanted locals to recruit hostesses who would "promote tolerance and appreciation" of servicemen of all racial and religious backgrounds.[94] Margaret Halsey was one of those hostesses. In a memo to racist white junior hostesses at the Philadel-phia sDC, Halsey boldly confronted some white women's fears of so-called predatory black men, as well as larger societal fears about miscegenation that formed the basis for objections to interracial dancing.[95]

> I don't believe any of you are very deeply concerned with Negro intel-ligence. What worries you more is the fear of rape. You unconsciously, but very arrogantly assume that no male Negro can so much as glance at you without wanting to get you with child. The truth is, that while you are an extremely attractive group of young women, there isn't one single one of you who's *that* good.
>
> Negro males react to you no more and no less than white males. As women, you know in your hearts that men of any description respond to you pretty much as you intend them to respond. This is especially true in the Canteen, which has hardly any points of resemblance at all to a lonely, moonlit shrubbery.
>
> The real basis of prejudice against Negroes is economic and historical, not sexual or psychological.

Halsey went on to say that those who contended that African American men sexually attacked white women did so only to subjugate African Americans and justify paying them lower wages than they did white workers. She strongly rebuked "prejudiced" white hostesses who refused to dance with black service-men. Halsey argued that intelligence had nothing to do with skin color. "If it had, you would all be much stupider when you are sunburned."[96] Her com-ment that men "respond to you pretty much as you intend them to respond" was not as daring as her comments on race, because her views on sexual conduct betrayed the commonly held assumption that women, not men, were responsible for sexual control.[97] While it is unclear what reaction Halsey's bold and nuanced analysis prompted from junior and senior hostesses, her memo might have been viewed by some as unfeminine and discourteous. Her comments encouraged junior hostesses to investigate the roots of their preju-dices and to rise above their misplaced arrogance.

While white uso clubs did not always treat African Americans with respect, clubs for black servicemen held their own dances, and those attending appre-ciated the efforts of the clubs to entertain them. The Coordinating Council for Colored Agencies, part of the Boston Soldiers and Sailors Recreation Committee, held a dance at Fort Devens for 100 servicemen and 60 hostesses.

As with most USO dances, the men outnumbered the women. At another Boston dance, 30 women entertained 75 men.[98] Writing from England General Hospital in Pennsylvania, Sergeant W. F. Fawkes thanked the SDC for entertaining all servicemen regardless of their race: "It [was] gratifying to know that you appreciate[d] our services in this struggle too."[99] The men of Company C, 11th ASF Training Regiment, in Camp Lee, Virginia, sent a letter of thanks to the South Broad Street USO in Philadelphia: "Your hostesses [were] incomparable, they [were] really TOPS. In all my travels I have yet to find as many in one place that were as gracious as yours."[100] Clubs like this, however, were not evenly distributed throughout the United States. In a harsh report on southern USO clubs, National Urban League representative William Y. Bell Jr. questioned the USO's inability to provide equal services for African American and white servicemen. Referring to the national USO's weak policy against segregation, Bell condemned the USO: "It will not compromise, for example, with local community wishes on beer or immoral hostesses. Is bigotry to be tolerated more than beer or racial immorality more than individual immorality?"[101] As historian Maryann Lovelace observes, the USO was a conservative organization.[102] While segregation was morally questionable in 1943, it was as conservative a tenet as female sexual respectability and temperance were. In this case, for women to embody sexual respectability, they needed to be white. Therefore, the USO was not contradicting its own conservative ideology when it refused to enforce integration and racial equality.

White Americans did not restrict their prejudices to African Americans during the war. They also discriminated against Mexican Americans in the streets and in USO clubs. In the infamous 1943 "Zoot Suit" riots, white servicemen beat hundreds of young Mexican American men on Los Angeles city streets; at the same time, public discrimination against Mexican American men and women was rampant in Texas. *Mañana*, a Mexican newspaper, criticized the Texas government: "The Nazis of Texas are not political partners of the Fuhrer of Germany but indeed they are slaves to the same prejudices."[103] As with interracial dancing in USO clubs throughout the country, interracial dating aggravated some Anglos in Texas. The USO in Texas discriminated against Mexican American women and the Anglo men with whom they kept company. Members of the Mexican American–operated Cosmopolitan Club of Del Rio, Texas, wrote a letter of protest to the national USO. Local business owners refused to serve Anglo soldiers from Laughlin Field who socialized with "Latin-American girls whose background, integrity and morale needs not [to be] question[ed]." The Cosmopolitan Club accused Mr. V. F. Rose, director of the Del Rio USO, of aiding this pattern of discrimination by not allowing Anglo men and Latin American women to enter the club. Rose likely relied on the common belief that respectable women were white and middle class. The Mexican American community took issue with these assumptions because families relied on chaperonage to safeguard and ensure the sexual reputations of their daughters.[104] Like many African American citizens during the war, members of the Cosmopolitan Club contended that in a time of war, "we, in every way equal those self styled true Americans." USO regional executive W. W. Jackson concluded that discrimination against Mexican Americans in Del Rio was "rather common to border towns." Jackson absolved the USO for its complicity in this when he stated, "The USO has been pulled into a local situation that has existed indefinitely."[105] This statement made it appear as though the USO director did not have the ability to end racial discrimination or to include Mexican American women as hostesses in his club. Rather, Director Rose chose to uphold this pattern of discrimination to send Anglo servicemen the message that they should not have associated with Mexican American women. By barring Mexican American women from attending USO functions with white servicemen, the USO limited the ways in which those women could demonstrate their commitment to the war and perpetuated white fears of miscegenation.

The physical act of dancing, whether it was a jitterbug or a waltz, brought together male and female bodies. This physical connection, however brief, gave servicemen and hostesses the opportunity to interact. For many hostesses, these interactions did not lead to dating or romance. For others, however, dancing at the USO was the logical channel by which they met and decided to pursue an acquaintance with particular servicemen. The USO tacitly encouraged this process by replicating the same system of ritualized courtship within its clubs that occurred among middle-class men and women during peacetime. The fact that USO clubs welcomed trustworthy women to entertain men of all classes, regions, and religions led to conflicts within these wartime relationships and to tensions built around racialized respectability.

Senior hostesses and the USO undercut their best efforts to keep servicemen and hostesses apart when they fostered a date-party atmosphere inside USO clubs that was predicated on heterosexual attraction. For example, sharing "box lunches" was a common activity at CDHC events for servicemen. Hostesses packed special lunches, and volunteers assigned each box a number.

Servicemen selected a number and enjoyed a meal with the hostess who brought that particular box. These mock dates encouraged male-female socialization under the supervision of one of the ten or more chaperones who accompanied approximately fifty hostesses to these dances. The USO wanted men and women to enjoy heterosexual companionship, but on its terms.[106] These box lunches could be a lot of fun for junior hostesses, because to make the "date" a success, they only had to prepare a nice meal and be a good conversationalist. Many young women likely welcomed the lack of sexual pressure that accompanied this contrived dating scenario. In a ploy to entice servicemen into its club, the Philadelphia USO Labor Plaza rewarded the "Millionth serviceman" to visit the Plaza with a $100 war bond and a kiss, or "lip service," from a junior hostess. Interestingly, in the Plaza's photograph of the kiss, junior hostess Marie Wall averted her face as the sailor, one whom she presumably did not know, tried to kiss her on the mouth.[107] In each of these instances, box lunch "dates" and "lip service," the USO manipulated servicemen and women into date settings or physically intimate, though sexually tame, situations to enhance the appeal of the club to servicemen and hostesses interested in dating. Clubs set couples up for potential conflicts, however, because the USO's orchestrated dating system paired carefully screened hostesses with men from unspecified social backgrounds.

In some USO clubs, rather than discourage dating, senior hostesses explicitly paired servicemen with juniors on dates. Director Vera Ruth Prentiss of the Montgomery, Alabama, USO club went so far as to act as a matchmaker for junior hostesses. She gave a serviceman of whom she approved a "formal introduction" to a hostess, and then he walked the hostess home.[108] The USO club in Phoebus, Virginia, managed a "date bureau" of reputable young women from the community available to date visiting servicemen.[109] Similarly, the USO club in Spartanburg, South Carolina, recorded interested servicemen's hometowns, educational backgrounds, and previous employment and then paired those men with young women from the community. A chosen serviceman went with a young woman, often another serviceman-hostess couple, and always a chaperone to her house for a home-cooked meal.[110] This chaste form of dating provided servicemen with feminine companionship and a good meal, but no promise of sexual intimacy with a stranger.

The USO's heterosocial atmosphere fostered competition among women to gain male soldiers' and sailors' attention. For instance, the Philadelphia USO Labor Plaza Executive Board distributed guest tickets to young women of their choosing who were not junior hostesses. This resulted in a conflict at the dances when the guests attended the events to "pick up a date and leave." The Labor Plaza Hostess Committee reduced the number of guest passes because guests had "none of the obligations of the regular hostesses on duty. These guests resent[ed] imposed restrictions, our girls resent[ed] their taking over, and bad public relations [came] about."[111] Female guests had the prerogative to leave with servicemen, whereas the Plaza confined junior hostesses to club premises. As a result, junior hostesses resented the presence of women who could freely date men without regard to appearances. As further evidence that women contended with one another to garner romantic attention from men, junior hostesses in Hattiesburg, Mississippi, stopped attending dances at the USO in high numbers when Army wives attended.[112] For these junior hostesses, their service was very much about associating with and potentially dating servicemen. When this was not a viable possibility, they lost interest in their patriotic service.

Competition for male attention extended to and ultimately defined the relationship between junior hostesses and servicewomen. One government representative found evidence that "civilian hostesses . . . resent[ed] having large groups of girls in uniform swell their ranks at dances." At a conference held by the YWCA of Boston, participants discussed the "sense of competition" between hostesses and Wacs at dances where hostesses were rude to servicewomen. The USO representative in attendance argued that the YWCA needed to "educate" hostesses about the needs of servicewomen.[113] The government held to the idea that Wacs and Waves deserved to participate in USO activities.[114] The sexual service component of hostessing, however, marginalized seemingly unfeminine Wacs and Waves who visited USO clubs designed for the pleasure of servicemen. By placing the perceived sexual needs of servicemen at its center, the USO forced servicewomen into the role of junior hostess, and this inevitably led to feelings of competition for men's attention between the two groups of women. Servicewomen remained out of place in an environment that encouraged a mock dating situation between traditionally feminine hostesses and masculine servicemen. A clear role outside this junior hostess/male soldier binary did not exist for servicewomen within the USO.

The USO was aware that the rules it created to guard the reputation of its hostesses fostered a contentious environment for hostesses and servicewomen. One fictional USO account confronted junior hostesses' competitive feelings toward servicewomen and praised hostess "Gracie Glick." She "had three Marines buzzing around her, and instead of trying to hang on to all of them, she called over a couple of Wistful Wacs, stranded without any men, and shared the wealth."[115] This passage implies that Wacs who passively waited for a dance partner naturally wanted to socialize with servicemen, and that male attention was "wealth." For their part, some Wacs concluded, "Hostesses were not interested in raising the morale of military personnel except of the marriageable variety."[116] The USO knew that some servicewomen used to be hostesses and advised current junior hostesses to welcome their positive contributions to USO activities.[117] Hostess-turned-Wave Marilyn Hale danced with servicemen as a Wave in Cleveland. She and her fellow servicewomen found a way to assuage junior hostesses' fears that the Waves would monopolize the attention of servicemen: "At first [the junior hostesses] were kind of mad and I got talking to one and she was jealous. [The hostess said,] 'You can walk out of here with the guys.' I said, 'Well there's no reason why you can't meet him outside. They [senior hostesses] don't have to know that.' Everything then changed. The girls treated us right [after that]. As soon as they found out they could [date the men] and we didn't care . . . if they liked somebody, really liked somebody." Marilyn knew that hostesses were "not supposed to date," but as a Wave, she could leave with a serviceman if she chose. Marilyn did not believe that leaving with one would have called her reputation into question, because doing so "did not mean we were going to shack up. A date was a date regardless of whether you're in a uniform or not." Marilyn did not feel the keen sense of competition with hostesses that they seemed to feel with her.[118] Despite media campaigns that called servicewomen's respectability into question,[119] Marilyn enjoyed the sense of liberation that came with her uniform. In her view, a strict code of appearances did not constrain her the way it did junior hostesses.

Many communities eliminated competition between junior hostesses and servicewomen by creating separate clubs for them. Lieutenant Colonel Katherine R. Goodwin, a Women's Army Corps (WAC) officer, found that servicewomen "prefer[red] mixed group activities, rather than having a special program set up for them alone."[120] Despite her findings, the USO in Milwaukee, Wisconsin, decided that including servicewomen in large-scale USO activities, presumably dances, had been "unsuccessful." Instead, the USO visited servicewomen in a "decentralized program."[121] The USO in Chattanooga, Tennessee, set up a servicewomen's club to entertain the 5,000 WAC trainees stationed at Fort Oglethorpe, while the USO helped to finance a club for 650

Wacs housed at Stephen F. Austin College in Nacogdoches, Texas.[122] Some female soldiers and sailors welcomed the USO's hospitality in whatever form it came. Mary E. Heagan, a servicewoman in Massachusetts, thanked Mrs. Hosmer of Concord for hosting a fine party for her and thirty-nine other servicewomen. Heagan enjoyed the "homey feeling that [she had] missed every once in a while" since joining the service.[123] Both servicemen and servicewomen wanted to participate in USO events, but local USO clubs were most comfortable isolating servicewomen from juniors, because they did not quite understand or know how to fit female soldiers and sailors whose femininity was doubtful[124] into their date-party style dances.

As the war continued, the USO's no-dating policies for junior hostesses deteriorated because they were not enforced, or because men and women violated them. This breakdown exposed more and more the conflict between the USO's mission to attract servicemen through sexual diversion and its condemnation of hostesses who understandably extended that mission by exiting the building with or dating those men. The national USO acknowledged that hostesses used clubs as places to "work and play with members of the opposite sex."[125] Prescriptive writers Alsop and McBride suggested that in many clubs, hostesses invariably dated soldiers because "human nature entered in and took charge," thereby nullifying restrictions against fraternization.[126] Public lore about the USO assumed and enjoyed the romantic image of dedicated USO hostesses as potential marriage partners for servicemen. In the film *Stage Door Canteen*, a love affair develops between Dakota, who does not have a hometown sweetheart, and Eileen, an ambitious young actress. After breaking fraternization rules and meeting outside the sanctuary of the canteen, Dakota and Eileen agree to marry, but at the end of the film, the army ships him and his buddies overseas before the hasty war marriage can occur.[127] The Hattiesburg, Mississippi, USO encouraged romance in the USO context when it showed *Stage Door Canteen* to servicemen on one of its movie nights.[128] Although it was a romantic story, *Stage Door Canteen* served as a warning to young women who might have become involved with servicemen by teaching them through Eileen and Dakota's lost romance that disobeying club rules could only come to a bad end. By perpetuating the notion that romance was synonymous with hostessing, the film highlighted the sexual tension present in dance and within USO service itself.

Excitement and the potential for romance characterized the experiences of some junior hostesses and servicemen, but there were many risks involved for both parties when they dated strangers. *Hints for Hostesses* highlighted several of the key issues hostesses faced as they considered dating servicemen. The manual listed the following as some of its "Acid Tests":

> Would you date this boy if he wore "civies" [*sic*]?
>
> Is he satisfied to be with you at the center until you know each other better?
>
> Can you discriminate? You know you can't date the whole army, navy and merchant marine — you can't give a chip off your heart often and at random and have any left for your "big" moment!

The manual also asked women if they were honest with men about their romantic connections and if they could be sure the men were also being honest about theirs. *Hints for Hostesses* ended its dating section by telling women, "You must learn to give service without giving too much of 'you.'" The manual encouraged women to "be on hand when [men] come back."[129] Hostesses ought to confine their companionship to the USO club, so they could give all of themselves to one man when he returned from the war. Besides, they needed to guard themselves against men who might lie to them and against lowering their prewar standards simply because a man was wearing a deceptively respectable uniform.

Sociologists and police blamed the "lure of the uniform" for the rise in female juvenile delinquency during the war, but this phenomenon was a tangible one for junior hostesses of good character as well.[130] Mrs. Dunaway, chairman of Home and Community Services, commented at the Florida State Defense Council meeting that for the "Khaki-wacky girl . . . the boys of her own age . . . [have] ceased to exist, as far as she [was] concerned — and he [didn't] like it."[131] As a hostess in the small community of Brawley, California, Barbara Emmons lost interest in high school boys her own age because male soldiers and sailors at the USO were much more enticing and exciting.[132] Hostess Norma Burris characterized the sailors who visited the San Diego USO as "clean, polite, good dancers, fun to talk to and good looking generally. Shiney [*sic*] . . . the cream of the crop."[133] The passage of time may have colored Norma's overly positive view of sailors. That the uniform, however, hid men's class and regional backgrounds and gave them all a polished appearance was a powerful factor. When a man was in uniform, only his racial identity could not be erased. Memphis junior hostess Alice Roby met and dated numerous servicemen and recognized that only the uniform made many of those men attractive to her. Alice learned that uniforms concealed men's class backgrounds: "A lot of these boys were from everywhere. [Hostesses] probably wouldn't [have] looked at them if they hadn't been in a snappy uniform. When in a uniform, they were gorgeous."[134] As veterans returned from overseas and attended uso dances out of uniform, senior hostesses at the uso Labor Plaza in Philadelphia had to "watch more closely" and deal with junior hostesses who rejected certain servicemen's request for a dance.[135] Veterans at the Plaza "complained" that hostesses snubbed them, and the young women admitted that they "never bothered with the ex-servicemen and the foreign boys."[136] Junior hostesses' habit of ignoring men who were out of uniform confirms that the uniform granted men a cover of respectability. The fact that junior hostesses met unknown servicemen who were sometimes older than them in the emotionally intense context of war added to the men's sexual appeal.

In addition to the mystique of the uniform, the uso dance hall provided men and women with remarkable anonymity. While inside the dance hall a serviceman, especially, could be anyone from anywhere and have any skills or attributes he chose. He could, and some did, tell junior hostesses stories that were "true" only for one night and sometimes were outright fabrications. In effect, the uso club of 1943 was comparable to the Internet chat room of the twenty-first century. At the Music Box Canteen in New York City, hostess Muriel Ross had an encounter with one soldier who hid from her the fact that he knew how to dance. Vaughn Monroe's band was performing one evening in the canteen, but there was no one on the dance floor. Muriel approached one of the uniformed soldiers who was sitting down and asked him if he would like to dance with her.

> He said, "I don't know how." I said, "Oh come on." I taught him the box step. . . . It's easy, and we danced and then the music stopped and I went over to someone else and danced. Well that night this soldier was introduced by somebody in the band [who said] that he was going to teach us all how to dance. He was a dance teacher! This was a big joke. I felt so foolish. I went over to him and said, "Now I don't think that's fair." He [stammered], "You don't mind, I just, you know . . ."
>
> He thought it was one big joke, I felt so foolish. I guess there were a lot of pretenses that [went] on.[137]

While he was having fun fooling her, this serviceman enjoyed the personal attention that Muriel offered him through the impromptu dance lessons.

Lying about his capabilities afforded him a few intimate minutes with a hostess who would spend the rest of the evening entertaining the many servicemen around her. She taught him simple dance steps, while he held the knowledge that her instruction was unnecessary. In this instance, he maintained a sense of power over Muriel and the situation because he withheld information from her. This story highlights the power differential between servicemen who passed though town briefly and trusting junior hostesses who took them at their word. His ploy embarrassed Muriel, but it did not do her any great harm.

Other servicemen's lies were not so innocuous and had the potential to harm the reputations of the hostesses they dated. Alice Roby's friend Roger, a soldier whom she met at the USO, introduced her to his friend Frank. Roger said Frank[138] was "very shy," but Alice later learned "he was about as shy as a barracuda." According to Alice, Frank's pretense of shyness "was a good come on you know; get somebody to feel sorry for your friend and go out with him. He used the sympathy ploy." Alice and a friend who was not a hostess double-dated the two men because they were "adventurous" and "fun." Whenever the two aviators were in Memphis, Alice and her girlfriend "were their girls; they didn't have any other girls, because we had so much fun together, so why bother?" Alice received a great shock one day, nonetheless, when she called the base and "asked to speak to Frank, and they said, 'Oh he had to go home, his wife's having a baby.'" Alice had dated and "necked with" this man many times; she went to dinner, the park, dancing, and the movies with him. When she learned that this so-called poor little timid man had led her to believe that he was single, she "just wouldn't see him again; [she] wouldn't go out with married men." Alice concluded that this sort of deception happened often during the war between hostesses and servicemen.[139] Indeed, a military study about VD revealed that as many as 50 percent of servicemen were unfaithful to their wives at some point during the war.[140] American GI's sang the oft-repeated "My wife doesn't understand me" song to British women throughout their tenure in England.[141] Both British and American women contended with deceitful or manipulative servicemen who used the anonymous and fleeting nature of their contact with these women to their advantage.

For hostesses who pursued steady relationships with servicemen, tensions within those relationships abounded over class and region — those very same markers that uniforms masked. One hostess manual advised juniors that "[service]men [were] a cross-section of American life representing the rich and the poor, the city and the country, the cultured and the uncultured."[142] This reference to the "democratic army" was entirely true, especially within USO dance halls that mixed men with women regardless of their regional or geographic backgrounds. Some hostesses found that some servicemen ranked below their usual standards for romantic partners. Alice Roby became engaged to a chief petty officer in the navy. Her fiancé, Henry,[143] looked "handsome in his uniform." During the war, Alice "liv[ed] from day to day, [she] just didn't think" about the future. As a result, Alice did not pay very much attention to Henry's background. This changed for Alice when the war was nearing an end. "Henry tactfully got across to me that he . . . had a farm and he expected me to milk cows! The closest I ever got to milk was in a milk bottle. It may sound like a ridiculous reason [to end an engagement], but on the contrary it really isn't. [His assumption that she would agree to milk cows] shows complete different lifestyles. I thought, 'You just don't understand me at all.' "[144] In another instance, Alice introduced one of her girlfriends to a "handsome" soldier, and the two began to date. When the war ended, "he came back and she took one look at him, the way he was dressed . . . the kind of shoes he wore, the kind of clothes he wore," and ended her relationship with him. According to Alice, her friend had "gone with the country club set all [her] life [and was] not exactly going to be interested in somebody right off the farm." Alice concluded that one could "take these boys off the farm or out of the filling station or something like that and dress them up and put them in an environment where they . . . are thrown with manners and all of that, all the time, they can pass. But you wouldn't want to marry them."[145] For men, their uniform allowed them to mix with women whom they otherwise might never have had the opportunity to date. These men likely understood marriage as a path to upward mobility and may have finessed the details of their social status to win the attention of junior hostesses.

For others, religion proved to be the primary unforeseen obstacle to long-lasting relationships. One Catholic bishop involved with the USO "wanted Catholic soldiers to dance only with Catholic girls," but circumstances within USO clubs that welcomed all servicemen regardless of religion stymied his wish.[146] Philadelphia junior hostess captain Norma Kane had a blond Jewish friend who hostessed with her. Her friend found herself dating a sailor whom she had met at the SDC who was "very much against Jewish people." The young woman did not know how to tell the anti-Semitic sailor that she was Jewish. When she finally did, their relationship ended.[147] Anti-Semitism plagued the USO throughout the country. The Winslow Street USO club in

Fayetteville, North Carolina, was initially known within the community as the "Jew USO and few gentiles visited the place." The volunteers at the club treated servicemen of all backgrounds with such great respect that the club itself earned the praise of Fayetteville's residents.[148] As with the case of Norma Kane's friend, society accepted romances within the same religion much more readily than it did interreligious dating.

Some women found men of the same religious and class backgrounds as their own at the USO, but their relationships collapsed because they came from different regions of the country and, as a result, held conflicting views regarding racial etiquette and hierarchies. Hostess Aileen Cooperman met a serviceman, Barry,[149] at the Chicago USO. With Aileen's consent, Barry asked her mother, a senior hostess, for permission to date Aileen. Her mother agreed, and the two began a relationship. After several months, Barry and Aileen considered marriage. At the request of his family, she traveled to Charleston, South Carolina, to spend three weeks sharing a room with his sister in the family house to become better acquainted with Barry. Aileen wanted "to see whether that was where I wanted to spend the rest of my life." The fact that both Aileen and Barry were Jewish made them acceptable partners to both sets of parents. After her three-week visit, Aileen decided that she "could not live in the south."

> My parents brought me up to be open and accepting of everyone. When I went to South Carolina I saw this tremendous . . . it was almost a hatred of the black people. I couldn't handle that. If Barry and I walked down the street and a black person was coming, they walked on the curb, and I said, "I can't believe this." He said, "Well that's the way it is down here." I couldn't handle it.
>
> We went to the beach and we spent all day at the beach and we were lying in the water. I have very dark skin, and I turned extremely dark. I didn't even know how dark I looked. Well, [it] came time to come home and we went to the bus and we got on. Barry [was] putting the money in and he said, "Ok there's a seat." The bus driver said, "You go to the back of the bus." I said, "Why?" He said, "Darkies go to the back of the bus." I said, "But I'm white, look at my hands." He said, "All the darkies have white hands." Barry said, "But she's with me." [The driver replied], "I don't care who she's with, she's not going to sit up front here, she's going to the back of the bus." So we got off the bus and Barry had to call his

father to come pick us up, because I wouldn't go to the back of the bus, and at least Barry wouldn't let me go to the back of the bus. That was the experience I had and I said, "I'm not going to live in this place, I cannot."

It bothered Aileen greatly that her boyfriend "was upset for me, not for the fact that black people had to go to the back of the bus." Barry refused to move to Chicago when Aileen asked him. Although they shared a common religion and middle-class upbringing, Aileen mused, "He was a southerner and I was a northerner and we just couldn't get together."[150] USO service gave Aileen the opportunity to meet someone from a different part of the country and then travel to that region to learn about its customs. She found that the USO was a good place to meet men whom she was interested in dating, but she could not commit to a man who was racist.

When they managed to fall in love with someone of the same social, religious, and regional background, compatible junior hostesses and servicemen often married. "Standards for USO Junior Hostess Groups" instructed, "USO clubs are neither date bureaus nor matrimonial agencies [but] the subject of war marriage is a real and vital one today," so the USO needed to include it in hostess training courses.[151] The USO was right to be concerned with war marriages. Marriages increased in number by 5.7 percent in 1940, 20 percent by 1941, and 50 percent immediately following the Japanese attack on Pearl Harbor. Birth rates increased accordingly.[152] The Baltimore USO club reported that "it was love-at-first-sight" for one serviceman and a visiting woman [not a hostess] whom the USO introduced. They married quickly after meeting each other in Baltimore in December 1943.[153] For hostess Irene Szuhay at the Dayton, Ohio, USO club a romance caused her to overlook the no-dating rules.

We were not allowed to leave the club with any of the male servicemen — but in March, 1945 I met a soldier who stole my heart. He walked in dripping wet from the rain outside — and I challenged him to a game of ping-pong (I won) — and then matched him for a coke. (I lost). I secretly slipped him my phone number — and he called shortly after I returned home from the club. We had a few dates before he left for Ft. Belvoir, Va. where he received his commission in the Corps of Engineers. I attended the commissioning — he proposed — and we married in Sept. 1945.[154]

Irene initially volunteered for the USO because she "worked long and hard hours at Wright Field [as a secretary], so this [hostessing] was a way [to] relax"

5.5. Margaret and Roger Fredrich's wedding portrait, 22 June 1946
(courtesy of Margaret and Roger Fredrich)

★ ★ ★

and "get together with servicemen."[155] Civilian men did not have the same allure that those in military uniforms possessed, even though they had been civilians recently themselves. Dancing and socializing with servicemen and, in Irene's case, playing Ping-Pong with one led to a romance. Irene overlooked the no-dating rules her club had in place because she believed Victor Hennig was an appropriate partner for her.[156] Peggy Campbell, whose father had forbidden her from joining the WAC, met Sergeant Roger Fredrich at a Birmingham, Alabama, USO dance. They married in 1946. While USO volunteers attempted to dismiss the impression that the organization was a "matrimonial agency," that was what it became for Peggy and her future husband. Junior hostesses took advantage of the USO as a logical place to meet and date men of their own age with similar interests, and some couples eventually married.

THE SATURDAY NIGHT dance was the centerpiece of the USO's entertainment schedule. The organization established contrived courtship scenarios that brought hostesses and servicemen together in a heterosocial space that soon led to genuine dating. The USO welcomed an economically and ethnically diverse military and, as a consequence of their own class-based selection processes, brought servicemen into contact with junior hostesses holding middle-class ideals. Junior hostesses competed with servicewomen to perform the sexual service that was an implicit part of their job. Meanwhile, this sexual service marginalized Waves and Wacs whose own uniforms set them apart from civilian women. Dancing served as a site of contestation and racial tension when African American servicemen and white hostesses engaged in it. The specter of miscegenation tainted all interracial dancing and dating, whether it was between whites and African Americans or between whites and Mexican Americans, because the USO predicated the selection of its hostesses on a racialized respectability rooted in white middle-class cultural mores. Inside integrated clubs, black men and white women dancing together challenged the basis for white women's social and sexual respectability. Couples who found commonalities in religion and social background and then dated sometimes found that race and racism undid their relationship. The excitement of wartime and of USO-inspired romance, however, led to long-lasting relationships for some couples.

Conclusion

Six weeks after eighteen-year-old junior hostess Phyllis Mayfield married Larry Baldridge, whom she had met at a USO dance, he received orders that the army was sending him overseas. Phyllis accompanied him to New York City, his departure point, where she anxiously said goodbye to her new husband. Phyllis returned to her former job at the Commerce Trust Company in Kansas City. She corresponded with her husband and traveled to Des Moines, Iowa, on a regular basis to spend time with his mother and two younger brothers. She wrote letters to his brother Don, stationed at the Pacific Kwajalein Island, and their father, a chief petty officer at the naval air base in Olathe, Kansas. On 17 March 1944, St. Patrick's Day, Phyllis commented to her friend that she "was going to have bad luck because [she] had on a blue velvet dress and had worn nothing green" to work that day. That evening as she slept, Phyllis thought she heard the "telephone ringing and that Larry was calling [her], but there was no one on the line." Several days later Phyllis received a War Department telegram telling her that her husband's plane was destroyed over Vienna, Austria, on 17 March 1944. One year later, Phyllis received the official news that her husband had been killed in action on that day. She endured the next few years by filling her time with work as a secretary and as a volunteer nurse's aide. After ending a yearlong romance with a naval officer, she visited her former mother-in-law in January 1947. For the first time, she met the brother-in-law with whom she had corresponded during the war. Don Baldridge "had hazel-brown eyes and a nice wide smile, was serious and steady and seemed to be a very considerate and good person." In the "only impulsive decision Don ever made," he proposed marriage to Phyllis six days after their first date. To become better acquainted with Don, Phyllis stayed in Des Moines and lived in her own room in the Baldridge family home. Phyllis and Don dated for the next five months and married on 1 June 1947.[1] The next year, USO operations concluded.[2]

The immediacy and urgency of wartime caused emotional turmoil and excitement in the lives of people like Phyllis, Larry, and Don as they contended with uncertain futures. World War II caused the geographic upheaval of millions of men and women as they entered military service or sought new employment opportunities throughout the country. These changes and emotions revealed tremendous social and gendered tensions throughout the United States. As a site where civilians met servicemen on a daily basis, the uso hosted and in some cases fostered many of these conflicts. But it also brought people together, as it did the Baldridges.

Through the uso, the state worked with private voluntary associations to create local institutions that managed social divisions sufficiently to maintain military morale and civilian support for the war. At the same time, the uso was unable fully to resolve social divisions such as segregation, and that failure left unsettled issues for the postwar period. The uso endeavor exposed how fears of interracial intimacy led white men and women to deny black people opportunities for full participation as citizens. The failure of the uso and the American citizenry successfully to resolve these issues calls the actions of the "Greatest Generation" into question.[3] This generation won the war overseas and brought stability to Europe but did not confront the realities of racial inequality and discrimination at home. That confrontation began in earnest with President Harry Truman's desegregation of the armed forces by Executive Order 9981 in 1948. Moreover, scores of African Americans acted on the emotional success of the Double V Campaign and harnessed the pain caused by injustices experienced within the military and the uso dance hall to launch a grassroots attack on segregation during the civil rights movement of the 1950s and 1960s.[4]

The uso's attempt to sort "good girls" from "bad" in an effort to entertain an army of men who could choose either reveals stress over gender and sexual codes that continued beyond the postwar period. Despite uso warnings, junior hostesses sought pleasure through casual socializing and, in some cases, sexual experimentation with the men they met through the uso. Their choices foretold women's agitation for greater sexual and ultimately greater economic independence during the 1960s and 1970s. During the Korean War, the uso re-created the dance halls of the World War II era, complete with chaperones and junior hostesses.[5] The organization dropped its chaperoned dance hall component in 1953 and focused on overseas entertainment for troops from the Vietnam War era to the present. Ideas about sexuality, chastity, and

chaperonage changed significantly between the Korean and Vietnam conflicts. In a new world filled with easily available antibiotics and the birth
control pill, screened hostesses and sexual continence were not as important
as they had been. Yet the armed forces and the civilian population at large
continued to perpetuate the sexual double standard that allowed, even encouraged, men to enjoy sex with numerous partners and criticized women
who made similar choices.[6]

The image of the uso-inspired "good girl" whose seductive chastity kept
men's morale on the upswing persists to the present. She continues to thrive in
popular culture, classroom advice guides, centerfolds, and beauty pageants.
Most dramatically, the feminist group New York Radical Women identified
her as Miss America, noting that the beauty queen possessed an "Unbeatable
Madonna-Whore Combination." At the 1968 Miss America pageant, these
protesters asserted that to "win approval, [women] must be sexy and wholesome, delicate but able to cope, demure yet titillatingly bitchy." The prizes for
such seemingly paradoxical behavior included heterosexual love, marriage,
and economic security. This analysis carries particular weight because as the
protesters pointed out, the uso ferried Miss America on morale-building
tours through Southeast Asia during the Vietnam War. As the ultimate good
girl, "she personifie[d] the unstained patriotic American womanhood our
boys [were] fighting for."[7] The protests at the Miss America pageant signified
that some American women were finished with symbolism. They hoped to
imbue the role of women in war and in civilian life with substance.

The civilian need to offer emotional and maternal support of service personnel, as well as government dependence on that support, did not disappear
on V-J Day 1945. Political scientist Cynthia Enloe details how the arm of
the state, through the military, reaches into women's kitchens, workplaces,
and bedrooms to procure their labor, often sexual, and affirmation for a
militarized state that undervalues their "invisible" contributions at the same
time that it regards those services as crucial underpinnings to its war-making
campaigns.[8] Throughout World War II, the military and the federal government used personal appeals that encouraged women to render vital unpaid
tangible and intangible services to the army and navy. These institutions
repeatedly thanked women for their mostly emotional labor but consigned
their work to the realm of voluntary service, therefore diminishing its public
importance within a society that measured the value of goods and services by
their cash equivalency.[9] For their part, senior and junior hostesses were not

C.1. Miss America Phyllis George on a USO tour in Vietnam, 1971
(courtesy of United Service Organizations, Inc.)

★ ★ ★

simply victims of the state; rather, they derived a corollary sense of emotional satisfaction, pleasure, and sometimes sexual companionship from entertaining and socializing with servicemen.

At present, the U.S. military relies on the emotional support of families and civilians both to lift the morale of troops and to supply them with essential products, including sunscreen, shampoo, lip balm, and phone cards. Care packages sent to troops by the USO and by members of networks such as Soldiers' Angels and the Airborne Angel Cadets of Texas embody both the monetary contributions of citizens to a military they already support with their tax dollars as well as the emotional sustenance the sunscreen and shampoo represent. The U.S. Army provides servicemen and servicewomen deployed in the Middle East with small amounts of generic sunscreen. The sunscreen that the USO and organizations like it send to soldiers is more readily available than the army product. By collecting, packaging, and mailing extra items to service personnel in the Middle East, volunteers on the home front bring comfort to themselves and to the troops. Much like the homemade cookies in a USO dance hall, sunscreen and phone cards represent the love and emotional support of civilians at home to servicemen and servicewomen stationed overseas.

Just as senior hostesses did during World War II, mothers of soldiers serving in Iraq play a key role in mustering emotional support on the home front for active-duty soldiers and sailors. For example, a "self-described ordinary mother of an ordinary young man turned hero" created Soldiers' Angels to send letters and cards to troops that did not receive any. She did this because she was a "caring and loving mother."[10] Not all mothers of children involved in the Iraq War reacted to the conflict in the same way. Cindy Sheehan, the mother of a fallen soldier, emerged in 2005 as an example of subversive motherhood that would not be contained by traditional volunteer work. Her patriotism manifested as protest against the Iraq War. Sheehan's activities were part of a larger effort by some Americans to end U.S. involvement in Iraq.[11] The desire to sustain troop morale with care packages during the Iraq War did not co-opt civilian support for the conflict as effectively as it had during World War II, given the distinctive scope and rationale for each war.

Each of these themes — racial conflict and reconciliation, gender and sexual codes, as well as support for service personnel during wartime — warrants further research and discussion beyond the World War II period, as does the story of the USO. For example, the organization's interaction with the federal government, the relationships between the member agencies, the role of religion in binding or creating conflict within the organization, and the ways in which local communities welcomed or rejected USO involvement promise to reveal much about the nature and framework of volunteer organizations. Exactly how the USO adapted its sexual and gender ideology to accommodate a changing military that included individuals of color on an equal footing with white service personnel, as well as an increasing number of female soldiers and sailors, promises to mirror or complicate much of what occurred in the civilian world. Equally interesting would be an examination of how the risqué humor of entertainers from USO Camp Shows, Inc., diverged from the dominant sexual code deployed within World War II dance halls. Learning how this form of entertainment for men overseas morphed into post–sexual revolution humor in a feminist era, and the ways entertainers from Bob Hope to Drew Carey finessed those boundaries, would most certainly prove engaging.

The sexualized banter and seductive performances of postwar USO bombshells like Marilyn Monroe and Nancy Sinatra departed from Phyllis Mayfield's waltzes and fox-trots in a Fort Leavenworth, Kansas, dance hall.[12] Most junior hostesses like her supported and found comfort in the USO's identification of itself as a safe, wholesome environment in which servicemen could meet "good girls" who would not have sex with them. Junior hostesses viewed USO rules as mutable boundaries, which they could cross when they chose to enjoy limited sexual intimacy with select servicemen. The USO worked to recast male soldiers and sailors as innocent boys in need of moral guidance, while uniforms granted men anonymity and allure and, for many women, inspired a degree of respect for their sacrifices. The USO fostered a heterosexual undercurrent in its activities in order to keep both junior hostesses and servicemen interested in attending club functions. Each of the USO's component goals came together, and in some cases clashed, on the dance floor itself as sexually respectable hostesses entertained and socialized with an economically, ethnically, and racially diverse male military. Many hostesses pursued relationships with servicemen, to positive or negative ends, with or without USO approval. Junior hostesses who danced their way through the war later measured their contributions to the period with memories of aching feet, warm conversations, and a nod to their patriotic service, a service that continues to resonate in relationships between women, men, war, and the military today.

Appendix

INTERVIEW/QUESTIONNAIRE TEMPLATE

1. Name
2. Current address
3. Birthplace and date
4. Where did you grow up?
5. What did your father do for a living?
6. What did your mother do for a living?
7. Where were you living during the war years, 1941–1945?
8. At the time of the war, did your family own or rent your home?
9. Were you in school? If yes, what was the name of the high school or college?
10. Did you work during the war? Where?
11. What was your marital status during the war?
12. How did you get involved with the USO?
13. What was the purpose of the USO in your opinion?
14. Why did you volunteer for the USO?
15. What was the application process like to become a USO hostess?
16. Describe the process, including interviews that you had to go through to become a hostess.
17. What type of volunteer work did you do for the USO?
18. Where did you do most of your volunteer work? (canteens, church halls, etc.)
19. How often did you volunteer for the USO each week?
20. What types of recreational activities did you engage in with the servicemen as part of your volunteer work?
21. How many USO dances with male servicemen did you attend?
22. In your estimation, what was the ratio of soldiers to hostesses at the dances?
23. What were the rules regarding hostesses and soldier behavior at the dances? Who enforced these rules? Did you agree with the rules?
24. Did you enjoy the USO dances? Why or why not?
25. What did you talk about with the servicemen?
26. What did you wear to USO events? What dress code did the USO enforce?

27. What were the senior hostesses like? Why, in your estimation, did senior hostesses volunteer for the USO?
28. What were the other junior hostesses like?
29. What rules did you have to follow as a hostess? What did you and the other hostesses think of the rules?
30. Were you allowed to date the servicemen, and were you interested dating them? Why or why not?
31. How many experiences did you have with servicemen of a race different than your own? What were those experiences?
32. What did your parents, neighbors, and community think of your volunteer work as a junior hostess?
33. Were there any girls who broke the USO rules, or who crossed any lines with servicemen? Describe these incidents.
34. What do you remember in particular about the servicemen or the things they said and did at the USO club?
35. What parts of the country were the servicemen who visited the USO club from?
36. As a USO hostess, how much contact did you have with industrial workers? With Wacs?
37. For how many months or years did you volunteer with the USO?
38. How did volunteering at the USO make you feel?
39. How would you assess your work with the USO? Was it enjoyable? Worthwhile?
40. How do you think your volunteer work at the USO contributed to the war effort?
41. What did you enjoy most about volunteering for the USO and what was your least favorite aspect of USO service?
42. What did you do after the war? (education, work, marriage, children, etc.)

Notes

ABBREVIATIONS

In addition to the abbreviations used in the text, the following appear in the notes.

CDHC Records	Records of the Concord Dance Hostess Committee, Concord Free Public Library, Concord, Mass.
Hattiesburg USO Records	Record Group M211, USO Club Records, University of Southern Mississippi, McCain Library and Archives, Hattiesburg, Miss.
JSH	Journal of Social Hygiene
NAACP Papers	National Association for the Advancement of Colored People Papers, Manuscript Division, Library of Congress, Washington, D.C.
NCCS Records	Records of the National Catholic Community Service, Archives of the Catholic University of America, Washington, D.C.
Neal Collection	Margaret Neal WWII Homefront Collection, P 151, Maryland Historical Society, Prints and Photographs Department, Baltimore, Md.
NUL Records	Records of the National Urban League, Manuscript Division, Library of Congress, Washington, D.C.
NUL-SRO Records	Records of the National Urban League — Southern Regional Office, Manuscript Division, Library of Congress, Washington, D.C.
RAC	Rockefeller Archive Center, North Tarrytown, N.Y.
RG 24	Record Group 24, Records of the Bureau of Navy Personnel, National Archives II, College Park, Md.
RG 215	Record Group 215, Records of the Office of Community War Services, National Archives II, College Park, Md.
RG 225	Record Group 225, Records of the Joint Army and Navy Boards and Committees, National Archives II, College Park, Md.

SA Papers   Salvation Army War Services Subject Files, 1939–1950, The
                       Salvation Army Archives and Research Center, Alexandria, Va.

WQ   Winchell Oral History Questionnaire

WWII Collection   World War II Collection, USO Series, Historical Society
                       of Pennsylvania, Philadelphia, Pa.

YMCA Collection   YMCA Collection, Archives and Special Materials Section,
                       Reference Department, Langsdale Library, University of
                       Baltimore, Md.

INTRODUCTION

1. Blake and Blake interview.

2. Meyer, *Creating GI Jane*; Anderson, *Wartime Women*; Hartmann, *Home Front and Beyond*.

3. Adams, *Best War Ever*, 70.

4. Fulton Oursler, *The People's Reporter*, 13 April 1944, RG III, 2 P, Office of the Messrs. Rockefeller Welfare Interests—General, 1942–45, box 50, folder 562, RAC; Coffey, *Always Home*, 3. The USO agreed to serve merchant marines but found that work problematic because merchant marines did not wear uniforms and soldiers, marines, and sailors did. The Baltimore USO did not know how to "fit them into the general picture." The USO in Baltimore, Md., was unsure what types of services seamen required; see Minutes, 6 November 1942, ser. 1, box 9, YMCA Collection. For a good description of the USO's creation, see Knapp, "Experimental Social Policy Making," 322–26.

5. "National USO Campaign Reaches Its Goal," *YMCA News*, September 1941, ser. 1, box 73, YMCA Collection; "USO Growth Rate Two Units a Day: Total Reaches 967," *USO News*, September 1942, box 53, folder 595, RAC. These numbers include clubs and mobile units.

6. *USO, Five Years of Service*, 5.

7. Blumin, *Emergence of the Middle Class*, 2.

8. Hatheway, *Gilded Age Construction of Modern American Homophobia*, 38; Dumenil, *Modern Temper*, 72–74, 78–81; Stock, *Main Street in Crisis*, 97; Wandersee, "Economics of Middle-Income Family Life," 47–48; Clement, *Love for Sale*, 7–8. Farmers and "petty producers" were members of the "old middle-class," according to Stock, *Main Street in Crisis*, 9.

9. For more information on USO Camp Shows, Inc., see Heberling, "Soldiers in Greasepaint," and Coffey, *Always Home*.

10. Coffey, *Always Home*, 6.

11. Harper Sibley, President of the USO, Proceedings, USO War Activities Conference, 12 April 1942, box 72, RG 24.

12. Mrs. Maurice T. Moore, Chairman of the Women's Committee of the USO, ibid.

13. Honorable Robert P. Patterson, Undersecretary of War, "We Need This Job Done," War Activities Conference, New York: USO, 1942, USO Series, General Welfare Files, RG III, box 54, folder 615, RAC.

14. Balbo, "Crazy Quilts," 51–53.

15. Address by Charles P. Taft, Assistant Coordinator of Health and Welfare, to Central Atlantic Area YMCA Convention, Atlantic City, N.J., 17 May 1941, box 1, RG 215; Knapp, "Experimental Social Policy Making," 323–25.

16. D'Emilio and Freedman, *Intimate Matters*, 184, 271; Meyer, *Creating GI Jane*, 36; Peiss, *Cheap Amusements*, 98–99; Muncy, *Creating a Female Dominion in American Reform*.

17. Brandt, *No Magic Bullet*, 162, 167; Hegarty, *Victory Girls, Khaki-Wackies, and Patriotutes*, 74–75; Fass, *Damned and the Beautiful*; Ware, *Holding Their Own*.

18. Hartmann, *Home Front and Beyond*, 2–3.

19. "A United Nation Backs Them Up," National USO Campaign, General Welfare Files, RG III, box 54, folder 615, RAC.

20. USO, Bulletin No. 9, "Guiding Considerations to Determine the Extent and Type of Need for USO Service," 30 October 1941, USO, Inc., New York, N.Y., box 75, RG 24; Knapp, "Experimental Social Policy Making," 325.

21. John D. Rockefeller Jr.'s radio address on Columbia Broadcasting Network, 8 July 1941, for the Parents-Neighbors Organization of the USO, General Welfare Files, ser. 3, box 53, folder 585, RAC.

22. Admiral Stark, proposed draft of four-minute radio speech that was not used, box 26, RG 24.

23. "Townsmen and Maneuvers: A Report of the Part Civilians Played in the Texas-Louisiana Maneuvers — 1942," OCWS-FSA, Division of Recreation, Region X, box 29, RG 215.

24. *Soldier Opinion about USO Clubs* (New York: USO, Inc., n.d.), SA Papers, 17.

25. "USO Growth Rate Two Units a Day: Total Reaches 967," *USO News*, September 1942, box 53, folder 595, RAC.

26. "Measures of Services in USO National Agency Operations since January 1944, Continental United States," USO, Inc., Department of Operations, Division of Statistical & Research Services, box 50, folder 562, RAC.

27. *USO General Operating Practice: A Manual of General Policies, Principal Organization Relationships, and the Main Lines of Procedure in USO Operations, Continental United*

States (New York: USO, Inc., 1944), SA Papers. In 1943, approximately 180 USO clubs or canteens served African Americans specifically, out of a total 1,326 sites. See Knapp, "Experimental Social Policy Making," 327.

28. "Scattering of Negro Troops in the Army," USO statement, 28 October 1943, box 37, RG 225.

29. William Y. Bell, Associate Regional Executive, Report Presented at Regional Staff Conference, December 1943, ser. 1, General Office Files, box A72, NUL-SRO Records.

30. "USO and the Negro Community," *Monthly Bulletin*, Atlanta, Ga., vol. 1, no. 8, July 1944, box A71, NUL-SRO Records. Ideas of racial uplift are also apparent in Charles C. Beckett, Executive Director, Proposal Submitted to Executive Committee of South Broad Street USO Club, ser. 6, box 7, NUL Records.

31. Gaines, *Uplifting the Race*; Gilmore, *Gender and Jim Crow*; Higginbotham, *Righteous Discontent*.

32. In an article published by the Phoenix-based *Arizona Republic*, I asked former USO hostesses to contact me if they were interested in discussing their USO experiences. Approximately 100 women responded to my request. I conducted telephone or oral interviews with about half of these women, and the remainder completed questionnaires about their USO experiences. Although currently residing in the Phoenix area, they served as USO hostesses in states throughout the country, including Illinois, New York, Virginia, Tennessee, Alabama, California, Washington, and many others. They relocated to Arizona for a variety of reasons not exclusively related to retirement. I have attempted to balance the accounts of the women who responded to this article, each of whom was white, with the exception of one woman of Lebanese descent, with written documentation about the experiences of hostesses of color. See Maureen West, "UA Student Seeks USO Hostesses," *Arizona Republic*, 20 February 2001, B3.

CHAPTER 1

1. Hoza, Hoza, Bowley, and Bowley interview.
2. Balbo, "Crazy Quilts," 63; Hochschild, *Managed Heart*, 11.
3. Boydston, *Home and Work*, 46–47.
4. D. Campbell, *Women at War with America*, 68–69, 71.
5. Ibid., 71.
6. Kerber, *No Constitutional Right to Be Ladies*, 250.
7. Cohen, *Consumers' Republic*, 75–79.
8. Ware, *Holding Their Own*, 2, 27–28.
9. Deutsch, *From Ballots to Breadlines*, 91–94.
10. Walker, *Shaping Our Mothers' World*, 76.

11. Alsop and McBride, *Arms and the Girl*, 263, 265.

12. *USO Bulletin*, 26 May 1941.

13. Address by Lilias H. Smith, opening of San Angelo Club, 16 March 1943, box 7, NCCS Records.

14. Summary of yearly totals, USO-YMCA Program and Services, 1 August 1941– 31 December 1945, Hattiesburg USO Records.

15. D. Campbell, *Women at War with America*, 66.

16. Ibid., 7.

17. Evans, *Born for Liberty*, 50, 114, 171.

18. *USO General Operating Practice: A Manual of General Policies, Principal Organization Relationships, and the Main Lines of Procedure in USO Operations, Continental United States* (New York: USO, Inc., 1944), SA Papers.

19. Shockley, *"We, Too, Are Americans,"* 41–42.

20. To NAACP from Mrs. Mallie B. Williams, 23 July 1943, Jacksonville, N.C., box A641, NAACP Papers.

21. Shockley, *"We, Too, Are Americans,"* 11, 41.

22. Charles C. Beckett, Executive Director, Proposal Submitted to Executive Committee of South Broad Street USO Club, ser. 6, box 7, NUL Records; "USO and the Negro Community," *Monthly Bulletin*, Atlanta, Ga., vol. 1, no. 8, July 1944, box A71, NUL-SRO Records; J. Saunders Redding, "Here's a New Thing Altogether," *Survey Graphic*, August 1944, box 7, RG 215.

23. Shockley, *"We, Too, Are Americans,"* 31.

24. To Walter White from Hazel Merrill-Branch, 5 June 1942, box B191, NAACP Papers.

25. To Walter White from Edward L. Bernays, 3 February 1942, and Ada McCormick, "An Open Letter," box B191, Legal File, NAACP Papers.

26. Sutherland, *Americans and Their Servants*, 12–13.

27. "Factors Influencing USO Services to Negroes in Region VII," presented by William Y. Bell, Associate Regional Executive, at the Regional Staff Conference, December 1943, ser. 1, General Office Files, box A72, NUL-SRO Records.

28. "Fayetteville Sums Up Importance of Negro Women in Wartime," *Information Sheet*, April 1943, box 6, WWII Collection.

29. *USO Manual, Community Conducted Operations*, box 19, RG 215; Elizabeth Cutter Morrow, Chairman, USO Institute, "USO Volunteer Training," *USO Reporter*, October 1943, box 55, folder 622, WWII Collection.

30. Minutes, Women's Committee of the Philadelphia SDC, 1 September 1945, box 9, WWII Collection.

31. *USO Manual, Community Conducted Operations*, box 19, RG 215.

32. D. Campbell, *Women at War with America*, 66.

33. Hartmann, *Home Front and Beyond*, 78.

34. *USO Manual, Community Conducted Operations*, box 19, RG 215.

35. Abel, *Cheers for Volunteers*, 15; Arthur Plaut, "The Story of the USO in Cincinnati," SA Papers, 23.

36. *USO Manual, Community Conducted Operations*, box 19, RG 215.

37. Miller interview.

38. Campbell interview.

39. *USO Manual, Community Conducted Operations*, box 19, RG 215, E 24.

40. Ibid.

41. Harrison G. Otis, San Antonio, Texas, "Hostess Corps Forms," 7 July 1941, box 5, RG 215.

42. Bailey, *From Front Porch to Backseat*, 15–16.

43. *USO Bulletin*, 30 February 1944.

44. Gorham, *So Your Husband's Gone to War!*, 53. Many former junior hostesses believed that this was why senior hostesses they knew volunteered for the USO. See Marjorie Hawkins Sloan, Alene Gwinn McKnight, Nora O. Robertson, Susan Collins [pseud.], Shirley L. Gippner, Mildred Reca Durnal, Elizabeth A. TePoorten, Shannon Kelley [pseud.], and Edith Richards [pseud.], all WQ.

45. *USO, Five Years of Service*, 28.

46. Address by Lilias H. Smith, opening of San Angelo Club, 16 March 1943, box 7, NCCS Records.

47. Proceedings, USO War Activities Conference, 12 April 1942, RG 24.

48. "At the Stage Door Canteen," *Reader's Digest*, July 1943, 108.

49. Proceedings, USO War Activities Conference, 12 May 1942, box 72, RG 24.

50. "Pats on the Back," *Information Sheet*, April 1943, box 6, WWII Collection.

51. Address by Lilias H. Smith, opening of San Angelo Club, 16 March 1943, box 7, NCCS Records.

52. Report of the Committee on Discharged Servicemen, Philadelphia USO Council, 8 March 1944, box 66, NUL Records. The USO expected its staff members to know how to counsel servicemen when called upon to do so. See "Dealing with Individual Problems in USO," *Community Conducted Operations Reporter*, vol. 2, no. 7, November 1944, box 4, WWII Collection.

53. "Conference RE: Counseling Training for USO Staff, 8 April 1942, Joint Army and Navy Committee on Welfare and Recreation (JANCWR)," box 44, RG 225. The Army and Navy Special Services Division hired and paid hostesses to coordinate recreational activities for soldiers and sailors in Army Service Clubs and Navy Ship's Service Clubs in camps. Approximately 350 senior, junior, and canteen hostesses, 3 per camp, worked with morale officers and with community volunteers to do this. These paid

hostesses coordinated the camp dances to which the USO and other civilian organizations sent busloads of hostesses. As of 1942, 22,000 women applied for these hostessing
jobs. The military trained hostesses at the Special Service School at Fort Meade,
Maryland. See Raymond B. Fosdick, "The Leisure Time of a Democratic Army,"
Survey Graphic, June 1942, General Welfare Files, ser. USO, RG III, box 54, RAC,
281–82, and "The Salvation Army in the United Service Organizations for National
Defense," listed Confidential, SA Papers. Relationships between USO and military
chaplains are also discussed in Barney Maticka, chairman, "Coordination with Army
and Navy in the USO," Report of Workshop Group — Regional Institute, Milwaukee,
Wisc., 28 February–2 March 1944, box 19, RG 215.

54. Herspring, *Soldiers, Commissars, and Chaplains*, 17. Military historian Robert L.
Gushwa recognizes the USO as a "helping agency" during World War II but does not
discuss senior hostesses or acknowledge their role as counselors; see *Best and Worst of
Times*, 175.

55. Pfau, "Miss Yourlovin," 14.

56. Ibid., 18.

57. Rogin, *"Ronald Reagan," the Movie*, 242.

58. Abel, *Cheers for Volunteers*, 5; Minutes, USO Labor Plaza, Evening Chairman Meeting, 16 August 1944, box 23, WWII Collection. John D. Rockefeller Jr.
complimented USO Women's Division chair Mrs. Maurice T. Moore in a thank-you
letter on the lack of "aggressiveness and domination" in her demeanor. Her attributes
of "modesty, tact, and human understanding" made her an agreeable woman for him
to work with. Her deference symbolized not only normative gender but the desired
relationship between women and the wartime state. See to Mrs. Moore from John D.
Rockefeller Jr., 14 October 1942, RG III, General Welfare Files, box 51, folder
571, RAC.

59. Hartmann, *Home Front and Beyond*, 177.

60. Brigadier William J. Parkins, national program director, Salvation Army, "The
USO Work of the Salvation Army," box 5, RG 215. This same sentiment is expressed in
"On the Job Day and Night, USO Hostesses Combine Mother, Nurse, and Advisor
Roles for Service Men," *Red Shield*, September 1942, SA Papers.

61. "USO Club Directors Solve Problem of Lonesome Boy," *Red Shield*, October
1942, SA Papers.

62. Lieutenant Commander F. S. Mathewson, "What Does the Navy Expect of the
USO," USO Volunteers Conference, Highland Park, Ill., box 26, RG 24.

63. "Women's War Work," *Red Shield*, October 1943, SA Papers.

64. Turner, *USO in Panama*, 110. This service center operated with the same set of
standards as USO clubs in the United States.

65. USO, *Five Years of Service*, 27.

66. Katherine Scarborough, "Servants of Service Men for More than 4 Years," Neal Collection.

67. A. N. Culbertson, aviation cadet, Maxwell Field, Alabama, "No Tough Situation Here," Prentiss Papers, Montgomery, Ala.

68. Turner, *USO in Panama*, 52.

69. Balbo, "Crazy Quilts," 52–53.

70. Wakefield interview.

71. *The Salvation Army War Service*, SA Papers, 6.

72. Brandt, *No Magic Bullet*, 164.

73. Ibid., 161–62. The federal government passed the May Act in July 1941 to make prostitution near military facilities a federal crime. The federal government threatened local communities with enforcement of the May Act if they did not eliminate prostitution, but the act was only enforced twice during the war, in Tennessee and North Carolina. See ibid., 162, 166; Hegarty, *Victory Girls, Khaki-Wackies, and Patriotutes*, 6.

74. Interdepartmental Committee on Venereal Disease, 12 August 1945, box 1, RG 215.

75. Evans, *Born for Liberty*, 181.

76. "The Hostess as Musician," *Red Shield*, September 1942, SA Papers.

77. Winston, *Red-Hot and Righteous*, 134.

78. "Plan Dealing with Reported 'Liquor Abuses' in the Vicinity of Army Camps," submitted by Frank R. Schwengel, Chairman, Executive Committee, Conference of the Alcoholic Beverage Industries, n.d., box 6, RG 225.

79. To Honorable Margaret Chase Smith, House of Representatives, from Frederick Osborn, Chairman, 12 March 1941, box 6, RG 225; Hegarty, *Victory Girls, Khaki-Wackies, and Patriotutes*, 135.

80. "A United Nation Backs Them Up," National USO Campaign, General Welfare Files, RG III, box 54, folder 615, RAC.

81. John D. Rockefeller Jr.'s radio address on Columbia Broadcasting Network, 8 July 1941, for the Parents-Neighbors Organization of the USO, General Welfare Files, ser. 3, box 53, folder 585, RAC.

82. Michael C. C. Adams develops the contradictions with regard to temperance and war in his work; see *Best War Ever*, 94.

83. Army and Navy Information for USO Program Publication, from JANCWR, 1943, box 44, RG 225. Soldiers most often listed beer and milk as their "favorite drinks." See speech given by Florence Taaffe, Director of Information and Reports, JANCWR, JANC Conference in Minneapolis, Minn., 5 February 1943, box 37, RG 225.

84. Jennings [pseud.] interview.

85. Adams, *Best War Ever*, 94.

86. *Soldier Opinion about USO Clubs* (New York: USO, Inc., n.d.), SA Papers, 1. This study is particularly useful because it focuses on soldiers' use of USO clubs, not camp shows, mobile services, or transit lounges.

87. Ibid., 3, 5. The USO attracted more young African American men as opposed to those over age thirty (64 percent).

88. Abel, *Cheers for Volunteers*, 3; Arthur Plaut, "The Story of the USO in Cincinnati," SA Papers.

89. Banner, *In Full Flower*, 292, 294.

90. Ibid., 308.

91. Pseudonym.

92. Letter to Mrs. Servais, 24 May 1943, and letter to Helen from Mrs. Servais, 18 May 1943, ser. 2, box 1, folder 3, CDHC Records.

93. Mary Agnes Usher to author, February 2001; Usher interview.

94. Usher interview.

95. Williams [pseud.] interview.

96. Kelly interview.

97. Cowan, " 'Industrial Revolution' in the Home," 380.

98. Abel, *Cheers for Volunteers*, 14.

99. Coffey, *Always Home*, 5.

100. "USO Kitchen Provides Lunch for Soldier Who Feared Dining Car," *Red Shield*, February 1943, SA Papers.

101. Some USO clubs did not follow this particular USO policy. Mayor Kelly's Servicemen's Center in Chicago became famous for its motto "Everything free." Some of the items it gave away to servicemen during the war included 7,946,710 hot dogs, 8,110,500 sandwiches and 9,550,200 pieces of cake. "Housewives," male and female members of local community groups, and stores contributed food to the club. See memo from Chicago Servicemen's Center, box 13, RG 215.

102. Abel, *Cheers for Volunteers*, 14; Bulletin #8, "Policies Regarding Services and Sales and Distribution of Materials in USO Clubs," USO, New York, N.Y., box 75, RG 24.

103. Hegland and Hegland, *USO, "The Heart of San Diego,"* 27.

104. Ibid., 12.

105. To Mark A. McCloskey, Federal Security Agency, from James D. McKinley, Field Recreation Representative, 27 May 1942, OCWS, box 13, RG 215. Most USO clubs held birthday parties for servicemen, since they were not able to celebrate with their families. See "Birthday Cakes, Candles, Are Part of USO Service," *USO Bulletin*, April 1944, box 4, WWII Collection.

106. Address by Lilias H. Smith, opening of San Angelo Club, 16 March 1943, box 7, NCCS Records.

107. "The Cookie Nook," *Red Shield*, August 1942, SA Papers.

108. Bentley, *Eating for Victory*, 102, 105.

109. "The Cookie Nook," *Red Shield*, September 1942, SA Papers.

110. Bentley, *Eating for Victory*, 39, 46.

111. "Proxy Sons from USO," *Red Shield*, June 1943, SA Papers.

112. Pleck, *Celebrating the Family*, 55.

113. Letter to VHC'er from Winfield Adam, Secretary of the Young Men's Division, Baltimore YMCA, 19 December 1941, ser. 1, box 75, folder 7, YMCA Collection.

114. "A Christmas Message from USO," USO Program Services Division, 1944, box 29, NCCS Records; Arthur Plaut, "The Story of the USO in Cincinnati," SA Papers.

115. Nickerson interview.

116. Marling, *Merry Christmas!*, 349. Similarly, Micaela Di Leonardo argues that women perform the "kin work" in families, including sending Christmas cards, hosting holiday dinners, and maintaining ties among relatives; see Di Leonardo, "Female World of Cards and Holidays."

117. Pleck, *Celebrating the Family*, 50.

118. "A Christmas Message from USO," USO Program Services Division, 1944, box 29, NCCS Records.

119. Christmas Planner, 1945, Program Department, box 29, NCCS Records. The USO in Cincinnati also had a shopping service and a "wrapping service . . . because [they] found out that most of the men [had] a pretty tough time with all of the fancy string and paper that goes around Christmas packages" (Arthur Plaut, "The Story of the USO in Cincinnati," SA Papers, 14).

120. Katcher, *US Army, 1941–45*, 16–17.

121. Ibid., 4.

122. Mollo, *Naval, Marine, and Air Force Uniforms of World War II*, 182–83.

123. Hoza, Hoza, Bowley, and Bowley interview.

124. "USO Policy and Procedures," in *USO Manual, Community Conducted Operations*, box 19, RG 215; "Suggested Press Release for September 9," in USO Publicity Kit, September, box 7, WWII Collection; "For Release on Wednesday, August 11," Publicity Kit, August, box 10, WWII Collection.

125. Chicago Service Men Center, 2 April 1945, box 13, RG 215.

126. "Friend and Counselor," *Red Shield*, September 1942, and "Women's War Work," *Red Shield*, October 1943, SA Papers; Narrative Report for July 1944, Army-Navy YMCA, Hattiesburg USO Records; *USO, Five Years of Service*, 28.

127. Williams [pseud.] interview.

128. "Repairs for Army Keep Navy Mothers Busy," *Information Sheet*, July 1943, box 6, WWII Collection.

129. Evans, *Born for Liberty*, 50, 114, 171.

130. Hegland and Hegland, *USO, "The Heart of San Diego,"* 20.

CHAPTER 2

1. Hutchings interview.

2. In her article on the Philadelphia USO, Maryann Lovelace argues that the USO placed limits on women's ability to "challenge prewar conventions." While I agree with Lovelace that the USO attempted to do this, I think hostesses played an active role in supporting and sometimes resisting those boundaries; see "Facing Change in Wartime Philadelphia," 156.

3. Ibid., 146.

4. Blake and Blake interview.

5. To Mickey from Ann, Philadelphia, 17 February 1944 (appears to be draft of a letter for publication), box 9, WWII Collection.

6. Gilligan, *Female Corporate Culture and the New South*, 12; Lowe, *Women in the Administrative Revolution*, 19–20; Benson, *Counter Cultures*, 209.

7. Minutes, 2 February 1942, Subcommittee on Dances, Cambridge Committee on Recreation, Civilian Defense, carton 9, Records of the Cambridge YWCA, Cambridge, Mass.

8. Wardman interview; Marjorie Hawkins Sloan, WQ. Sloan also joined with college friends.

9. Hartmann, *Home Front and Beyond*, 103.

10. Nadine Thomas Cothrun, WQ. Also, Susan Collins [pseud.], Shannon Kelley [pseud.], Julia Currie [pseud.], Carol Brooks [pseud.], Donna Smith [pseud.], and Shirley L. Gippner, all WQ; Pantaz interview.

11. Beverly Littlejohn, WQ.

12. "Standards for USO Junior Hostess Groups," USO Field Service Bulletin #29, box 18, WWII Collection.

13. Manual, Hostess Training Institute, Madison, Wisc., Recreation Committee of the Dane County Civilian Defense Council, box 5, RG 215.

14. *Volunteer Hostess Club News Notes*, Central YMCA, 25 June 1941, YMCA Collection.

15. Hoza, Hoza, Bowley, and Bowley interview; Jewish Welfare Board Captains Minutes, 21 June 1945, box 18, WWII Collection.

16. "Standards for USO Junior Hostess Groups," USO Field Service Bulletin #29, box 18, WWII Collection.

17. Luckow [pseud.] interview.

18. Collins, *Black Feminist Thought*, 130.

19. Of the women interviewed for this project, the primary occupations they held while hostessing included secretary/office clerk/bookkeeper/stenographer (23), student (11), store clerk (7), social service employee (6), and entertainer/entertainment support (4). Junior hostesses in this pool also babysat (1), joined the WAVES (1), worked in factories (2), and were writers (1).

Twenty-five hostesses had fathers employed in the trades, law enforcement, or blue-collar work. Twenty fathers enjoyed white-collar status in fields such as engineering, medicine, education, and sales. Several were also military officers. The fathers of eight hostesses were farmers, ranchers, or plantation owners. Five men owned their own businesses.

Of the former junior hostesses interviewed for this project, 46 had mothers who were primarily homemakers and in some cases also assisted with the family business, such as a grocery store. When mothers worked they were employed in the trades (1), in the food service industry (4), in agriculture (3), in sales (4), in clerical work (1), or as a telephone operator (1).

20. Stock, *Main Street in Crisis*, 9.

21. "Standards for USO Junior Hostess Groups," USO Field Service Bulletin #29, box 18, WWII Collection.

22. *Girls Service Organization Manual*, Saratoga Street USO, Neal Collection, 9; Girls in Montgomery, Alabama, went through a similar process. See "Constitution-Girls Service Organization," Prentiss Papers, Montgomery, Ala.

23. Minutes of Hostess Committee Meeting, USO Labor Plaza, 14 June 1944, box 23, WWII Collection.

24. "The USO in Philadelphia," box 19, WWII Collection.

25. To Anne from Laura P. Servais, 4 March 1943, and to Julie Anne from Ethel Hutchinson, 28 February 1943, ser. 2, box 1, CDHC Records.

26. June Program Report, USO Club, 1942, Hattiesburg USO Records.

27. "Standards for USO Junior Hostess Groups," USO Field Service Bulletin #29, box 18, WWII Collection.

28. Bristow, *Making Men Moral*, 1–2; Clement, *Love for Sale*, 114–15.

29. Address by James J. Norris, Executive Director of NCCS, 18 May 1941, box 7, NCCS Records.

30. "Personal and Strictly Confidential," 26 May 1941, Welfare Interests General, RG III, box 51, folder 566, RAC.

31. "Betty Ward Accorded USO Title of 'Regiment Sweetheart' at Center," Betty Ward Collection, Tempe, Ariz.

32. Baldridge interview.

33. Marian Richardson, WQ.

34. "Willie Gillis at the USO," in Sommer, *Norman Rockwell*, 35.

35. Honey, "Maternal Welders," 511; Melissa Dabakis also makes this argument in "Gendered Labor," 186.

36. Summary of events, 15 January 1945, box 9, WWII Collection.

37. "SDC Adds Thirty Colored Girls to Staff," *Afro-American News*, 24 March 1944, box 9, WWII Collection.

38. To Executive Director of SDC, from Barbara Stix, 10 March 1945, box 9, WWII Collection.

39. Lovelace, "Facing Change in Wartime Philadelphia," 155.

40. "Wanted at Once: 100 Japanese American Hostesses," *USO, Five Years of Service*, 13.

41. Memo to Mr. Francis Keppel, Secretary, JANCWR, from Karl W. Marks, Major AGD, Asst. Executive Officers, Special Services Division, October 1944, box 44, RG 225. Just as the federal government chose not to intern Hawaiians of Japanese descent, the USO in Hawaii likely disregarded the JANCWR policy on hiring Japanese Americans. See Bailey and Farber, *First Strange Place*, 5.

42. Bailey and Farber, *First Strange Place*, 53.

43. *USO General Operating Practice: A Manual of General Policies, Principal Organization Relationships, and the Main Lines of Procedure in USO Operations, Continental United States* (New York: USO, Inc., 1944), SA Papers, 46.

44. Memo to Ray Johns from Henry W. Pope, 4 March 1944, RG III 2 P, Office of the Messrs. Rockefeller Welfare Interests — General, 1942–1945, box 50, folder 562, RAC.

45. To Walter White, Secretary, NAACP, from Matthew W. Bullock, 22 October 1943, General Office Files, box A641, NAACP Papers.

46. To Walter White, Secretary, NAACP, from Ray W. Guild, President of the Coordinating Council of Colored Clubs for National Defense, member of the USO, Inc., 29 September 1943, box A641, NAACP Papers.

47. Hale, *Making Whiteness*; Gilmore, *Gender and Jim Crow*; Higginbotham, *Righteous Discontent*.

48. Maryann Lovelace draws this same conclusion about race relations and the USO in Philadelphia in "Facing Change in Wartime Philadelphia," 170.

49. To Walter White, Secretary, NAACP, from Ray W. Guild, President of the Coordinating Council of Colored Clubs for National Defense, member of the USO, Inc., 29 September 1943, box A641, NAACP Papers.

50. Gilmore, *Gender and Jim Crow*, 177; Higginbotham, *Righteous Discontent*, 89.

51. Cohen, *Consumers' Republic*, 43–44.

52. *Pittsburgh Courier*, 7 February 1942, 1. Megan Taylor Shockley, in *"We, Too, Are Americans,"* 26, argues that black women used wartime volunteerism to advance their claims to citizenship.

53. "Standards for USO Junior Hostess Groups," USO Field Service Bulletin #29, rev. 26 April 1944, box 18, WWII Collection.

54. To Helen Albertson, Women's Page, Philadelphia Record, from Stella Moore, Philadelphia SDC, 23 June 1943, box 9, WWII Collection; Constitution, Girls Service Organization, Prentiss Papers, Montgomery, Ala. Other organizations also followed the age limits set by the national USO; see CDHC, Agenda for Meeting of Fort Devens Area Dance Hostess Committees, 15 May 1942, ser. 2, box 1, CDHC Records; Girls Service Organization in Baltimore, *Girls Service Organization Manual*, Saratoga Street USO, Neal Collection; Madison Hostess Units, *Madison Hostess Units Manual*, box 5, RG 215.

55. To Barbara from Laura P. Servais, 11 January 1943, box 2, CDHC Records.

56. In her letter, Servais did not specify Mrs. Jeanson's ethnicity but said she did not "speak English very well." See to Julianne from Laura P. Servais, 5 March, 19 February, ser. 2, box 1, CDHC Records.

57. Wardman interview.

58. Rader interview.

59. "Standards for USO Junior Hostess Groups," USO Field Service Bulletin #29, rev. 26 April 1944, box 18, WWII Collection; Girls Service Organization in Baltimore, *Girls Service Organization Manual*, Saratoga Street USO, Neal Collection, 10.

60. Church and Church interview.

61. Alene Eva Gwinn McKnight, WQ.

62. Constitution Girls Service Organization, Prentiss Papers, Montgomery, Ala.; agenda for meeting of Fort Devens Area Dance Hostess Committees, 15 May 1942, ser. 2, box 1, CDHC Records; Girls Service Organization in Baltimore, *Girls Service Organization Manual*, Saratoga Street USO, Neal Collection; Madison Hostess Units, *Madison Hostess Units Manual*, box 5, RG 215.

63. Dorothy Cheyne, "It Happened Here," in *Serving the Armed Services: A Look Through the Window of a Salvation Army Service Club*, Fayetteville, N.C., SA Papers.

64. Narrative Program Report for July 1943, Hattiesburg USO Records.

65. Narrative Program Report for May 1943, ibid.

66. Arthur Plaut, "The Story of the USO in Cincinnati," SA Papers.

67. Meyer, *Creating GI Jane*, 55, 66.

68. To Commander J. L. Reynolds, Director of WR Division, U.S. Navy, from Bertha F. Stone, Executive Director of the ATW SDC of Washington Lafayette Square, 14 April 1943, box 44, RG 225. The SDC also enforced this rule in Philadelphia; see Women's Committee Minutes of the SDC, Philadelphia, 27 June 1944, box 9, WWII Collection.

69. To Commander J. L. Reynolds from Lt. Commander C. L. P. Nichols, USNR, 23 April 1943, box 44, RG 225.

70. Minutes of the Women's Committee of the SDC, Philadelphia, 21 December 1942, 1 February 1943, box 34, WWII Collection.

71. Stage Door Canteen, WWII Collection; Weinstock and Weinstock interview; Blake and Blake interview; Hale interview; *USO, Five Years of Service*; Coffey, *Always Home*, 13.

72. Sumner Blake was a doorman at the Hollywood Canteen; see Blake and Blake interview.

73. Weinstock and Weinstock interview.

74. Hale interview.

75. Speech by Francis Keppel, Secretary of JANCWR, USO Club, Washington, D.C., 15 December 1942, box 44, RG 225.

76. "Report of Trip to Pacific Coast," Pearl Case Blough, Jan–Feb 1944, box 45, RG 225.

77. Ibid.

78. Pearl Case Blough, "Clubs Welcome Service Women," *USO Reporter* (Community Conducted Operations), August 1943, box 4, WWII Collection; Minutes of Conference of Joint Army and Navy Committee on Welfare and Recreation, OCWS, USO Committee on Services to Women and Girls, 16 May [no year], box 45, RG 225; to Commander John L. Reynolds, Director, WR Division, from John Schoolcraft, USO Area Representative, Washington, D.C., box 44, RG 225.

79. YWCA of Philadelphia, Report, 17 December 1942, box 2, WWII Collection.

80. In 1944, the national USO decided to add "and Service Women" to their official welcome signs and publicity; see "USO Signs Will Welcome US Service Women, Too," *USO Bulletin*, August 1944, box 4, WWII Collection.

81. Linda Kerber argues that the public did not believe women in the military served their country in an appropriate fashion throughout the post-1945 period; see *No Constitutional Right to Be Ladies*, 287.

82. "Colonel Martha Hamon Resumes USO Activity," *Red Shield*, January 1945, SA Papers. Leisa Meyer argues that the Women's Army Corps also held this opinion; see *Creating GI Jane*, 55.

83. "Report of Trip to Pacific Coast," Pearl Case Blough, Jan–Feb 1944, box 45, RG 225.

84. Minutes of Conference of Joint Army and Navy Committee on Welfare and Recreation, OCWS, USO Committee on Services to Women and Girls, May 16 [no year], box 45, RG 225.

85. "Report of Trip to Pacific Coast," Pearl Case Blough, Jan–Feb 1944, box 45, RG 225.

86. Meyer, *Creating GI Jane*, 3.

87. Monthly Program Bulletin, vol. 2, no. 1, NCCS Records, 6.

88. "Hostess Standards Reflect Human Needs Emphasized by War," *Information Sheet*, February 1943, box 6, WWII Collection.

89. Ibid.

90. Interview with May Edward Hill, in *The Black Women's Oral History Project*, ed. Ruth Edmonds Hill (Westport, Conn.: Meckler, 1991), 6:23; "Elaborate USO Center, Better Than Whites', Stirs Army Curiosity," Series Legal File, box B191, NAACP Papers; Shockley, *"We, Too, Are Americans."*

91. Narrative Report, Negro Club, Wilmington, N.C., to John I. Neasmith, Regional Recreation Rep., Defense Health and Welfare Services, from Harry M. Wellott, Field Recreation Rep., 17 August 1942, box 4, RG 215.

92. Memo: RE Charleston, SC, 4–5 May 1943, General Office Files, box A66, NUL-SRO Records.

93. Craig, *Ain't I a Beauty Queen?*, 31–35.

94. "Hostess Standards Reflect Human Needs Emphasized by War," *Information Sheet*, February 1943, box 6, WWII Collection.

95. Higginbotham, *Righteous Discontent*, 14–15; Craig, *Ain't I a Beauty Queen?*, 33.

96. Wong, "War Comes to Chinatown," 179–80.

97. Madison Hostess Units, *Madison Hostess Units Manual*, box 5, RG 215.

98. "Junior Hostesses' Rules," American Theatre Wing War Service, Inc., Philadelphia SDC, box 10, WWII Collection.

99. Brumberg, *Fasting Girls*, 13, 246; Bordo, *Unbearable Weight*, 159.

100. *USO Manual, Community Conducted Operations*, box 19, RG 215, 48. This document duplicates sections from USO Field Service Bulletin #29, "Standards for USO Junior Hostess Groups," rev. 26 April 1944, box 18, WWII Collection.

101. Minutes of the Meeting of Junior Captains, 18 October 1945, box 18, WWII Collection.

102. *Volunteers in the War Emergency Services of the Salvation Army*, SA Papers.

103. Madison Hostess Units, *Madison Hostess Units Manual*, box 5, RG 215.

104. Brumberg, *Fasting Girls*, 69.

105. Peiss, *Hope in a Jar*, 239, 245.

106. *Hints for Hostesses in Service Clubs*, box 5, RG 215.

107. Madison Hostess Units, *Madison Hostess Units Manual*, box 5, RG 215.

108. Peiss, *Hope in a Jar*, 244.

109. Delano, "Making Up for War," 41, 43.

110. Peiss, *Hope in a Jar*, 244.

111. *Hints for Hostesses in Service Clubs*, box 5, RG 215.

112. Blake and Blake interview.

113. Weinstock and Weinstock interview.

114. *Girls Service Organization Manual*, Saratoga Street USO, Neal Collection. The Madison, Wisc., clubs also encouraged hostesses to accessorize; see *Madison Hostess Units Manual*, box 5, RG 215.

115. *Girls Service Organization Manual*, Saratoga Street USO, Neal Collection, 12.

116. Hegland and Hegland, *USO, "The Heart of San Diego,"* 41.

117. "Rules of Soldier's Center," Prentiss Papers, Montgomery, Ala.; "Standards for USO Junior Hostess Groups," USO Field Service Bulletin #29, rev. 26 April 1944, box 18, WWII Collection; also specified in *Girls Service Organization Manual*, Saratoga Street USO, Neal Collection, and *Madison Hostess Units Manual*, box 5, RG 215.

118. Boston Soldiers and Sailors Committee: Dances and Social Events Committee, YMCA, 1 June 1942, carton 9, Records of the Cambridge YWCA, Cambridge, Mass.; Narrative Program Report of July 1943, Hattiesburg USO Records.

119. To CDHC from Sarah Mongeon, Program Assistant, Ayer USO, ser. 2, box 1, CDHC Records.

120. Marling, *Debutante*, 101.

121. Helen A. Gosnell, WQ; Penska interview.

122. Hartmann, *Home Front and Beyond*, 194.

123. Grossman and Assyia interview.

124. Baldridge interview. *Life* magazine instructed women how to apply "bottled stockings" in a pictorial spread; see "Bare-Leg Make-Up," *Life*, 5 July 1943, 86–90.

125. Pinky King purchased stockings when they were available but had no qualms about wearing bare legs to USO dances when she could not find them in Spokane, Washington. See King interview.

126. Girls Service Organization in Baltimore, *Girls Service Organization Manual*, Saratoga Street USO, Neal Collection, 12.

127. Roby [pseud.] interview.

128. The SDC required its hostesses to "look [their] prettiest," even while they wore blue aprons with red and white pockets. Junior hostess captains wore red aprons with the same decoration. See "Junior Hostesses' Rules," American Theatre Wing War Service, Inc., Philadelphia SDC, box 10, and to Helen Albertson, Philadelphia Record, from Stella Moore, 23 June 1943, box 9, WWII Collection. The USO held a Conference on Standardized Dress at Lord and Taylor's in New York City to view and discuss proposed uniforms for USO paid staff. The USO wanted the uniforms to be distinguishable from military uniforms. The women's uniform included a blue dress and jacket. See memo to Major HD McKeige from K. Kenneth-Smith, 14 February 1942, box 26, RG 24.

129. To Mrs. Favorite from Marjorie Simson [last name is handwritten and difficult to read], 8 April 1945, box 9, WWII Collection. Captains reported junior hostesses

who broke the rules to the "checkers" who sat at the front desk. The checkers marked their "junior hostess book" as follows: S, Wore Sweater; B, Bad Attitude; P, Forgot Pass; M, Left with service man. Junior captains "warned" those women who disobeyed the rules, "suspended" the second-offenders, and removed third-time offenders from the canteen roster. See "Captains," SDC, box 10, WWII Collection. The Junior Hostess Committee of the USO in Baltimore was responsible for "screening" and monitoring hostesses as well as expelling "undesirable hostesses." See "Work Analysis Sheet of Miss Sally Loudon, Assistant Director, Baltimore USO," from Baltimore USO Staff Plan and Organizations, ser. 1, box 59, YMCA Collection.

130. Labor Plaza Evening Chairman and Hostess Committee Meeting, 21 February 1945, box 23, WWII Collection.

131. Weinstock and Weinstock interview.

132. *USO Bulletin*, August 1946, 2.

133. Abel, *Hail Hostesses*, 4.

134. Westbrook, " 'I Want a Girl,' " 595, 600.

135. Grossman and Assyia interview.

136. Lovelace, "Facing Change in Wartime Philadelphia," 168.

137. Grossman and Assyia interview. Though the Music Box Canteen was not an official USO organization, the woman in charge, a former opera singer, used similar class-based selection processes to screen hostesses and enforced the same types of rules that the USO did. For example, the Music Box Canteen did not allow hostesses to leave with servicemen. The canteen was also alcohol-free. Servicemen danced with hostesses, played cards and Ping-Pong, and chatted with them at the Music Box.

138. To Walter White, Secretary, NAACP, from Theodore R. Senior and Edgar B. Anderson, 20 December 1943; "Lonely Soldiers in South Pacific Want Colored Pin-Up Girls," 6 January 1944; to Sir from Ozell E. Bryant, 15 January 1944, box A650, NAACP Papers.

139. Meyerowitz, "Women, Cheesecake, and Borderline Material," 17, 20.

CHAPTER 3

1. To Sir from Geraldine Stansbery, 21 May 1943, box 23, WWII Collection. Response from Samuel H. Rosenberg, Secretary to the Mayor, to Geraldine Stansbery, ibid., indicates that Stansbery wrote to Acting Mayor Bernard Samuel.

2. D. Campbell, *Women at War with America*, 67–69.

3. Ibid., 34.

4. Marjorie Hawkins Sloan, WQ.

5. Irene Szuhay Hennig, WQ.

6. Byko interview. Other women expressed a similar desire to socialize with servicemen and with other women; see Susan Collins [pseud.], WQ; Penska interview; Pantaz interview; Beverly Littlejohn, WQ.

7. Penksa interview.

8. "Salute to Miss Jones, Miss Brown, Miss Smith, from the USO," USO Club, 131 S. Wabash Avenue, Chicago, Ill., box 10, WWII Collection.

9. Bailey, *From Front Porch to Backseat*, 42–43.

10. Mildred Reca Durnal, WQ. The majority of men who attended USO functions came from urban backgrounds, often had a high school or a college degree, and visited clubs on a regular basis. See *Soldier Opinion about USO Clubs* (New York: USO, Inc., n.d.), SA Papers, 6, 12.

11. *Hints for Hostesses in Service Clubs*, box 5, RG 215.

12. June Elkin, WQ.

13. Marjorie Hawkins Sloan, WQ.

14. Dumenil, *Modern Temper*, 81.

15. While hostessing, Ann manufactured *Sears* and *Montgomery Ward's* catalogs for R. R. Donnelly. She also worked in a newspaper office. Her father was unemployed and later sold groceries on commission. Her mother was a homemaker, and her parents owned their own home. See Luckow [pseud.] interview.

16. "Junior Hostesses' Rules," American Theatre Wing War Service, Inc., and "Rules for Hostesses," Philadelphia SDC, box 10, WWII Collection.

17. Women's Committee of the Philadelphia SDC, 22 February 1943, box 10, and 28 September 1942, box 34, WWII Collection.

18. Minutes of Meeting of Junior Captains, JWB, 18 October 1945, box 18, WWII Collection.

19. The numbers were 5,077 in 1944 and 2,812 in 1945; see Summary of Yearly Totals, USO-YMCA Program and Services, 1 August 1941–31 December 1945, Hattiesburg USO Records.

20. Form letter from Personnel Committee addressing first absence, Philadelphia SDC, and form letter from Philadelphia SDC addressing second absence, box 10, WWII Collection.

21. Form letter to Junior Hostess from Mrs. Van Horn Ely Jr., Philadelphia SDC, box 10, WWII Collection.

22. Carolyn Mullin, "To The Hostesses," *USO Labor Plaza News*, box 25, WWII Collection.

23. Hostesses had the option to appeal their dismissal to the Labor Plaza Grievance Committee. See USO Labor Plaza, Hostess Committee and Evening Chairman Meeting, 25 July 1945, box 23, WWII Collection.

24. "Recreation for Women in War Areas," box 6, RG 215.

25. To Miss Miller from Emily [handwritten last name impossible to decipher], 27 November 1942, and to Miss Miller from Emily, n.d., ser. 2, box 1, CDHC Records.

26. Woods interview.

27. Weinstock and Weinstock interview.

28. Blumer, "Morale," 209; Pope, "How Can Individuals Keep a Healthy Morale in Wartime?," 252.

29. Paul McNutt, "Proposals for United Services of National Private Agencies in the Morale Aspects of the National Service Program," December 1940, SA Papers.

30. "General Gavin Praises USO," November 1946, box 29, NCCS Records.

31. Reverend Edward V. Stanford, *The Serviceman and Sex* (1940; 7th printing, 1964), NCCS Records, 4; "A Study of Protective Measures in the City of Boston," *JSH*, no. 7 (1942): 410; "Building Morale in the US Army and Navy," *JSH*, no. 5 (1941): 227; Dr. Joseph Earle More, Chief of Syphilis Division of the Medical Clinic, Johns Hopkins University, Chairman of the Subcommittee on VD, National Research Council, in address to Joint Army and Navy Committee, Conference of Morale Officers, 25–28 February 1941, box 1, RG 215; Costello, *Virtue under Fire*, 89.

32. John D. Rockefeller Jr.'s radio address on Columbia Broadcasting Network, 8 July 1941, for the Parents-Neighbors Organization of the USO, General Welfare Files, ser. 3, box 53, folder 585, RAC.

33. Commander John L. Reynolds, Director, Welfare and Recreation Section, Bureau of Navigation, United States Navy, "Relaxation—The USO's Business," War Activities Conference, General Welfare Files, USO Series, box 54, RAC.

34. Arthur Plaut, "The Story of the USO in Cincinnati," SA Papers, 23.

35. Blake and Blake interview.

36. Wardman interview.

37. Blake and Blake interview.

38. Arthur Plaut, "The Story of the USO in Cincinnati," SA Papers, 38.

39. D. Campbell, *Women at War with America*, 71.

40. Hutchings interview. The same sentiment was expressed in Donna Smith [pseud.], WQ.

41. Cohen, *Consumers' Republic*, 139.

42. Press release from United Service Organizations, Inc., New York, N.Y., 19 March 1942, box B191, folder "USO, 1942," NAACP Papers.

43. To Helen Albertson, Women's Page, Philadelphia Record, from Stella Moore, Philadelphia SDC, 23 June 1943, box 9, WWII Collection.

44. *Soldier Opinion about USO Clubs* (New York: USO, Inc., n.d.), SA Papers, 18.

45. Carolyn Mullin, "To the Hostesses," *USO Labor Plaza News*, box 25, WWII Collection, 3.

46. Raymond B. Fosdick, "The Leisure Time of a Democratic Army," *Survey Graphic*, June 1942, General Welfare Files, ser. USO, RG III, box 54, RAC, 281–82. The federal government set up a subcommittee on hostesses in 1941 to establish educational qualifications for senior and junior army hostesses. See to Miss Mildred McAfee, President of Wellesley College, from Mrs. Francis Keppel, Secretary of Joint Army and Navy Committee on Welfare and Recreation, 12 August 1941, box 32, RG 225. A subcommittee that included Sarah Blanding, dean of the School of Domestic Sciences, Cornell University; Grace Coyle, professor of Group Work Activities, Western Reserve University; and others recommended that hostesses should have been college graduates with three to five years of experience in the field of recreation planning. See Memorandum to JANCWR from Subcommittee on Hostesses, 25 August 1941; to Frederick Osborn, Chairman, Joint Army and Navy Committee on Welfare and Recreation, from Reverend M. R. Hamsher, Central Pa. Synod, Harrisburg, Pa., 19 March 1941; and to Reverend M. R. Hamsher from Frederick Osborn, 22 March 1941, box 32, RG 225.

47. Meyer, *Creating GI Jane*, 33.

48. To Frederick Osborn, Chairman, Joint Army and Navy Committee on Welfare and Recreation, from Reverend M. R. Hamsher, Central Pa. Synod, Harrisburg, Pa., 19 March 1941, and to Reverend M. R. Hamsher from Frederick Osborn, 22 March 1941, box 32, RG 225.

49. Raymond B. Fosdick, "The Leisure Time of a Democratic Army," *Survey Graphic*, June 1942, General Welfare Files, ser. USO, RG III, box 54, RAC, 283–84.

50. "Salute to Miss Jones, Miss Brown, Miss Smith, from the USO," USO Club, 131 S. Wabash Avenue, Chicago, Ill., box 10, WWII Collection.

51. To Helen Albertson, Women's Page, Philadelphia Record, from Stella Moore, Philadelphia SDC, 23 June 1943, box 9, WWII Collection.

52. July 1942 Program Report, Hattiesburg USO Records.

53. Madison Hostess Units, *Madison Hostess Units Manual*, box 5, RG 215.

54. Manual, Hostess Training Institute, Madison, Wisc., Recreation Committee of the Dane County Civilian Defense Council, box 5, RG 215. This document does not have "USO" printed on it. According to the "Service Men's Centers" folder in box 10, RG 215, two USOs were located in Madison: USO Center, 16 E. Doty Street, operated by the YMCA, and USO Center, Unitarian Church, Wisconsin and Dayton Streets, operated by the YMCA. List of centers from 5 January 1944.

55. Hoza, Hoza, Bowley, and Bowley interview.

56. Comments from Lieutenant Russell B. Becktell, Chaplain at Bedford, 16 July 1942, ser. 2, box 1, CDHC Records.

57. Bailey, *From Front Porch to Backseat*, 110, 115.

58. Katherine Scarborough, "Servants of Service Men for More Than Four Years," newspaper clipping, Neal Collection.

59. "Dancing for Our Boys," *American Dancer*, November 1942, 31.

60. "Hostess Standards Reflect Human Needs Emphasized by War," *Information Sheet*, February 1943, box 6, WWII Collection.

61. *Stage Door Canteen* filled the number 10 spot on *Film Daily*'s "10 Best List" and "became one of the 24 top grossing films of 1942–43" (Fetrow, *Feature Films, 1940–1949*, 476).

62. *Stage Door Canteen*.

63. Narrative Program Report, January 1945, Hattiesburg USO Records.

64. Soldiers most often danced, "met girls," and read magazines in USO clubs, but they also played games, listened to music, sang, participated in sports, wrote letters, made sketches, and learned new activities like photography. See *Soldier Opinion about USO Clubs* (New York: USO, Inc., n.d.), SA Papers. The CDHC often asked hostesses to bake cookies for the cookie jar at the Concord Service Men's Center; see Announcements, 9 August 1942, ser. 3, box 2, CDHC Records. Hostesses and servicemen went on "mystery outings . . . to private homes in the suburbs" of Baltimore where they enjoyed dinner and outdoor sports, while CDHC members participated in bingo parties where prizes for servicemen included cartons of cigarettes, a long-distance telephone call, and "a manicure by a beautiful blonde." See YMCA Minutes, 8 June 1942, ser. 1, box 9, YMCA Collection, and USO-Shirley, Bingo Party (report), 17 November, ser. 1, box 1, CDHC Records. Junior hostesses from the USO–National Catholic Community Services in San Francisco, Calif., sang at a memorial service to commemorate Navy Day in 1946; see "Memorial Service Held at Sea," December 1946, box 29, CUA, NCCS Records.

65. Alsop and McBride, *Arms and the Girl*, 272.

66. "Salute to Miss Jones, Miss Brown, Miss Smith, from the USO," USO Club, 131 S. Wabash Avenue, Chicago, Ill., box 10, WWII Collection.

67. Wilson, *Charm*, 25. The same advice was given in *Madison Hostess Units Manual*, box 5, RG 215.

68. *Hints for Hostesses in Service Clubs*, box 5, RG 215.

69. Ibid.

70. Hochschild, *Managed Heart*, 11.

71. Alsop and McBride, *Arms and the Girl*, 276.

72. Girls Service Organization in Baltimore, *Girls Service Organization Manual*, Saratoga Street USO, Neal Collection, 13.

73. Manual, Hostess Training Institute, Madison, Wisc., Recreation Committee of the Dane County Civilian Defense Council, box 5, RG 215.

74. Abel, *Hail Hostesses*, 8; "Salute to Miss Jones, Miss Brown, Miss Smith, from the USO," USO Club, 131 S. Wabash Avenue, Chicago, Ill., box 10, WWII Collection.

75. Memo to Junior Hostesses, RE: Dancing with Negro servicemen at the Stage

Door Canteen, from Margaret Halsey, author, captain of junior hostesses at SDC, General Office Files, box A641, NAACP Papers. Reprinted with her permission.

76. Memo for Lt. Col. Stanton Hall, 13 April 1943, box 41, RG 225. The military provided poor facilities for black troops in Norfolk, Virginia. See to the Commandant, Eight Naval District, New Orleans, La., from the Commanding Officer, U.S. Naval Training Station, Norfolk, Va., 19 February 1942, box 26, RG 24.

77. To Wheeler from William Bell Jr., Investigation of New Orleans, 27 May 1944, box A72, NUL-SRO Records.

78. Ibid.

79. Lee, *Employment of Negro Troops*, 100–106.

80. William Y. Bell, Associate Regional Executive, paper presented at Regional Staff Conference, December 1943, ser. 1, General Office Files, box A72, NUL-SRO Records. It was more difficult for black men and women to organize USO clubs and programs, given the racism that they often battled simply to secure funds and space; see J. Saunders Redding, "Here's a New Thing Altogether," *Survey Graphic*, August 1944, box 7, RG 215.

81. William Y. Bell, Associate Regional Executive, report presented at Regional Staff Conference, December 1943, scr. 1, General Office Files, box A72, NUL-SRO Records.

82. "NAACP Asks for Statement of USO Policy," 6 June 1944, telegram, Legal Files, box B191, NAACP Papers; memorandum for Lt. Col. L. F. Nickel from Francis Keppel, Secretary, 11 November 1942, box 37, RG 225.

83. To Joshua Bell, Grand Rapids, Mich., from Secretary of NAACP, 27 May 1943, General Office Files, box A641, NAACP Papers.

84. To Ned Pope, Director of Services to Negroes, USO, from Assistant Secretary, 8 October 1943; to Roy Wilkins from Effa Manley, Newark USO, 7 October 1943; to Roy Wilkins from Henry Pope, Director of Services to Negroes, USO, 13 October 1943, General Office Files, box A641, NAACP Papers. Similar circumstances existed in Salinas, Calif., where black citizens wanted to create a USO club for black servicemen; see to Walter White, NAACP, from Mrs. Alma A. Bains, Branch Secretary, Salinas NAACP, 8 February 1943, General Office Files, box A650, NAACP Papers. The NAACP branch in Hutchinson, Kans., also did not know how to respond when white USO officers would not allow black servicemen into their clubs. The branch knew that black troops needed recreation, but they were hesitant to perpetuate segregation by opening a separate club for them. See to Walter White, NAACP, from [handwritten name unreadable], 11 May 1943, NAACP Papers; to Mr. White from Mr. Konvitz; to Walter White from Joshua Bell, 23 May 1943; to Sirs from Clifton Pope, Secretary of Hutchinson Branch, 10 May 1943, vol. 2, General Office Files, box A641, NAACP Papers.

85. Wardman interview.

86. Donna Smith [pseud.] and Elizabeth A. TePoorten, WQ. Also, Mildred Reca Durnal, Julia Currie [pseud.], and Nadine Thomas Cothrun, all WQ.

87. June Elkin, WQ.

88. Alene Eva Gwinn McKnight, WQ.

89. Gubar, " 'This Is My Rifle,' " 240. D'Ann Campbell, *Women at War with America*, 71, also discusses the danger of gossip during the war.

90. *Hints for Hostesses in Service Clubs*, box 5, RG 215; "Standards for USO Junior Hostess Groups," USO Field Service Bulletin #29, rev. 26 April 1944, box 18, WWII Collection.

91. "Junior Hostesses" and "Junior Hostesses' Rules," American Theatre Wing War Service, Inc., Philadelphia SDC, box 10, WWII Collection.

92. Blake and Blake interview.

93. Mary E. Hester, National Catholic Community Service Volunteer Services, "Suggested Procedures for the Organization of Junior Hostesses," box 9, NCCS Records.

94. Nickerson interview.

95. Mary E. Hester, National Catholic Community Service Volunteer Services, "Suggested Procedures for the Organization of Junior Hostesses," box 9, NCCS Records.

96. Annual Report, Army and Navy Comm. JWB, 4 March 1945, box 18, WWII Collection.

97. *Volunteers in the War Emergency Services of the Salvation Army*, SA Papers; to Mrs. William F. Hurter from Helen Morton, 6 February 1942, box 13, Records of the Cambridge YWCA, Cambridge, Mass. The Massachusetts USO State Committee held a group discussion on junior hostess training at the Fort Devons Area Conference in Fitchburg, Mass.; see series 2, box 1, CDHC Records. The USO Labor Plaza taught women about the Philadelphia area and about the history of the Labor Plaza; see Labor Plaza Minutes, 15 May 1946, box 22, WWII Collection.

98. Madison Hostess Units, *Madison Hostess Units Manual*, box 5, RG 215; membership application, Volunteer Hostess Club, Young Men's Division, Central YMCA, Baltimore, Md., ser. 1, box 75, YMCA Collection; Carol Brooks [pseud.], WQ.

99. Donna Hendrickson [pseud.], WQ.

100. Minutes of Meeting of Junior Captains, 18 October 1945, box 18, WWII Collection. The no-smoking rule was also specified in the *Madison Hostess Units Manual* and *Hints for Hostesses in Service Clubs*, box 5, RG 215. The GSO in Baltimore forbade gum chewing and smoking in its club; see *Girls Service Organization Manual*, Saratoga Street USO, Neal Collection.

101. Junior Hostess Rules, ATW — Philadelphia SDC, box 10, WWII Collection.

102. "Standards for USO Junior Hostess Groups," USO Field Service Bulletin #29, rev. 26 April 1944, box 18, WWII Collection.

103. Announcements, 1 July 1942, ser. 3, box 2, CDHC Records. The same sentiment was expressed in Announcements, 9 August 1942, ibid.

104. "Salute to Miss Jones, Miss Brown, Miss Smith, from the USO," USO Club, 131 S. Wabash Avenue, Chicago, Ill., box 10, WWII Collection.

105. "Standards for USO Junior Hostess Groups," USO Field Service Bulletin #29, rev. 26 April 1944, box 18, WWII Collection; "USO Junior Hostess Orientation," newspaper clipping, 10 April 1945, box 13, RG 215; "USO Welcomes Them Home," *Information Sheet*, October 1944, box 6, WWII Collection.

106. Hegland and Hegland, *USO, "The Heart of San Diego,"* 35.

107. Cushing General Hospital, "Tips to Hostesses for Dances, Parties, Open House," series 2, box 2, CDHC Records. See similar discussion in report, 21 December 1942, New Station Hospital, Fort Devons, Square Dancing, ser. 1, box 1, CDHC Records.

108. Cushing General Hospital, "Tips to Hostesses for Dances, Parties, Open House," ser. 2, box 2, CDHC Records.

109. Monaco and Musumeci interview.

110. Kane interview.

111. Minutes of the Meeting of Junior Captains, 18 October 1945, Jewish Welfare Board, box 18, WWII Collection.

112. "Captains," Stage Door Canteen, box 10, WWII Collection.

113. "Scope of Responsibility," in "Work Analysis Sheet of Miss Sally Loudon Assistant Director, Baltimore USO," from Baltimore USO Staff Plan and Organizations, ser. 1, box 59, YMCA Collection.

114. USO Labor Plaza, Hostess Committee Meeting, 25 July 1944, box 23, WWII Collection.

115. USO Labor Plaza, Evening Chairman Meeting, 16 August, 21 September 1944, and USO Labor Plaza, Minutes of Hostess Committee Meeting, 17 September 1945, box 23, WWII Collection.

116. Florence Williams, "Junior Hostesses Want More Voice in Program," *Information Sheet*, July 1944, box 6, WWII Collection. The Cincinnati USO reported that its junior hostesses enjoyed a spirit of unity as a hostess corps; see Arthur Plaut, "The Story of the USO in Cincinnati," SA Papers, 36.

117. "20,000 G.S.O. Girls Soon," *Army Navy YMCA Bulletin*, January 1942, box 75, RG 24.

118. "Constitution — Girls Service Organization," Prentiss Papers, Montgomery, Ala. The National Defense Recreation and Service Committee of San Antonio, Tex., created a similar structure for its hostess corps; see "National Defense Hostess Corps of the Alamo City," box 5, RG 215.

119. Newspaper Committee of GSO, *Girls Service Organization Manual*, Saratoga Street USO, 1945, Neal Collection.

120. Phyllis Mayfield Baldridge, "Images" (2001), unpublished manuscript in Baldridge's possession; Baldridge interview.

121. Fredrich and Fredrich interview.

122. Rosenberg interview.

123. Shannon Kelley [pseud.], WQ; Johnson interview.

124. "Volunteers Pile Up Long Work Records, Qualify for National USO's Award Pins," *Information Sheet*, June 1945, box 5, WWII Collection. Volunteers in Hattiesburg, Mississippi, earned USO award pins; see Narrative Program Report for March 1944, Hattiesburg USO Records.

125. Kane interview; Weinstock and Weinstock interview.

126. Letter to CDHC from Boston Soldiers and Sailors Committee, 28 March 1944, ser. 2, box 2, CDHC Records.

127. To Mrs. Herbert Buttrick Hosmer from Charles B. Taylor, Captain AC, 370th Fighter Squadron, Mitchel Field, New York, 3 June 1943, box 2, CDHC Records.

128. Beverly Littlejohn, WQ.

129. Julia Currie [pseud.], WQ.

130. Wardman interview.

131. D. Campbell, *Women at War with America*, 67.

CHAPTER 4

1. Woods interview.

2. Foucault, *Discipline and Punish*, 199.

3. Eliot Ness, speech, 1941, RG 215.

4. Brandt, *No Magic Bullet*, 161–62. See also Hegarty, *Victory Girls, Khaki-Wackies, and Patriotutes*, 37–40.

5. Bristow, *Making Men Moral*, 1–2.

6. Scholars who have made this argument include Lovelace, in "Facing Change in Wartime Philadelphia," 164; Hegarty, in *Victory Girls, Khaki-Wackies, and Patriotutes*; and Brandt, in *No Magic Bullet*.

7. Foucault, *History of Sexuality*, 11.

8. Brandt, *No Magic Bullet*, 38; "Suggestions for Organizing a Community Hygiene Program," *JSH*, no. 2 (1939): 98.

9. Report to Eliot Ness, OCWS, and Memorandum to the Recipient of this Report, both from Walter Clarke, Md., Executive Director of ASHA, 9 November 1944, and Outline of Activities of Federal Security Agency, Community War Services, Social Protection Division, box 1, RG 215.

10. "Personal and Strictly Confidential," 26 May 1941, Welfare Interests General, RG III, box 51, folder 566, RAC.

11. Letter to J. P. Morgan, head of Markle Foundation, from John D. Rockefeller, 29 May, 10 July 1941, box 51, folder 566, RAC. When John D. Rockefeller donated $200,000 to the USO in 1942, he requested that the organization give $75,000 to ASHA to investigate prostitution around military camps. See Letter to Mr. Spencer Robertson from John D. Rockefeller Jr., 27 April 1942, ibid.

12. Lindsley F. Kimball, Recommendation Respecting the Service of National Voluntary Agencies — USO or Equivalent — in the Event of a New Military Emergency, March 1948, General Welfare Files, RG III, box 51, folder 573, RAC.

13. Spongberg, *Feminizing Venereal Disease*, 2; Hegarty, *Victory Girls, Khaki-Wackies, and Patriotutes*, 3.

14. Brandt, *No Magic Bullet*, 72.

15. "The Prostitution Racket," *JSH*, no. 5 (1939): 212.

16. "The Relation of the National Defense Program to Social Hygiene," *JSH*, no. 8 (1940): 359.

17. Brandt, *No Magic Bullet*, 94; Clement, *Love for Sale*, 240–58.

18. Hobson, *Uneasy Virtue*, 3.

19. "Prostitution and Quackery in Relation to Syphilis Control," *JSH*, no. 1 (1940): 7.

20. Brandt, *No Magic Bullet*, 162; Hegarty, *Victory Girls, Khaki-Wackies, and Patriotutes*, 6.

21. "National Events," *JSH*, no. 2 (1941): 83.

22. Brandt, *No Magic Bullet*, 166.

23. Ibid.

24. "Best Traditions of the Service," *JSH*, no. 1 (1942): 24.

25. Brandt, *No Magic Bullet*, 168.

26. Editorial, "This Way Out," *JSH*, no. 5 (1944): 309.

27. Hegarty, *Victory Girls, Khaki-Wackies, and Patriotutes*, 9.

28. Reverend Edward V. Stanford, *The Serviceman and Sex* (1940; 7th printing, 1964), NCCS Records, 4.

29. Bristow, *Making Men Moral*, 48.

30. "'Send Up Those USO-ers,' Shipboard Officers Shout," *Red Shield*, February 1943, SA Papers.

31. "A Study of Protective Measures in the City of Boston," *JSH*, no. 7 (1942): 410; Hegarty, *Victory Girls, Khaki-Wackies, and Patriotutes*, 87–88.

32. "Building Morale in the U.S. Army and Navy," *JSH*, no. 5 (1941): 227.

33. Charles P. Taft, address to the Central Atlantic Area YMCA Convention, Atlantic City, N.J., 17 May 1941, box 1, RG 215.

34. Dr. Joseph Earle More, Chief of Syphilis Division of the Medical Clinic, Johns Hopkins University, Chairman of the Subcommittee on VD, National Research Council, address to Joint Army and Navy Committee, Conference of Morale Officers, 25–28 February 1941, box 1, RG 215.

35. "Fit to Fight . . . and Fit for Life," *JSH*, no. 1 (1942): 5; Wallace, *Military Sanitation*, 23–25.

36. Navy Department, Bureau of Medicine and Surgery, "Navy Venereal Disease Contact Investigation," 3rd quarter, 1944, Report No. 1, box 4, RG 215.

37. Costello, *Virtue under Fire*, 89.

38. "The Sexual Aspects of Military Personnel," *JSH*, no. 3 (1941): 114, 117.

39. Costello, *Virtue under Fire*, 91–92, 126, 149; Goldstein, *War and Gender*, 334; Gubar, "'This Is My Rifle,'" 255; Meyer, *Creating GI Jane*; Hegarty, *Victory Girls, Khaki-Wackies, and Patriotutes*; Cameron, *American Samurai*.

40. *Yank: The Army Weekly*, 19 November 1943.

41. Ibid., 10 March 1944, 11.

42. Ibid.

43. Westbrook, "'I Want a Girl,'" 596.

44. Meyerowitz, "Women, Cheesecake, and Borderline Material," 15.

45. Ibid.; Westbrook, "'I Want a Girl,'" 603.

46. Westbrook, "'I Want a Girl,'" 605; Grossman and Assyia interview.

47. Release forms for pinup girl contest, Philadelphia SDC, 25 May 1944, World War II Collection, and Women's Committee Minutes, Philadelphia SDC, 25 May 1944, box 9, WWII Collection.

48. Gubar, "'This Is My Rifle,'" 251–52.

49. War Department, *So You've Got a Furlough*, June 1944, box 1, RG 215.

50. Costello, *Virtue under Fire*, 152.

51. Bailey and Farber, *First Strange Place*, 28.

52. Ibid., 97, 104. Hawaiian authorities chose not to enforce the May Act because the middle class and elites in Hawaii believed that it was better for servicemen to have sex with prostitutes than with respectable Hawaiian women. See ibid., 99.

53. Williams [pseud.] interview; Wallace, *Military Sanitation*, 26–27.

54. To Eliot Ness, Director, Division of Social Protection, from James S. Owens, Regional Social Protection Representative, Subject: West Virginia and Virginia, 1 September 1944, box 1, RG 215; "Number of Girls in Quarantine Clinic from February 1942 to April 1943 in Age Groups by Color," San Antonio, Tex., box 4, RG 215; "Statistical Reporting System of Contact Reporting," box 3, RG 215; Hegarty, *Victory Girls, Khaki-Wackies, and Patriotutes*, 6; Anderson, *Wartime Women*, 108.

55. Third Air Force, *Believe It or Not by Ripley*, box J5, NUL-SRO Records. The

military also warned servicemen about various kinds of women in the pamphlet *So You've Got a Furlough*, War Department, June 1944, box 1, RG 215.

56. Hegarty, *Victory Girls, Khaki-Wackies, and Patriotutes*, 9.

57. Third Air Force, *Believe It or Not by Ripley*, box J5, NUL-SRO Records.

58. "Social Hygiene and Youth in Defense Communities," *JSH*, no. 8 (1942), 440.

59. Hegarty, *Victory Girls, Khaki-Wackies, and Patriotutes*, 106.

60. Report of the Social Protection Section RE: Sub-Committee of House Naval Affairs Committee, Newport, R.I., 20 April 1943, box 8, RG 215.

61. Hegarty, *Victory Girls, Khaki-Wackies, and Patriotutes*, 22.

62. "Junior Hostess Groups, Organization and Rules," Shirley, Mass., USO Club, box 2, CDHC Records.

63. Bailey, *From Front Porch to Backseat*, 27; Kunzel, *Fallen Women*; Solinger, *Wake Up Little Susie*.

64. Simmons, "Modern Sexuality and the Myth of Victorian Repression," 160–61.

65. Alexander, *"Girl Problem,"* 61–62.

66. Odem, *Delinquent Daughters*, 189; Dumenil, *Modern Temper*, 134.

67. New Jersey State Department of Health, *To Womanhood for Girls and Teens*, U.S. Public Health Service, box 5, RG 215.

68. Speech about CDHC given at a fund-raiser, 1941–1946, box 1, ser. 2, folder 3, CDHC Records.

69. Letter to Miss Helen Deacon from Mrs. Laura P. Servais, 14 February [1944–1946], CDHC Records.

70. To Helen from Mrs. Eleanor Holden Greenman, ser. 2, box 1, folder 3, CDHC Records.

71. To Anne from Laura P. Servais, 15 October, ibid.

72. *Hints for Hostesses in Service Clubs*, box 5, RG 215.

73. Newspaper Committee of GSO, *Girls Service Organization Manual*, Saratoga Street USO, 1945, Neal Collection; Julia Currie [pseud.], Marian Richardson, Helen A. Gosnell, June Elkin, Carol Brooks [pseud.], Shirley L. Gippner, and Susan Collins [pseud.], all WQ; Marilla Barlow Bagby, WQ and personal narrative.

74. "Step Out Soldier," *American Dancer*, November 1942, 31.

75. Comments from Lieutenant Russell B. Becktell, Chaplain at Bedford, Meeting Minutes, 16 July 1942, ser. 2, box 1, CDHC Records.

76. Photograph with caption identifying hostesses and servicemen sitting on the floor in a circle playing spin the bottle in "Biography of a Canteen," box 16, WWII Collection; "Junior Hostesses' Rules," American Theatre Wing War Service, Inc., Philadelphia SDC, box 10, WWII Collection.

77. YMCA Volunteer Hostess Club Membership Application, series 1, box 75,

YMCA Collection. This rule was also enforced by other clubs, including those discussed in the following collections: box 1, folder 10, CDHC Records; box 9, folder 368,
Records of the Cambridge YWCA, Cambridge, Mass.; *Madison Hostess Units Manual*,
box 5, RG 215; "Junior Hostesses' Rules," American Theatre Wing War Service, Inc.,
Philadelphia SDC, box 10, WWII Collection.

78. USO Club, Shirley, Mass., identification card, ser. 5, 1942 and 1943, box 2,
CDHC Records. The Philadelphia SDC also forbade hostesses from leaving with
servicemen and from joining them "outside in the vicinity of the canteen"; see their
"Rules for Hostesses," June 1942, box 10, WWII Collection. CDHC chaperones
required junior hostesses to "stay inside the building; you may go up or down stairs only
with your chaperons [*sic*] permission"; see "Announcements," 22 July 1942, ser. 3, box
2, CDHC Records, and Brigadier William J. Parkins, National Program Director,
Salvation Army, "The USO Work of the Salvation Army," box 5, RG 215.

79. "Junior Hostess Groups, Organization and Rules," ser. 3, box 2, CDHC Records.

80. Alexander, *"Girl Problem,"* 61–62.

81. "Salute to Miss Jones, Miss Brown, Miss Smith, from the USO," USO Club, 131
S. Wabash Avenue, Chicago, Ill., box 10, WWII Collection.

82. Kelly interview.

83. Roby [pseud.] interview. The Cincinnati USO speculated that its hostesses saw
the value of USO rules over time; see Arthur Plaut, "The Story of the USO in Cincinnati," SA Papers, 36.

84. Alice Roby [pseud.] to author, 20 February 2001.

85. Roby [pseud.] interview. Other women also expressed the idea that men who
visited USO clubs were "gentlemen." See Jean Cohen, Elizabeth A. TePoorten, Alene
Eva Gwinn McKnight, Marjorie Hawkins Sloan, June Elkin, and Mildred Reca Durnal, all WQ.

86. Woods interview.

87. Mapstead interview.

88. Williams [pseud.] interview. The USO was aware that its wholesome image did
not appeal to all servicemen. One survey introduced by USO president Chester Barnard asked soldiers to agree or disagree with the statement, among others, "The staff is
too 'goody-goody' to suit me" (survey number 46, box 45, RG 225).

89. "Rules at Soldiers Center," Prentiss Papers, Montgomery, Ala.

90. "No Tough Situation Here," ibid.

91. Narrative Program Report for August 1942, USO Club Operated by Army
YMCA, Hattiesburg, Miss., Hattiesburg USO Records.

92. "Community Safeguards in the Protection of Childhood and Youth," *JSH*, no. 5
(1940): 201. See also Peiss, *Cheap Amusements*, and Hegarty, *Victory Girls, Khaki-
Wackies, and Patriotutes*.

93. Meyer, *Creating GI Jane*, 585.

94. For occupations of the women interviewed for this project, see n. 19, Chapter 2.

95. *USO Bulletin*, 16 June 1941.

96. Norma Carson, speech to Regional Health Institute, Washington, Pa., 17 November 1943, box 25, WWII Collection.

97. Norma Carson, "Reports Received at the USO Council Office from the Policewomen's Unit of the Bureau of Police Dealing with the USO Labor Plaza," ibid.

98. Norma Carson, speech to Regional Health Institute, Washington, Pa., 17 November 1943, ibid.

99. Bailey, *From Front Porch to Backseat*, 7.

100. Bristow, *Making Men Moral*, 82.

101. Hegland and Hegland, *USO, "The Heart of San Diego,"* 38, 41.

102. Bailey, *From Front Porch to Backseat*, 16–17.

103. Fredrich and Fredrich interview.

104. Meyer, *Creating GI Jane*, 36–38.

105. Bailey and Farber, *First Strange Place*, 178.

106. Bailey, *From Front Porch to Backseat*, 94.

107. Woods interview.

108. Rosenberg interview.

109. Roby [pseud.] interview.

110. Toni Chapman [pseud.], WQ.

111. Hegarty, *Victory Girls, Khaki-Wackies, and Patriotutes*, 112.

112. Nickerson interview.

113. "USO Report," box 9, RG 215. Additional reports that list USO clubs as sites where servicemen met women who presumably gave them VD include "Report on Program Conducted by Social Protection Committee in Trenton, New Jersey," to Thomas Devine, Director, SPD, from Jule T. Bouchard, Social Protection Representative, 18 April 1945, box 13, RG 215, in which 5 of 170 men in Trenton, N.J., between January and December 1944 named unspecified USO clubs as sites where they met women who later gave them VD. Servicemen listed a white USO club once out of thirty "places of procurement" in "Venereal Disease Infections among Military Personnel Contracted in Mobile, Alabama," July 1942–January 1943, box 2, RG 215. Between May and December 1944 two servicemen named women whom they met at the white USO club as sources of VD; see "Field Report for Panama City, Florida, and Tyndall Field," 7 March 1944, to Eliot Ness, Director, SPD, from David Strong, Social Protection Representative, box 2, RG 215. Three servicemen named the white USO club as the place where they met infected women; see "Master Chart for New England, State Health Department Information, Source of Venereal Infections as Named by Men in the Armed Forces, July 1943," box 1, RG 215.

114. Women's Committee Minutes, 15 February 1943, box 34, WWII Collection.

115. Social Corps Manual, Fort Dix Community Service, Pointville, N.J., box 5, RG 215.

116. Brandt, *No Magic Bullet*, 158.

117. Kryder, *Divided Arsenal*, 69, 138.

118. To Brigadier General William H. Hobson, Fort Benning, Ga., from E. E. Farley, Director of the USO Colored Army-Navy YMCA, Columbus, Ga., 11 May 1944, box 2, Nelson Jackson Papers, NUL-SRO Records. Soldiers named other African American USO clubs as places where they met infected women, including those discussed in the following reports: "Pro-Station Report, 27 December 1943–16 July 1944, Chattanooga, Tennessee," to Eliot Ness, Federal Security Agency, from Nelson C. Jackson, box 3, Nelson Jackson Papers, NUL-SRO Records; "Trend of Infections of Military Personnel in Montgomery, Alabama, during First Seven Months of 1943," box 2, RG 215; "Venereal Disease Infections among Military Personnel Contracted in Mobile, Alabama, July 1942–January 1943," box 2, RG 215; "Special Study Relative to VD Contacts in Ten Selected Cities," April, May, June 1943, box 3, RG 215.

119. To Eliot Ness, Federal Security Agency, from Nelson C. Jackson, Field Representative, 3 December 1943, "Field Report, Columbus, Georgia, 22 and 23 November 1943," box 2, Nelson Jackson Papers, NUL-SRO Records.

120. To Harry T. Baker, Army and Navy Department YMCA, from F. E. Farley, USO Colored Army and Navy YMCA, 16 March 1943, box 2, Nelson Jackson Papers, NUL-SRO Records.

121. Solinger, *Wake Up Little Susie*, 54, 137.

122. Kunzel, *Fallen Women*, 146.

123. Toni Chapman [pseud.], WQ.

124. Rosenberg interview.

125. Roby [pseud.] interview. Other former hostesses had similar views of the USO or discussed friends who shared Alice's point of view; see Johnson interview; Susan Collins [pseud.], WQ; and Marilla Barlow Bagby, WQ and personal narrative.

126. Helen A. Gosnell, WQ.

127. Lovelace, "Facing Change in Wartime Philadelphia," 168.

128. Ibid.

129. Shannon Kelley [pseud.], Julia Currie [pseud.], Betty M. Pyper, Donna Hendrickson [pseud.], Marian Richardson, Grace Scully Marconi, Dorothy Wirtz, all WQ.

CHAPTER 5

1. As was customary at USO events, the Shirley USO in Massachusetts offered cigarettes as bingo prizes, "ranging from two packs for some of the quick games to a

carton for covering the board," and other USO clubs in the area asked hostesses to donate the cigarettes. See USO Shirley, Bingo and Dance Party, 11 July 1944, ser. 1, and to CDHC from Shirley USO, 20 March 1944, ser. 2, box 1, CDHC Records.

2. Baldridge interview; Phyllis Baldridge, "Images" (2001), unpublished manuscript in Baldridge's possession.

3. For a personal description of this process, see Richard White's biography of his mother, *Remembering Ahanagran*, 239–40.

4. Higginbotham, *Righteous Discontent*, 205.

5. Driver, *Century of Dance*, 144–45.

6. Fass, *Damned and the Beautiful*, 300–306.

7. Ibid., 201; Erenberg, *Steppin' Out*, 11.

8. "Asks Girls to Aid with Dance Program," *Chronicle*, Camden, S.C., 17 October 1941, box 3, RG 215.

9. "Dancing for Our Boys," *American Dancer*, November 1942, 13.

10. October Program Report, 1942, Hattiesburg USO Records.

11. "You are Cordially Invited to attend a Formal Christmas Dance"; "Won't You Be Our Valentine?"; to V.C.H.'er, from The Committee, 29 December 1941; and The Dancer's Guide, Summer Edition, Young Men's Division, Central YMCA, Baltimore, Md., 3 July 1941, all in ser. 1, box 75; "Oh Boy, Oh Boy — AND GIRL Dances, Dances, Dances!" *YMCA News*, May 1943, and "Dundalk USO-YMCA," *YMCA News*, March 1944, both in ser. 1, box 73; "Military Dance Every Saturday Night," *YMCA News*, September 1941, ser. 1, box 75, all in YMCA Collection.

12. "Keep 'em Dancing," *American Dancer*, March 1942, 3C; "Military Recreation Committee Report," *American Dancer*, April 1942, 26.

13. "Dance and War," *American Dancer*, September 1942, 20; Bernard J. Shaw, "Dancing Is My Business," *American Dancer*, March 1942, 40; "What Are We Waiting For?" *American Dancer*, April 1942, 8B; Anna M. Greene, President, Dancing Masters of America, Inc., "Dance Teachers of America," *American Dancer*, April 1942, 8A; "Dancing with Our Boys," *American Dancer*, June 1943, 13.

14. Aviation Cadet L. T. Carr, "Step Out, Soldier!" *Dance Magazine*, October 1942, 20.

15. Ibid.

16. Memo to Mr. Frank E. Cane from Mr. F. J. McGahren, 19 June 1944, box 7, NCCS Records.

17. Narrative Program Report for February 1946, Hattiesburg USO Records.

18. "Paul Jones," Central YMCA, *Volunteer Hostess Club News Notes*, 13 August 1941, ser. 1, box 75, YMCA Collection.

19. Social Corps Manual, Fort Dix Community Service, Pointville, N.J., box 5, RG 215.

20. "Square Dancing Seen as True Americana," *Information Sheet*, April 1943, box 6, WWII Collection.

21. Driver, *Century of Dance*, 217.

22. Nickerson interview.

23. Dannett and Rachel, *Down Memory Lane*, 116–17; Driver, *Century of Dance*, 137.

24. "Records, for Our Fighting Men, Inc," 1942, box 41, RG 225. The following document discusses the importance of music in wartime and specifically what Ohio residents could do to encourage civilians' and servicemen's enjoyment of music during the war: Lloyd W. Reese, Field Recreation Representative, Community War Services, Cleveland, Ohio, "Music in Wartime," box 6, RG 215.

25. "Informal Dancing" (report), 13 July 1944, ser. 1, box 1, CDHC Records. For more information about All Girl Orchestras, see Tucker, *Swing Shift*.

26. Hegland and Hegland, *USO, "The Heart of San Diego,"* 41.

27. Dannett and Rachel, *Down Memory Lane*, 79.

28. Driver, *Century of Dance*, 31.

29. Ibid., 15–16.

30. Erenberg, *Steppin' Out*, 150.

31. Driver, *Century of Dance*, 15–16.

32. Back, "Syncopated Synergy," 171; Dannett and Rachel, *Down Memory Lane*, 136.

33. Irene Szuhay Hennig, WQ.

34. Back, "Syncopated Synergy," 171–72.

35. Driver, *Century of Dance*, 141, 143.

36. Back, "Syncopated Synergy," 172.

37. Social Corps Manual, Fort Dix Community Service, Pointville, N.J., box 5, RG 215.

38. Back, "Syncopated Synergy," 172.

39. "No Tough Situation Here," Prentiss Papers, Montgomery, Ala.

40. Reba N. Muller, WQ.

41. Beverly Littlejohn, WQ.

42. Historian Pete Daniel explores the continuation of generational disputes over race, dance, and music in the South, in *Lost Revolutions*, 148.

43. To Miss Morton from Mrs. A. Clark Woodard, Chairman, Dance and Social Events Committee, Boston Soldiers and Sailors Recreation Committee, 29 August 1941, box 9, Records of the Cambridge YWCA, Cambridge, Mass.

44. Bailey, *From Front Porch to Backseat*, 31.

45. Report, 4–5 July 1942, ser. 1, box 1, CDHC Records. Female volunteers chaperoned all of the dances in which CDHC members participated. See to Mrs. Turner from Miss Muriel Alexander et al., 17 October 1942, ser. 2, box 1, CDHC Records.

46. To Joan from Ruth Hill, box 2, CDHC Records. According to the CDHC

correspondence file, the chairman of the CDHC sent a thank-you note to every chaperone after each dance. Chaperones likely appreciated and expected this formality when they donated their time to the club. See to Mrs. Fitzpatrick from Julie Anne Foote, Chairman of the CDHC, 3 March 1943, ser. 2, ibid.

47. *Hints for Hostesses in Service Clubs*, box 5, RG 215.

48. Lt. Commander F. S. Mathewson, District Welfare and Recreation Officer, "What Does the Navy Expect of the USO," report given to the USO Volunteers Conference, Highland Park, Ill., 1943, box 26, RG 24.

49. Carol Brooks [pseud.], WQ.

50. "Biography of a Canteen," box 16, WWII Collection.

51. Charles C. Beckett, Executive Director, South Broad Street USO Club, "The Function of Senior Hostesses," box 10, WWII Collection.

52. USO Labor Plaza, Evening Chairman Meeting, 16 August 1944, and Labor Plaza Hostess Committee Minutes, 2 August 1944, box 23, WWII Collection.

53. *Volunteer Hostess Club News Notes*, Central YMCA, 16 July, 6 August 1941, scr. 1, box 75, YMCA Collection.

54. Ibid., 17 September 1941. Senior hostesses at the South Broad Street USO Club for African American servicemen also took "the lead in getting service men and hostesses together." See Charles C. Beckett, Executive Director, South Broad Street USO Club, "The Function of the Senior Hostess," box 10, WWII Collection.

55. Social Corps Manual, Fort Dix Community Service, Pointville, N.J., box 5, RG 215.

56. USO Labor Plaza, Hostess Committee and Evening Chairmen Meeting, 25 July 1945, box 23, WWII Collection.

57. Minutes of Hostess Committee Meeting, USO Labor Plaza, 14 June 1944, ibid.

58. Hegland and Hegland, *USO, "The Heart of San Diego,"* 41. Most of the dances held at the Hattiesburg USO Club in Mississippi were formal, with the club issuing 600 invitations to servicemen from Camp Shelby and 300 to hostesses. See Program Report, March 1942, Hattiesburg USO Records.

59. Aviation Cadet L. T. Carr, "Step Out, Soldier!" *Dance Magazine*, October 1942, 20; Juanita Eastman, "Partners in Uniform," *Dance Magazine*, July 1944, 16.

60. With 18,000 men stationed at Camp Shelby, those who were invited felt fortunate to attend. See June Program Report, 1942, Hattiesburg USO Records.

61. Elizabeth A. TePoorten, WQ.

62. To Mr. Mark McCloskey from the City of Cincinnati Public Recreation Commission, 28 April 1942, box 5, RG 215. Not enough servicemen to provide partners for junior hostesses attended a dance for the 101st cavalry; see ser. 1, box 1, CDHC Records, and Narrative Program Report for January 1944, Hattiesburg USO Records.

63. To USO Shirley from B. Miller, 1 December 1942, and to Shirley USO from CDHC, 2 March 1943, ser. 2, box 1, CDHC Records.

64. Marjorie H. Foster, "The Philadelphia Stage Door Canteen," article submitted first to Mrs. Favorite for review before being submitted for potential publication. See to Mrs. Favorite from Marjorie H. Foster, 4 March 1945, box 9, WWII Collection.

65. Bailey, *From Front Porch to Backseat*, 35; McComb, "Rate Your Date," 47.

66. Nora O. Robertson, WQ. The gender ratio inside the USO is similar to that of "gold rush" California, in which bachelor men vastly outnumbered marriageable women. See Hurtado, *Intimate Frontiers*.

67. Alsop and McBride, *Arms and the Girl*, 272.

68. "Rules for Hostesses," Philadelphia SDC, box 10, WWII Collection. The rules are prefaced by the instructions, "PLEASE READ THESE RULES CAREFULLY AND KEEP THEM!!" *Hints for Hostesses in Service Clubs*, box 5, RG 215, also discouraged juniors from socializing with one another at the expense of servicemen.

69. Johnson interview.

70. This is similar to Westbrook's conclusion in "'I Want a Girl,'" 603, that pinups inspired sacrifice for "American women."

71. Abel, *Hail Hostesses*, 8.

72. Carroll [pseud.] interview.

73. Roby [pseud.] interview.

74. Nora O. Robertson, Grace Scully Marconi, Donna Smith [pseud.], all WQ.

75. Marjorie H. Foster, "The Philadelphia Stage Door Canteen," article submitted first to Mrs. Favorite for review before being submitted for potential publication. See to Mrs. Favorite from Marjorie H. Foster, 4 March 1945, box 9, WWII Collection.

76. Neal Collection.

77. USO Labor Plaza, Hostess Committee and Evening Chairman Meeting, 28 July 1945, box 23, WWII Collection; Social Corps Manual, Fort Dix Community Service, Pointville, N.J., box 5, RG 215.

78. McQuirter, "Awkward Moves," 94.

79. "Rules for Hostesses," June 1942, Philadelphia SDC, box 10, WWII Collection.

80. Someone used a pencil to cross out the portion of this statement regarding junior hostesses. See Women's Committee Minutes of the SDC, 28 February 1943, box 10, WWII Collection.

81. "Attitudes of Negro Troops in Six CPBC Quartermaster Companies," Research Branch Information—Education Section, Central Pacific Base Command, Excerpts from Report #7, November 1944, box 45, RG 225; 981 black soldiers on Oahu participated in this survey.

82. Bailey and Farber, *First Strange Place*, 133, 150, 162.

83. Report about incident, box 9, WWII Collection. This aspect of the story is discussed in Chapter 3.

84. Letter to Mrs. Upton Favorite from "U.S.M.M." n.d., box 9, WWII Collection. Racial tension was also evident in factories. See Boris, "'You Wouldn't Want One of 'em Dancing with Your Wife,'" 79, and Archibald, *Wartime Shipyards*, 77.

85. Dance report, 22 July 1944, box 1, CDHC Records.

86. Back, "Syncopated Synergy," 181, 187; Roeder, *Censored War*, 57.

87. Gardiner, *"Over Here,"* 141, 152, 155–56.

88. Back, "Syncopated Synergy," 181, 187; Roeder, *Censored War*, 57.

89. Gardiner, *"Over Here,"* 152. Government officials in Australia strongly opposed the stationing of African American troops in the country because its administration, along with many white Australians, was racist. The Australian military chastised any white Australian soldier who fraternized with African American servicemen, and many white Australians condemned white women who danced or associated with African American servicemen. See Barker and Jackson, *Fleeting Attraction*, 177–88.

90. USO Labor Plaza, Hostess Committee Meeting, 25 July 1944, box 23, WWII Collection.

91. Minutes of Meeting of Executive Committee, USO Labor Plaza, 16 August 1944, box 6, WWII Collection.

92. Lovelace, "Facing Change in Wartime Philadelphia," 172.

93. To Stage Door Canteen from U.S.M.M. (United States Merchant Marine), n.d., box 9, WWII Collection.

94. "Standards for Junior Hostess Groups," USO Field Service Bulletin #29, rev. 26 April 1944, box 18, WWII Collection.

95. Higginbotham, *Righteous Discontent*, 189; Gilmore, *Gender and Jim Crow*, 72; Williamson, *Crucible of Race*.

96. Memo to Junior Hostesses, RE: Dancing with Negro servicemen at the Stage Door Canteen, from Margaret Halsey, author, captain of Junior Hostesses at SDC, General Office Files, box A641, NAACP Papers. Reprinted with her permission.

97. Beth Bailey argues and fully develops this point in *From Front Porch to Backseat*, 88.

98. Seventeenth Meeting of the Committee on Dances and Social Events of the Boston Soldiers and Sailors Recreation Committee, Boston YMCA, 5 January 1942, box 9, Records of the Cambridge YWCA, Cambridge, Mass. For more on dances for black servicemen, see Meeting of the Dance and Social Events Committee of the Boston Soldiers and Sailors Committee, 2 March 1942, ibid., and "Number of Service Men Expected Still a Mystery," *Charlotte Observer* (N.C.), 9 November 1941, box 3, RG 215.

99. Letter to "Ladies" from Sgt. W. F. Fawkes, box 9, WWII Collection. Another African American serviceman expressed his appreciation for black USO clubs in a letter: to Mr. Becket from John H. Hersey, ser. 6, box 7, NUL Records.

100. To Sirs (South Broad Street USO, Philadelphia) from Pvt. Norwood Ewell et al., 5 May 1944, ser. 6, box 7, NUL Records.

101. "Extension Services to Negroes, Regions VIII and IX," 3 September 1943, to W. Noel Hudson from William Y. Bell Jr., Series General Office Files, box A66, NUL-SRO Records.

102. Lovelace, "Facing Change in Wartime Philadelphia," 155.

103. Takaki, *Different Mirror*, 394.

104. Vicki Ruiz argues that Mexican American chaperonage eventually declined in these years; see "Flapper and the Chaperone," 207, 219.

105. The Cosmopolitan Club mistakenly believed that Nelson Rockefeller was the head of the national USO. He was in charge of the separate Better Understanding among Latin Americans program. Rockefeller's office forwarded the Cosmopolitan Club's letter to the USO. See to Nelson Rockefeller, Executive Director for USO, from Members of Cosmopolitan Club, 22 September 1943; to Texas Good Neighbor Commission from Members of Cosmopolitan Sorority, 22 September 1943; to Miss Pérez from Arthur W. Packard, 29 September 1943; to Chester Barnard and Anne Spock from Arthur Packard, 28 September 1943; to Arthur Packard from Ray Johns, Director of Operations, Continental United States, USO, 15 October 1943; to Ray Johns from W. W. Jackson, Regional Executive, USO, San Antonio, Tex., 12 October 1943; and to Arthur Packard from Chester Barnard, President, USO, 1 October 1943, General Welfare Files, RG III, box 50, folder 562, RAC.

106. Report by Concord Dance Hostess Committee, 19 August 1942, and report by CDHC, 21 April 1942, ser. 1, box 1, folder I, CDHC Records. Box lunches are also discussed in letter to Miss Joan Miller from Helen F. Hawke, Program Assistant-USO-YWCA, 7 July 1942, ser. 2, box 1; to Joan Miller from Helen F. Hawke, Program Assistant, USO-YWCA, 15 June 1942, ser. 2, box 1; and Service Club (report), 13 August 1944, ser. 1, box 1, CDHC Records.

107. "'Lip' Service," caption and photograph, USO Labor Plaza News, box 25, WWII Collection.

108. "No Tough Situation Here," Prentiss Papers, Montgomery, Ala.

109. "Phoebus, VA, USO Club," *Red Shield*, July 1942, SA Papers, 2.

110. "Uncle Sam's Nieces Aid in Recreation," *USO News*, 10 February 1942, NCCS Records.

111. USO Labor Plaza, Minutes of the Hostess Committee Meeting, 17 September 1945, box 23, WWII Collection.

112. Narrative Program Report for March 1944, Hattiesburg USO Records.

113. Minutes of a Conference between Logan, Kuauth, Goddard, Seeber, Leggett, 27 October 1943, box 28, Records of the Boston YWCA, Cambridge, Mass.; "Standards for USO Junior Hostess Groups," USO Field Service Bulletin #29, rev. 26 April 1944, box 18, WWII Collection; Mary E. Hester, National Catholic Community Service Volunteer Services, "Suggested Procedures for the Organization of Junior Hostesses," box 9, NCCS Records.

114. "Recreation for Women in War Areas," box 6, RG 215.

115. Abel, *Hail Hostesses*.

116. Treadwell, *Women's Army Corps*, 198.

117. "Standards for USO Junior Hostess Groups," USO Field Service Bulletin #29, rev. 26 April 1944, box 18, WWII Collection.

118. Hale interview.

119. Meyer, *Creating GI Jane*, 41–42.

120. Minutes of Conference of JANCWR, OCWS, USO Committee on Services to Women and Girls with Representatives of Women's National Organizations, 16 May, New York City, box 45, RG 225.

121. "Work with Women and Girls in the USO," Mary Louise Vetter, Chairman, Report of Workshop Group—Regional Institute, Milwaukee, Wisc., 28 February–2 March 1944, box 19, RG 215.

122. "The Servicewoman and Her Leisure Time in the Community," box 45, RG 225, in folder USO-Blough, perhaps written by Pearl Case Blough. The USO–Greater Boston Soldiers and Sailors Committee also set up a separate club for servicewomen; see photograph of servicewoman standing in a doorway below the sign "Service Woman's USO Club, sponsored by USO–Greater Boston Soldiers and Sailors Committee, financed by Greater Boston United War Fund," carton 132, folder 3344, Records of the Boston YWCA, Cambridge, Mass. Also, "Service Women's USO Will Open Sunday at YWCA," *Boston Herald*, 23 June 1943, carton 13, Records of the Boston YWCA, Cambridge, Mass.

123. To Mrs. Hosmer from Mary E. Heagan, 9 May 1943, ser. 2, box 1, CDHC Records.

124. Meyer, *Creating GI Jane*, 55, 66; to Commander J. L. Reynolds, Director of WR Division, U.S. Navy, from Bertha F. Stone, Executive Director of the ATW SDC of Washington Lafayette Square, 14 April 1943, box 44, RG 225; Women's Committee Minutes of the SDC, Philadelphia, 27 June 1944, box 9, WWII Collection.

125. "Hostess Standards Reflect Human Needs Emphasized by War," *Information Sheet*, February 1943, box 6, WWII Collection

126. Alsop and McBride, *Arms and the Girl*, 273.

127. *Stage Door Canteen*.

128. Narrative Program Report for May 1944, Hattiesburg USO Records.

129. *Hints for Hostesses in Service Clubs*, box 5, RG 215. Similar advice given in Abel, *Hail Hostesses*, and *Madison Hostess Units Manual*, box 5, RG 215.

130. "Barometers of Wartime Influences on the Behavior of Children and Youth," U.S. Department of Labor, CB, 1 February 1943, entry 19, RG 215; memo to Miss Eleanor Ten Broeck, Martinez Junior High School, Martinez, Calif., from George R. Vestal, Field Recreation Representative, entry 19, RG 215; "Curfews and the Teen Age Girl," reprinted from Techniques of Law Enforcement against Prostitution, FSA, OCWS, SPD, 1943, entry 19, RG 215.

131. Florida State Defense Council Meeting on Juvenile Delinquency, May 1943, entry 19, RG 215.

132. Emmons interview.

133. Norma Burris Rethwish, WQ.

134. Roby [pseud.] interview. During the war, British women were also attracted to American servicemen in uniform. They agreed that the outfits "fitted in all the right places" (Gardiner, *"Over Here,"* 110). Irish women also found American uniforms enticing; see McCormick, " 'One Yank and They're Off,' " 232–33.

135. USO Labor Plaza, Evening Chairman Meeting, 21 September 1944, box 23, WWII Collection.

136. Ibid., 16 August 1944.

137. Grossman and Assyia interview.

138. Pseudonyms.

139. Roby [pseud.] interview; Donna Smith [pseud.], WQ.

140. Brandt, *No Magic Bullet*, 165.

141. Gardiner, *"Over Here,"* 142.

142. Manual, Hostess Training Institute, Madison, Wisc., Recreation Committee of the Dane County Civilian Defense Council, box 5, RG 215.

143. Pseudonym.

144. Roby [pseud.] interview.

145. Ibid.

146. Memorandum on the USO, 1942, General Welfare Files, RG III, box 51, RAC.

147. Kane interview.

148. Bi-Monthly Report, 26 April 1942 to 11 May 1942, to John I. Neasmith, Acting Regional Recreation Representative, Washington, D.C., from RC Robinson, Field Recreation Representative, Fayetteville, N.D. [*sic*], box 4, folder "Fayetteville, North Carolina," RG 215.

149. Pseudonym.

150. Rosenberg interview.

151. "Standards for USO Junior Hostess Groups," USO Field Service Bulletin #29, rev. 26 April 1944, box 18, WWII Collection.

152. Gordon, *Woman's Body, Woman's Right*, 356. There was also a large international group of war brides who married American men. One million women immigrated to the United States as war brides following World War II. The federal government passed legislation in December 1945 known as the War Brides Act. This law exempted war brides from immigration quotas. In 1952, the government admitted Japanese war brides when it ended the Oriental Exclusion Act. See Shukert and Scibetta, *War Brides of World War II*, 46, 2.

153. "Romance via USO-YMCA," *YMCA News*, February 1944, ser. 1, box 73, YMCA Collection.

154. To author from Irene Szuhay Hennig, 21 February 2001.

155. Irene Szuhay Hennig, Donna Smith [pseud.], Reba N. Muller, Donna Hendrickson [pseud.], and Shannon Kelley [pseud.], all WQ; Church and Church interview; Fredrich and Fredrich interview; Baldridge interview.

156. Irene and Victor were married for thirty-nine years until his death in 1984; see Irene Szuhay Hennig, WQ. Of the sixty-three junior hostesses interviewed for this project, forty-one married servicemen or men who entered the armed service following the war.

CONCLUSION

1. Baldridge interview; Phyllis Mayfield Baldridge, "Images" (2001), unpublished manuscript in Baldridge's possession.

2. USO operations began to wind down after V-J Day when the organization shifted focus from entertaining troops to assisting them with the reconversion process. The WWII USO concluded operations on 9 January 1948. See Coffey, *Always Home*, 45, and "USO Rejoices over News of Long Awaited Peace," *Information Sheet*, September 1945, box 6, WWII Collection.

3. Brokaw, *Greatest Generation*.

4. Shockley, *"We, Too, Are Americans"*; Estes, *I Am a Man!*

5. Coffey, *Always Home*, 51 52.

6. Douglas, *Where the Girls Are*. The Prelinger Archive houses educational shorts from the 1950s that emphasized the "do's and don'ts of dating" and attempted to help boys and girls distinguish between good and bad influences of all kinds; see <http://www.archive.org/details/prelinger>.

7. "No More Miss America!," 584–88; Douglas, *Where the Girls Are*; <http://www.archive.org/details/prelinger>. Hugh Hefner labeled the Playboy Bunny "the girl next door." See Bailey, *From Front Porch to Backseat*, 108.

8. Enloe, *Maneuvers*.

9. Hochschild, *Managed Heart*, 11.

10. <http://soldiersangels.org/>, accessed 30 May 2007; <http://www.operationuso carepackage.org/>, accessed 25 May 2007; <http://www.airborneangelcadets.com/ whatisrequested.html>, accessed 30 May 2007; <http://opgratitute.com/>, accessed 30 May 2007.

11. Sheehan, *Peace Mom*.

12. Coffey, *Always Home*, 66–67, 106.

Bibliography

PRIMARY SOURCES

MANUSCRIPT COLLECTIONS

Alexandria, Va.
    Salvation Army Archives and Research Center
        Salvation Army War Services Subject Files, 1939–1950
Baltimore, Md.
    Maryland Historical Society, Prints and Photographs Department
        Margaret Neal WWII Homefront Collection, P 151
    University of Baltimore, Langsdale Library, Reference Department
        Archives and Special Materials Section, YMCA Collection
Cambridge, Mass.
    Radcliffe Institute for Advanced Study, Harvard University, Schlesinger Library
        Records of the Boston YWCA
        Records of the Cambridge YWCA
College Park, Md.
    National Archives II
        Record Group 24, Records of the Bureau of Navy Personnel
        Record Group 215, Records of the Office of Community War Services
        Record Group 225, Records of the Joint Army and Navy Boards and
            Committees
Concord, Mass.
    Concord Free Public Library
        Records of the Concord Dance Hostess Committee
Hattiesburg, Miss.
    University of Southern Mississippi, McCain Library and Archives
        Record Group M211, USO Club Records
Minneapolis, Minn.
    University of Minnesota, History Archives
        YWCA National Board/United Service Organization Records, 1941–1975, So-
        cial Welfare

Montgomery, Ala.
    State of Alabama Department of Archives and History
        Vera Ruth Prentiss Papers, 1941–1979
North Tarrytown, N.Y.
    Rockefeller Archive Center, Rockefeller Family Archives
        General Welfare Subject Files, United Service Organizations,
            General, 1941–1961
Philadelphia, Pa.
    Historical Society of Pennsylvania, Philadelphia
        World War II Collection, USO Series
Tempe, Ariz.
    Betty Ward Collection
        Private Collection of Ward O'Connell
Tucson, Ariz.
    University of Arizona Library
        American Social Hygiene Association
            Account of History, Purpose and Work of the Association,
                1914–1916, microfilm 4300, no. 992
Washington, D.C.
    Archives of the Catholic University of America
        Records of the National Catholic Community Service
    Library of Congress, Manuscript Division
        National Association for the Advancement of Colored People Papers
        Records of the National Urban League
        Records of the National Urban League — Southern Regional Office

JOURNALS AND NEWSPAPERS

American Dancer   *Pittsburgh Courier*
Dance Magazine   *Reader's Digest*
Journal of Social Hygiene   *USO Bulletin*
Life Magazine   *Yank: The Army Weekly*

LETTERS

Carson, Dorothy, Phoenix, Ariz., to Meghan Winchell, Tucson, Ariz., 24 March 2001.
    In author's possession.
Rogers, Mary Ellen [pseud.], Parker, Ariz., to Meghan Winchell, Tucson, Ariz., 19
    April 2001. In author's possession.

ORAL AND TELEPHONE INTERVIEWS

All interviews were conducted and recorded by the author and are currently in the author's possession.

Baldridge, Phyllis Mayfield. 16 March 2001, Apache Junction, Ariz.

Bernstein, Hannah [pseud.]. 27 September 2001, Scottsdale, Ariz.

Blake, Nancy Brown, and Sumner Blake. 15 March 2001, Scottsdale, Ariz.

Byko, Barbara. 26 March 2001, Glendale, Ariz.

Calvaruso, Marianne. 18 September 2001, Paradise Valley, Ariz.

Campbell, Helen. Telephone interview, 17 April 2001.

Canaday, Lee. Telephone interview, 2 April 2001.

Carroll, Helen. 5 March 2001, Mesa, Ariz.

Church, Anne Rodriguez, and John H. Church. 16 March 2001, Sun City, Ariz.

Emmons, Barbara. 3 March 2001, Tucson, Ariz.

Fredrich, Margaret Campbell, and Roger Fredrich. 14 March 2001, Phoenix, Ariz.

Gercke, Frances. 27 March 2001, Scottsdale, Ariz.

Goodman, Rhoda. Telephone interview, 23 April 2001.

Grossman, Muriel Ross, and Sylvia Ross Assyia. 26 March 2001, Sun City, Ariz.

Habecker, Catherine. 26 February 2001, Gilbert, Ariz.

Hale, Marilyn. 18 September 2001, Phoenix, Ariz.

Hodge, Ralph [pseud.]. Telephone interview, 20 May 2001.

Hoza, Helen Scheidel, John S. Hoza, Margaret Scheidel Bowley, and Don Bowley. 26 March 2001, Phoenix, Ariz.

Hutchings, Doretta Cloyed. 2 October 2001, Sun City, Ariz.

Jennings, Gordon [pseud.]. 12 June 2001, Davenport, Iowa.

Johnson, Doris Machado. 4 September 2001, Phoenix, Ariz.

Kane, Norma Williams. 6 March 2001, Phoenix, Ariz.

Kaufman, Roberta. 17 September 2001, Phoenix, Ariz.

Kelly, John S., Sr. Telephone interview, 6 March 2001.

King, Maretta "Pinky." 15 March 2001, Scottsdale, Ariz.

Luckow, Anne [pseud.]. 5 March 2001, Tempe, Ariz.

Mapstead, Rosemary Anderson. 27 September 2001, Phoenix, Ariz.

Masland, Miki [pseud.]. 2 October 2001, Sun City, Ariz.

McBride, Lu. Telephone interview, 4 April 2001.

Miller, Joella. Telephone interview, 4 April 2001.

Monaco, Dolly, and Frank Musumeci. 14 March 2001, Phoenix, Ariz.

Nickerson, Peggy Jane Peebler. 5 March 2001, Scottsdale, Ariz.

Pantaz, Mary I. Telephone Interview, 2 April 2001.

Penska, Ann Gushue. Telephone interview, 9 November 2001.

Roby, Alice [pseud.]. 6 March 2001, Phoenix, Ariz.

Rader, Janice Assaff. 14 March 2001, Scottsdale, Ariz.

Rosenberg, Aileen Cooperman. 4 September 2001, Phoenix, Ariz.

Shanahan, Catherine. 27 March 2001, Peoria, Ariz.

Usher, Mary Agnes Goodson. 17 September 2001, Goodyear, Ariz.

Wakefield, Larry. Telephone interview, 18 March 2001.

Wardman, Bettelee Zahn. 17 September 2001, Mesa, Ariz.

Warren, Barbara. 3 March 2001, Tucson, Ariz.

Weinstock, Dorothy Goldstein, and Warren Weinstock. 26 February 2001, Mesa, Ariz.

Williams, Robert [pseud.]. Telephone interview, 3 June 2001.

Woods, Audrey Armstrong. 15 March 2001, Fountain Hills, Ariz.

WINCHELL QUESTIONNAIRE

All questionnaires are in the author's possession.

Bagby, Marilla Barlow, 5 April 2001.

Brooks, Carol [pseud.], 16 March 2001.

Chapman, Toni [pseud.], 10 March 2001.

Cohen, Jean, 8 March 2001.

Collins, Susan [pseud.], 6 May 2001.

Cothrun, Nadine Thomas, 12 April 2001.

Currie, Julia [pseud.], 28 March 2001.

Durnal, Mildred Reca, 15 March 2001.

Elkin, June, 8 March 2001.

Gippner, Shirley L., 26 March 2001.

Gosnell, Helen A., May 2001.

Hendrickson, Donna [pseud.], 14 April 2001.

Hennig, Irene Szuhay, 11 March 2001.

Kelley, Shannon [pseud.], 28 March 2001.

Littlejohn, Beverly, May 2001.

Marconi, Grace Scully, 9 March 2001.

McKnight, Alene Eva Gwinn, 20 March 2001.

Muller, Reba N., 7 May 2001.

Pyper, Betty M., 23 March 2001.

Rethwish, Norma Burris, 7 April 2001.

Richards, Edith [pseud.], 23 April 2001.

Richardson, Marian, 8 March 2001.

Robertson, Nora O., 13 March 2001.

Sloan, Marjorie Hawkins, 24 March 2001.

Smith, Donna [pseud.], 19 May 2001.

TePoorten, Elizabeth A., 1 March 2001.

Wirtz, Dorothy, 8 March 2001.

SECONDARY SOURCES

Abel, Barbara. *Cheers for Volunteers*. USO Committee on Volunteer Service, Archives
of the National Board of the YWCA, Empire State Building, New York, N.Y., n.d.

——. *Hail Hostesses*. USO Committee on Volunteer Service, Archives of the National
Board of the YWCA, Empire State Building, New York, N.Y., n.d.

Adams, Michael C. C. *The Best War Ever: America and World War II*. Baltimore: Johns
Hopkins University Press, 1994.

Agnew, Elizabeth N. *From Charity to Social Work: Mary E. Richmond and the Creation of
an American Profession*. Chicago: University of Illinois Press, 2004.

Alexander, Ruth. *"The Girl Problem": Class Inequity and Psychology in the Remaking of
Female Adolescence, 1900–1930*. Ithaca: Cornell University Press, 1995.

Allison, Anne. *Nightwork: Sexuality, Pleasure, and Corporate Masculinity in a Tokyo Hostess Club*. Chicago: University of Chicago Press, 1994.

Alsop, Gulielma, and Mary F. McBride. *Arms and the Girl: A Guide to Personal Adjustment in War Work and War Marriage*. New York: Vanguard, 1943.

Anderson, Karen. "The Victory Girl in Wartime America: Sexual Conformist or
Rebel?" Paper presented at the Southeastern Women's Studies Association Conference, Johnson City, Tenn., 1979.

——. *Wartime Women: Sex Roles, Family Relations, and the Status of Women during
World War Two*. Westport, Conn.: Greenwood Press, 1981.

Anthony, Susan B. *Out of the Kitchen — into the War: Woman's Winning Role in the
Nation's Drama*. New York: Stephen Daye, 1943.

Archibald, Katherine. *Wartime Shipyards: A Study in Social Disunity*. Urbana: University of Illinois Press, 2006.

Back, Les. "Syncopated Synergy: Dance, Embodiment, and the Call of the Jitterbug."
In *Out of Whiteness: Color, Politics, and Culture*, edited by Vron Ware and Les Back,
169–95. Chicago: University of Chicago Press, 2002.

Bailey, Beth. *From Front Porch to Backseat: Courtship in Twentieth Century America*. Baltimore: Johns Hopkins University Press, 1988.

Bailey, Beth, and David Farber. *The First Strange Place: Race and Sex in World War Two
Hawaii*. New York: Free Press, 1992.

Balbo, Laura. "Crazy Quilts: Rethinking the Welfare State Debate from a Woman's

Point of View." In *Women and the State: The Shifting Boundaries of Public and Private*, edited by Anne Showstack Sassoon, 45–67. London: Routledge, 1992.

Banner, Lois. *In Full Flower: Aging Women, Power, and Sexuality*. New York: Alfred A. Knopf, 1992.

Barker, Anthony, and Lisa Jackson. *Fleeting Attraction: A Social History of American Servicemen in Western Australia during the Second World War*. Nedlands: University of Western Australia Press, 1996.

Benson, Susan Porter. *Counter Cultures: Saleswomen, Managers, and Customers in American Department Stores, 1890–1940*. Chicago: University of Illinois Press, 1986.

Bentley, Amy. *Eating for Victory: Food Rationing and the Politics of Domesticity*. Chicago: University of Illinois Press, 1998.

Blackwelder, Julia Kirk. *Women of the Depression: Caste and Culture in San Antonio, 1929–1939*. College Station: Texas A&M University Press, 1984.

Blumer, Herbert. "Morale." In *American Society in Wartime*, edited by William Fielding Ogburn, 207–31. Chicago: University of Chicago Press, 1943.

Blumin, Stuart M. *The Emergence of the Middle Class: Social Experience in the American City, 1760–1900*. New York: Cambridge University Press, 1989.

Bock, Gisela, and Susan James, eds. *Beyond Equality and Difference: Citizenship, Feminist Politics, and Female Subjectivity*. New York: Routledge, 1992.

Bond, Chrystelle Trump. "Homefront Heroes: Jitterbugging in Wartime Baltimore." *Maryland Historical Magazine* 88 (Winter 1993): 462–72.

Bordo, Susan. *Unbearable Weight: Feminism, Western Culture, and the Body*. Berkeley: University of California Press, 1993.

Boris, Eileen. " 'You Wouldn't Want One of 'em Dancing with Your Wife': Racialized Bodies on the Job in World War II." *American Quarterly* 50, no. 1 (March 1998): 77–108.

Boydston, Jeanne. *Home and Work: Housework, Wages, and the Ideology of Labor in the Early Republic*. New York: Oxford University Press, 1990.

Brandt, Allan. *No Magic Bullet: A Social History of Venereal Disease in the United States since 1880*. New York: Oxford University Press, 1987.

Bredbenner, Candice Lewis. *A Nationality of Her Own: Women, Marriage, and the Law of Citizenship*. Los Angeles: University of California Press, 1998.

Bremner, Robert H. *Giving: Charity and Philanthropy in History*. New Brunswick: Transaction Publishers, 1994.

Bristow, Nancy K. *Making Men Moral: Social Engineering during the Great War*. New York: New York University Press, 1996.

Brokaw, Tom. *The Greatest Generation*. New York: Random House, 1998.

Brown, Dorothy. *Setting a Course: American Women in the 1920s*. Boston: Twayne, 1987.

Brumberg, Joan Jacobs. *The Body Project: An Intimate History of American Girls*. New York: Random House, 1997.

——. *Fasting Girls: The History of Anorexia Nervosa*. New York: Vintage, 2000.

Cameron, Craig M. *American Samurai: Myth, Imagination, and the Conduct of Battle in the First Marine Division, 1941–1951*. New York: Cambridge University Press, 1994.

Campbell, D'Ann. *Women at War with America: Private Lives in a Patriotic Era*. Cambridge: Harvard University Press, 1984.

Campbell, Julie A. "Madres y Esposas: Tucson's Spanish-American Mothers and Wives Association." *Journal of Arizona History* 31 (Summer 1990): 161–82.

Carson, Julia M. H. *Home away from Home: The Story of the USO*. New York: Harper and Brothers, 1946.

Chafe, William. *The Paradox of Change: American Women in the 20th Century*. New York: Oxford University Press, 1991.

Clement, Elizabeth Alice. *Love for Sale: Courting, Treating, and Prostitution in New York City, 1900–1945*. Chapel Hill: University of North Carolina Press, 2006.

Coffey, Frank. *Always Home: 50 Years of the USO — The Official Photographic History*. New York: Brassey's (US), Inc., 1991.

Cohen, Elizabeth, Frances Newman, Patricia Tobin, and Gail MacPherson. "Historical Perspectives on the Study of Female Prostitution." In *Prostitution*, edited by Nancy Cott, 99–105. London: K. G. Saur, 1993.

Cohen, Lizabeth. *A Consumers' Republic: The Politics of Mass Consumption in Postwar America*. New York: Vintage, 2004.

Collins, Patricia Hill. *Black Feminist Thought: Knowledge, Consciousness, and the Politics of Empowerment*. New York: Routledge, 2000.

Corrigan, Philip, and Derek Sayer. *The Great Arch: English State Formation as Cultural Revolution*. London: Basil Blackwell, 1985.

Costello, John. *Virtue under Fire: How World War Two Changed Our Social and Sexual Attitudes*. Boston: Little, Brown, 1985.

Cott, Nancy. *Public Vows: A History of Marriage and the Nation*. Cambridge: Harvard University Press, 2000.

Cowan, Ruth Schwartz. "The 'Industrial Revolution' in the Home: Household Technology and Social Change in the Twentieth Century." In *Women's America: Refocusing the Past*, 6th ed., edited by Jane Sherron DeHart and Linda K. Kerber, 399–410. New York: Oxford University Press, 1991.

——. *More Work for Mother: The Ironies of Technology from the Open Hearth to the Microwave*. New York: Basic Books, 1983.

——. "Two Washes in the Morning and a Bridge Party at Night: The American Housewife between the Wars." *Women's Studies* 2 (1976): 447–68.

Craig, Maxine Leeds. *Ain't I a Beauty Queen? Black Women, Beauty, and the Politics of Race*. New York: Oxford University Press, 2002.

Cressey, Paul G. *The Taxi-Dance Hall: A Sociological Study in Commercialized Recreation and City Life*. Chicago: University of Chicago Press, 1932.

Crompton, Rosemary, and Gareth Jones. *White Collar Proletariat: Deskilling and Gender in Clerical Work*. London: Macmillan, 1984.

Dabakis, Melissa. "Gendered Labor: Norman Rockwell's Rosie the Riveter and the Discourses of Wartime Womanhood." In *Gender and American History since 1890*, edited by Barbara Melosh, 182–204. New York: Routledge, 1993.

Daniel, Pete. *Lost Revolutions: The South in the 1950s*. Chapel Hill: University of North Carolina Press, 2000.

Dannet, Sylvia G. L., and Frank R. Rachel. *Down Memory Lane: Arthur Murray's Picture Story of Social Dancing*. New York: Greenberg, 1954.

Davis, Nanette J., ed. *Prostitution: An International Handbook on Trends, Problems, and Policies*. Westport, Conn.: Greenwood Press, 1993.

Decades of Discontent: The Women's Movement, 1920–1940. Edited by Lois Scharf and Joan M. Jensen. Westport, Conn.: Greenwood Press, 1983.

Delano, Page Dougherty. "Making Up for War: Sexuality and Citizenship in Wartime Culture." *Feminist Studies* 26, no. 1 (2000): 33–68.

D'Emilio, John, and Estelle B. Freedman. *Intimate Matters: A History of Sexuality in America*. New York: Harper and Row, 1988.

Deutsch, Sally J. *From Ballots to Breadlines: American Women, 1920–1940*. New York: Oxford University Press, 1994.

DeVault, Marjorie. *Feeding the Family: The Social Organization of Caring as Gendered Work*. Chicago: University of Chicago Press, 1991.

Dijkstra, Bram. *Evil Sisters: The Threat of Female Sexuality and the Cult of Manhood*. New York: Alfred A. Knopf, 1996.

Di Leonardo, Micaela. "The Female World of Cards and Holidays: Women, Families, and the Work of Kinship." *Signs* 12, no. 3 (Spring 1987): 440–53.

Doane, Mary Ann. *The Desire to Desire: The Woman's Film of the 1940s*. Bloomington: Indiana University Press, 1987.

Doherty, Thomas. *Projections of War: Hollywood, American Culture, and World War II*. New York: Columbia University Press, 1993.

Douglas, Susan. *Where the Girls Are: Growing Up Female with the Mass Media*. New York: Times Books, 1995.

Driver, Ian. *A Century of Dance*. London: Octopus Publishing Group Limited, 2000.

Dumenil, Lynn. *The Modern Temper: American Culture and Society in the 1920s*. New York: Hill and Wang, 1995.

Ellis, Susan J., and Katherine H. Noyes. *By the People: A History of Americans as Volunteers*. San Francisco: Jossey-Bass, 1990.

Enloe, Cynthia. *Maneuvers: The International Politics of Militarizing Women's Lives*. Los Angeles: University of California Press, 2000.

Erenberg, Lewis A. *Steppin' Out: New York Nightlife and the Transformation of American Culture, 1890–1930*. Westport, Conn.: Greenwood Press, 1981.

Escobedo, Elizabeth. "Mexican American Home Front: The Politics of Gender, Culture, and Community in World War II Los Angeles." Ph.D. diss., University of Washington, 2004.

Estes, Steve. *I Am a Man! Race, Manhood, and the Civil Rights Movement*. Chapel Hill: University of North Carolina Press, 2005.

Evans, Sara M. *Born for Liberty: A History of Women in America*. New York: Free Press, 1989.

Fass, Paula. *The Damned and the Beautiful: American Youth in the 1920's*. New York: Oxford University Press, 1977.

Faue, Elizabeth. *Community of Suffering and Struggle: Women, Men, and the Labor Movement in Minneapolis, 1915–1945*. Chapel Hill: University of North Carolina Press, 1991.

Fee, Elizabeth. "Venereal Disease: The Wages of Sin?" In *Passion and Power: Sexuality in History*, edited by Kathy Peiss and Christina Simmons, 178–98. Philadelphia: Temple University Press, 1989.

Feldstein, Ruth. *Motherhood in Black and White: Race and Sex in American Liberalism, 1930–1965*. Ithaca: Cornell University Press, 2000.

Fetrow, Alan G. *Feature Films, 1940–1949: A United States Filmography*. Jefferson, N.C.: McFarland, 1994.

Filene, Peter. *Him/Her/Self: Sex Roles in Modern America*. Baltimore: Johns Hopkins University Press, 1986.

Foucault, Michel. *Discipline and Punish: The Birth of the Prison*. New York: Vintage, 1979.

——. *The History of Sexuality* Vol. 1, *An Introduction*. New York: Vintage, 1990.

Frisch, Michael. *A Shared Authority: Essays on the Craft and Meaning of Oral and Public History*. Albany: SUNY Press, 1990.

Gaines, Kevin K. *Uplifting the Race: Black Leadership, Politics, and Culture in the Twentieth Century*. Chapel Hill: University of North Carolina Press, 1996.

Gardiner, Juliet. *"Over Here": The GI's in Wartime Britain*. London: Collins & Brown, 1992.

Gavin, Lettie. *American Women in World War I: They Also Served*. Niwot: University of Colorado Press, 1997.

Gayne, Mary K. "Japanese Americans at the Portland YWCA." *Journal of Women's History* 15, no. 3 (Autumn 2003): 197–203.

Gere, Anne Ruggles. *Intimate Practices: Literacy and Cultural Work in U.S. Women's Clubs, 1880–1920*. Chicago: University of Illinois Press, 1997.

Giddings, Paula. *In Search of Sisterhood: Delta Sigma Theta and the Challenge of the Black Sorority Movement*. New York: William Morrow, 1988.

Gilligan, Maureen Carroll. *Female Corporate Culture and the New South*. Edited by Stuart Bruchey. Garland Studies in the History of American Labor. New York: Garland, 1999.

Gilmore, Glenda Elizabeth. *Gender and Jim Crow: Women and the Politics of White Supremacy in North Carolina, 1896–1920*. Chapel Hill: University of North Carolina Press, 1996.

Glenn, Evelyn Nakano, Grace Chang, and Linda Rennie Forcey, eds. *Mothering: Ideology, Experience, and Agency*. New York: Routledge, 1994.

Gluck, Sherna Berger. *Rosie the Riveter Revisited*. New York: Meridian, 1987.

———. *Women, the War, and Social Change*. New York: Meridian, 1988.

Goldstein, Joshua S. *War and Gender: How Gender Shapes the War System and Vice Versa*. New York: Cambridge University Press, 2001.

Goodman, Jack, ed. *While You Were Gone: A Report on Wartime Life in the United States*. New York: Simon and Schuster, 1946.

Goossen, Rachel Waltner. *Women against the Good War: Conscientious Objection and Gender on the American Home Front, 1941–1947*. Chapel Hill: University of North Carolina Press, 1997.

Gordon, Linda. *Woman's Body, Woman's Right: A Social History of Birth Control in America*. New York: Penguin, 1988.

Gorham, Ethel. *So Your Husband's Gone to War!* Garden City, N.Y.: Doubleday, Doran, 1942.

Gruenberg, Sidonie, ed. *The Family in a World at War*. New York: Harper and Brothers, 1942.

Gubar, Susan. " 'This Is My Rifle, This Is My Gun': World War II and the Blitz on Women." In *Behind the Lines: Gender and the Two World Wars*, edited by Margaret Randolph Higonnet, Jane Jenson, Sonya Michel, and Margaret Collins Weitz, 227–59. New Haven: Yale University Press, 1987.

Gushwa, Robert L. *The Best and Worst of Times: The United States Army Chaplaincy, 1920–1945*. Vol. 4. Washington, D.C.: Office of the Chief of Chaplains, Department of the Army, 1977.

Haiken, Elizabeth. *Venus Envy: A History of Cosmetic Surgery*. Baltimore: Johns Hopkins University Press, 1997.

Hale, Grace Elizabeth. *Making Whiteness: The Culture of Segregation in the South, 1890–1940*. New York: Pantheon, 1998.

Harris, Mark Jonathan, Franklin D. Mitchell, and Steven Schechter. *The Homefront: America during World War II*. New York: G. P. Putnam's Sons, 1984.

Hartmann, Susan. *The Home Front and Beyond: American Women in the 1940's*. Boston: Twayne, 1982.

Hatheway, Jay. *The Gilded Age Construction of Modern American Homophobia*. New York: Palgrave Macmillan, 2003.

Heberling, Lynn O'Neal. "Soldiers in Greasepaint: USO Camp Shows, Inc., during World War Two." Ph.D diss., Kent State University, 1989.

Hedges, Elaine, ed. *Ripening: Selected Work, Meridel Lesueur*. New York: Feminist Press, 1990.

Hegarty, Marilyn. "Patriot or Prostitute? Sexual Discourses, Print Media, and American Women during World War Two." *Journal of Women's History* 10, no. 2 (Summer 1998): 112–36.

———. *Victory Girls, Khaki-Wackies, and Patriotutes: The Regulation of Female Sexuality during World War Two*. New York: New York University Press, 2008.

Hegland, Edwina Kenney, and Sheridan Hegland. *USO, "The Heart of San Diego": A History of USO in San Diego City and County, 1941–1946*. San Diego: San Diego USO Council, 1946.

Herspring, Dale R. *Soldiers, Commissars, and Chaplains: Civil-Military Relations since Cromwell*. New York: Rowan & Littlefield, 2001.

Hester, Harriet. *300 Sugar Saving Recipes*. New York: M. Barrows, 1942.

Higginbotham, Evelyn Brooks. *Righteous Discontent: The Women's Movement in the Black Baptist Church, 1880–1920*. Cambridge: Harvard University Press, 1993.

Hobson, Barbara Meil. *Uneasy Virtue: The Politics of Prostitution and the American Reform Tradition*. New York: Basic Books, 1987.

Hochschild, Arlie Russell. *The Managed Heart: Commercialization of Human Feeling*. Berkeley: University of California Press, 1983.

Holloway, Pippa. *Sexuality, Politics, and Social Control in Virginia, 1920–1945*. Chapel Hill: University of North Carolina Press, 2006.

Honey, Maureen. *Creating Rosie the Riveter: Class, Gender, and Propaganda during World War Two*. Amherst: University of Massachusetts Press, 1984.

———. "Maternal Welders: Women's Sexuality and Propaganda on the Homefront during World War Two." *Prospects: An Annual of American Cultural Studies* 22 (1997): 479–519.

———. "Remembering Rosie: Advertising Images of Women in World War Two." In

The Homefront War: World War II and American Society, edited by Kenneth Paul O'Brien and Lynn H. Parsons, 83–106. Westport, Conn.: Greenwood Press, 1995.

————, ed. *Bitter Fruit: African American Women in World War Two*. Columbia: University of Missouri Press, 1999.

Hurtado, Albert. *Intimate Frontiers: Sex, Gender, and Culture in Old California*. Albuquerque: University of New Mexico Press, 1999.

Imber, Michael. "Analysis of a Curriculum Reform Movement: The American Social Hygiene Association's Campaign for Sex Education, 1900–1930." Ph.D. diss., Stanford University, 1980.

Inness, Sherrie A., ed. *Delinquents and Debutantes: Twentieth-Century American Girls' Cultures*. New York: New York University Press, 1998.

Kaminer, Wendy. *Women Volunteering: The Pleasure, Pain, and Politics of Unpaid Work from 1830 to the Present*. Garden City, N.Y.: Anchor Press, 1984.

Katcher, Philip. *The U.S. Army, 1941–45*. Edited by Martin Windrow. Men at Arms Series. London: Osprey, 1995.

Kennedy, David M. *Freedom from Fear: The American People in Depression and War, 1929–1945*. New York: Oxford University Press, 1999.

Kerber, Linda K. *No Constitutional Right to Be Ladies: Women and the Obligation of Citizenship*. New York: Hill and Wang, 1998.

Knapp, Gretchen. "Experimental Social Policymaking during World War II: The United Service Organizations (USO) and American War-Community Services (AWCS)." *Journal of Policy History* 12, no. 3 (2000): 321–38.

Koppes, Clayton. "Hollywood and the Politics of Representation: Women, Workers, and African Americans in World War Two Movies." In *The Homefront War: World War Two and American Society*, edited by Kenneth Paul O'Brien and Lynn H. Parsons, 25–40. Westport, Conn.: Greenwood Press, 1995.

Kryder, Daniel. *Divided Arsenal: Race and the American State during World War II*. New York: Cambridge University Press, 2000.

Kunzel, Regina G. *Fallen Women, Problem Girls: Unmarried Mothers and the Professionalization of Social Work, 1890–1945*. New Haven: Yale University Press, 1993.

Landis, Carole. *Four Jills in a Jeep*. New York: Random House, 1944.

Lee, Ulysses. *The Employment of Negro Troops*. Washington, D.C.: U.S. Government Printing Office, 1966.

Linehan, Mary. "Vicious Circle: Prostitution, Reform, and Public Policy in Chicago, 1830–1930." Ph.D. diss., University of Notre Dame, 1991.

Lingeman, Richard R. *Don't You Know There's a War On? The American Homefront, 1941–1945*. New York: G. P. Putnam's Sons, 1970.

Litoff, Judy Barrett, and David C. Smith, eds. *American Women in a World at War*. Wilmington, Del.: Scholarly Resources, 1997.

——. *Since You Went Away: World War Two Letters from American Women on the Home-front*. New York: Oxford University Press, 1991.

Lovelace, Maryann. "Facing Change in Wartime Philadelphia: The Story of the Philadelphia USO." *Pennsylvania Magazine of History and Biography* 123 (July 1999): 143–75.

Lovette, Leland P. *Naval Customs, Traditions, and Usage*. Annapolis, Md.: U.S. Naval Institute, 1939.

Lowe, Graham S. *Women in the Administrative Revolution: The Feminization of Clerical Work*. Oxford: Polity Press, 1987.

Lunbeck, Elizabeth. *The Psychiatric Persuasion: Knowledge, Gender, and Power in Modern America*. Princeton: Princeton University Press, 1994.

Marin, Christine. "La Asociacion Hispano-Americana de Madres y Esposas: Tucson's Mexican American Women in World War Two." *Renato Rosaldo Lecture Series Monograph* 1 (Summer 1985): 5–18.

Marling, Karal Ann. *Debutante: Rites and Regalia of American Debdom*. Lawrence: University of Kansas Press, 2004.

——. *Merry Christmas! Celebrating America's Greatest Holiday*. Cambridge: Harvard University Press, 2000.

McCarthy, Kathleen D., ed. *Lady Bountiful Revisited: Women, Philanthropy, and Power*. New Brunswick: Rutgers University Press, 1990.

McComb, Mary C. "Rate Your Date: Young Women and the Commodification of Depression Era Courtship." In *Delinquents and Debutantes: Twentieth-Century American Girls' Cultures*, edited by Sherrie A. Inness, 40–60. New York: New York University Press, 1998.

McCormick, Leanne. " 'One Yank and They're Off': Interaction between U.S. Troops and Northern Irish Women, 1942–1945." *Journal of the History of Sexuality* 15, no. 2 (May 2006): 228–57.

McInosh, William Alex, and Mary Zey. "Women as Gatekeepers of Food Consumption: A Sociological Critique." *Food and Foodways* 3, no. 4 (1989): 317–32.

McKinley, E. H. *Marching to Glory: The History of the Salvation Army in the United States, 1880–1992*. Grand Rapids: William B. Eerdmans, 1995.

——. *Somebody's Brother: The History of the Salvation Army Men's Social Service Department*. Lewiston: Edwin Mellen Press, 1986.

McQuirter, Marya Annette. "Awkward Moves: Dance Lessons from the 1940's." In *Dancing Many Drums: Excavations in African American Dance*, edited by Thomas F. DeFrantz, 81–103. Madison: University of Wisconsin Press, 2002.

Melnick, Jane F. "When Women Went from Good to Bad: Gender, Narrative, and Cultural Politics in New York, 1890–1935." Ph.D. diss., New York University, 1991.

Meyer, Leisa D. *Creating GI Jane: Sexuality and Power in the Women's Army Corps during World War Two*. New York: Columbia University Press, 1996.

Meyerowitz, Joanne. "Women, Cheesecake, and Borderline Material: Responses to Girlie Pictures in the Mid-Twentieth-Century U.S." *Journal of Women's History* 8, no. 3 (Fall 1996): 9–35.

Michel, Sonya. "American Women and the Discourse of the Democratic Family in World War Two." In *Behind the Lines: Gender and the Two World Wars*, edited by Margaret Randolph Higonnet, Jane Jenson, Sonya Michel, and Margaret Collins Weitz, 154–67. New Haven: Yale University Press, 1987.

Mjagkij, Nina, and Margaret Spratt, eds. *Men and Women Adrift: The YMCA and the YWCA in the City*. New York: New York University Press, 1997.

Mollo, Andrew. *Naval, Marine, and Air Force Uniforms of World War II*. New York: Macmillan, 1975.

Mumford, Kevin. *Interzones: Black/White Sex Districts in Chicago and New York in the Early Twentieth Century*. New York: Columbia University Press, 1997.

Muncy, Robyn. *Creating a Female Dominion in American Reform, 1890–1935*. New York: Oxford University Press, 1991.

Nantais, Cynthia Lynn. "Images of American Women in War: Protector or Protected?" M.A. thesis, University of Windsor, Canada, 1996.

"No More Miss America!" In *Sisterhood Is Powerful: An Anthology of Writings from the Women's Liberation Movement*, edited by Robin Morgan, 521–24. New York: Vintage, 1970.

Odem, Mary E. *Delinquent Daughters: Protecting and Policing Adolescent Female Sexuality in the United States, 1885–1920*. Chapel Hill: University of North Carolina Press, 1995.

Odendahl, Teresa, and Michael O'Neill, eds. *Women and Power in the Nonprofit Sector*. San Francisco: Jossey-Bass, 1994.

Palmer, Nancy B. "Gender, Sexuality, and Work: Women and Men in the Electrical Industry, 1940–1955." Ph.D. diss., Boston College, 1995.

Palmer, Phyllis. *Domesticity and Dirt: Housewives and Domestic Servants in the United States, 1920–1945*. Philadelphia: Temple University Press, 1989.

Parker, Kathleen Ruth. "Law, Culture, and Sexual Censure: Sex Crime Prosecutions in a Midwest, County-Circuit Court, 1850–1950." Ph.D. diss., Michigan State University, 1993.

Peiss, Kathy. *Cheap Amusements: Working Women and Leisure in Turn-of-the-Century New York*. Philadelphia: Temple University Press, 1986.

———. *Hope in a Jar: The Making of America's Beauty Culture*. New York: Metropolitan Books, 1998.

Peiss, Kathy, and Christina Simmons, eds. *Passion and Power: Sexuality in History*. Philadelphia: Temple University Press, 1989.

Perks, Robert, and Alistair Thomson, eds. *The Oral History Reader*. New York: Routledge, 1998.

Pfau, Ann Elizabeth. "Miss Yourlovin: Women in the Culture of American World War Two Soldiers." Ph.D. diss., Rutgers University, 2001.

Pivar, David J. *Purity and Hygiene: Women, Prostitution, and the "American Plan," 1900–1930*. Westport, Conn.: Greenwood Press, 2002.

Pleck, Elizabeth. *Celebrating the Family: Ethnicity, Consumer Culture, and Family Rituals*. Cambridge: Harvard University Press, 2000.

Pope, Arthur Upham. "How Can Individuals Keep a Healthy Morale in Wartime?" In *America Organizes to Win the War: A Handbook on the American War Effort*, 250–65. New York: Harcourt, Brace, 1942.

Renov, Michael. *Hollywood's Wartime Women: Representations and Ideology*. Ann Arbor: University Microfilms, 1988.

Ritchie, Donald A. *Doing Oral History*. New York: Twayne, 1995.

Roeder, George H., Jr. *The Censored War: American Visual Experience during World War Two*. New Haven: Yale University Press, 1993.

Rogin, Michael. *"Ronald Reagan," the Movie and Other Episodes in Political Demonology*. Berkeley: University of California Press, 1987.

Rosebury, Theodor. *Microbes and Morals: The Strange Story of Venereal Disease*. New York: Viking, 1971.

Rosen, Ruth. *The Lost Sisterhood: Prostitution in America, 1900–1918*. Baltimore: Johns Hopkins University Press, 1982.

Ruiz, Vicki. "The Flapper and the Chaperone: Cultural Constructions of Identity and Heterosexual Politics among Adolescent Mexican American Women, 1920–1950." In *Delinquents and Debutantes: Twentieth-Century American Girls' Cultures*, edited by Sherrie A. Inness, 199–226. New York: New York University Press, 1998.

——. *From out of the Shadows: Mexican Women in Twentieth Century America*. New York: Oxford University Press, 1998.

Rupp, Leila. *Mobilizing Women for War: German and American Propaganda, 1939–1945*. Princeton: Princeton University Press, 1978.

Scharf, Lois. *To Work and to Wed: Female Employment, Feminism, and the Great Depression*. Westport, Conn.: Greenwood Press, 1980.

Schneider, Carl J., and Dorothy Schneider. *Into the Breach: American Women Overseas in World War I*. New York: Viking, 1991.

Schur, Edwin. *Labeling Women Deviant. Gender, Stigma, and Social Control*. New York: McGraw-Hill, 1984.

Sheehan, Cindy. *Peace Mom: A Mother's Journey through Heartache to Activism*. New York: Atria Books, 2006.

Shockley, Megan Taylor. *"We, Too, Are Americans": African American Women in Detroit and Richmond, 1940–1954*. Chicago: University of Illinois Press, 2004.

Shukert, Elfrieda Berthiaume, and Barbara Smith Scibetta. *War Brides of World War II*. Novato, Calif.: Presidio Press, 1988.

Simmons, Christina. "Modern Sexuality and the Myth of Victorian Repression." In *Passion and Power: Sexuality in History*, edited by Kathy Peiss and Christina Simmons, 157–77. Philadelphia: Temple University Press, 1989.

Solinger, Rickie. *Wake Up Little Susie: Single Pregnancy and Race before Roe v. Wade*. New York: Routledge, 1992.

Sommer, Robin Langley. *Norman Rockwell: A Classic Treasury*. New York: Barnes and Noble, 1997.

Spongberg, Mary. *Feminizing Venereal Disease: The Body of the Prostitute in Nineteenth Century Medical Discourse*. New York: New York University Press, 1997.

Stage Door Canteen. Edited by Frank Borzage. Burbank Video, 1943. Videocassette.

Stock, Catherine McNicol. *Main Street in Crisis: The Great Depression and the Old Middle Class on the Northern Plains*. Chapel Hill: University of North Carolina Press, 1992.

Sullivan, Barbara. *The Politics of Sex: Prostitution and Pornography in Australia since 1945*. New York: Cambridge University Press, 1997.

Summerfield, Penny. *Reconstructing Women's Wartime Lives: Discourse and Subjectivity in Oral Histories of the Second World War*. New York: Manchester University Press, 1998.

Sutherland, Daniel E. *Americans and Their Servants: Domestic Service in the United States from 1800 to 1920*. Baton Rouge: Louisiana State University Press, 1981.

Takaki, Ronald. *A Different Mirror: A History of Multicultural America*. New York: Little, Brown, 1993.

Terkel, Studs. *The Good War: An Oral History of World War Two*. New York: Pantheon, 1984.

Terry, Jennifer, and Jacqueline Urla, eds. *Deviant Bodies: Critical Perspectives on Difference in Science and Popular Culture*. Bloomington: Indiana University Press, 1995.

Thomas, Mary Martha. *Riveting and Rationing in Dixie: Alabama Women in the Second World War*. Tuscaloosa: University of Alabama Press, 1987.

Treadwell, Mattie E. *The United States Army in World War II, Special Studies: The Women's Army Corps*. Washington D.C.: Office of the Chief of Military History, 1954.

Tucker, Sherrie. *Swing Shift: "All-Girl" Bands of the 1940s*. Durham: Duke University Press, 2000.

Turner, George W. *USO in Panama, 1942–1947*. Panama: USO, 1947.

Tuttle, William M., Jr. *"Daddy's Gone to War": The Second World War in the Lives of America's Children*. New York: Oxford University Press, 1993.

Ullman, Sharon R. *Sex Seen: The Emergence of Modern Sexuality in America*. Los Angeles: University of California Press, 1997.

USO, Five Years of Service: Report of the President. New York: United Service Organizations, Inc., 1946.

Van Til, Jon, ed. *Critical Issues in American Philanthropy: Strengthening Theory and Practice*. San Francisco: Jossey-Bass, 1990.

Vogel, Ursula, and Michael Moran, eds. *The Frontiers of Citizenship*. London: Macmillan, 1991.

Walker, Nancy A. *Shaping Our Mothers' World: American Women's Magazines*. Jackson: University Press of Mississippi, 2000.

Wallace, Andrew. *Military Sanitation, War Department Field Manual*. Washington, D.C.: U.S. Government Printing Office, 1945.

Wandersee, Winifred. "The Economics of Middle-Income Family Life: Working Women during the Great Depression." In *Decades of Discontent: The Women's Movement, 1920–1940*, edited by Lois Scharf and Joan M. Jensen, 45–58. Westport, Conn.: Greenwood Press, 1983.

Ware, Susan. *Holding Their Own: American Women in the 1930s*. Boston: Twayne, 1982.

Ware, Vron, and Les Back. *Out of Whiteness: Color, Politics, and Culture*. Chicago: University of Chicago Press, 2002.

Weatherford, Doris. *American Women and World War Two*. New York: Facts on File, 1990.

Weeks, Jeffrey. *Sex, Politics, and Society: The Regulation of Sexuality since 1800*. New York: Longman, 1981.

Westbrook, Robert B. "Fighting for the American Family: Private Interests and Political Obligations in World War Two." In *The Power of Culture: Critical Essays in American History*, edited by Richard Wightman Fox and T. J. Jackson Lears. Chicago: University of Chicago Press, 1993.

———. " 'I Want a Girl, Just Like the Girl That Married Harry James': American Women and the Problem of Political Obligation in World War Two." *American Quarterly* 42, no. 4 (December 1990): 587–614.

White, Marion. *Sweets without Sugar*. New York: M. S. Mill, 1942.

White, Richard. *Remembering Ahanagran: Storytelling in a Family's Past*. New York: Hill and Wang, 1998.

Willett, Julie A. *Permanent Waves: The Making of the American Beauty Shop*. New York: New York University Press, 2000.

Williamson, Joel. *The Crucible of Race: Black-White Relations in the American South since Emancipation*. New York: Oxford University Press, 1984.

Wilson, Margery. *Charm*. New York: Frederick A. Stokes, 1934.

Winston, Diane. *Red-Hot and Righteous: The Urban Religion of the Salvation Army*. Cambridge: Harvard University Press, 1999.

Wise, Nancy Baker, and Christy Wise. A *Mouthful of Rivets: Women at Work in World War II*. San Francisco: Jossey-Bass, 1994.

Wong, K. Scott. "War Comes to Chinatown: Social Transformation and the Chinese of California." In *The Way We Really Were: The Golden State in the Second Great War*, edited by Roger Lotchin, 164–86. Chicago: University of Illinois Press, 2000.

Wylie, Philip. *Generation of Vipers*. New York: Holt, Rinehart and Winston, 1955.

Young, Agatha Brooks. *Recurring Cycles of Fashion, 1760–1937*. New York: Cooper Square Publishers, 1966.

Yow, Valerie Raleigh. *Recording Oral History: A Practical Guide for Social Scientists*. Thousand Oaks, Calif.: Sage, 1994.

Acknowledgments

I am grateful for the support of numerous colleagues and institutions in assisting me with the completion of this book. The Academic Affairs Office at Nebraska Wesleyan University and the Ameritas Foundation provided vital financial assistance in the final stages of publication. The Southwest Oral History Association awarded a grant that helped me conduct oral interviews with women and men in the Phoenix area. A grant from the University of Arizona Social and Behavioral Sciences Research Institute and fellowships from the University of Arizona Graduate College and History Department allowed me to complete archival research in Washington, D.C., Philadelphia, and Boston.

I thank those men and women who took the time to recall their wartime experiences in oral interviews and questionnaires. Their memories added a key component to my research and writing. I also thank Jeff Bridgers at the Library of Congress, John Shepherd at the American Catholic History Research Center and University Archives of the Catholic University of America, Leslie Perrin Wilson at the Concord Free Public Library, Ellen Shea and Sarah Hutcheon at the Schlesinger Library, Thomas Hollowak at the University of Baltimore's Langsdale Library, Kelly Clegg at the Historical Society of Pennsylvania, Susan Mitchem at the Salvation Army Archives and Research Center, and the archivists at the National Archives in College Park, Maryland, for assistance in locating and navigating various collections. Archivists at the Rockefeller Archive Center, the McCain Library and Archives at the University of Southern Mississippi, and the State of Alabama Department of Archives and History also provide me with invaluable assistance.

Colleen Griffin, Tania Woolcock, and Tanya and Bill Marks supplied lodging and friendship during various research trips. Joe McCartin and Diane Reis opened their home to my family and me so we could spend extra time together as I conducted research.

Karen Anderson, Sarah Deutsch, and Beth Bailey offered crucial advice and insight throughout the research and writing process. Each of these superb scholars taught me how to examine sources and shape my writing in the most effective way possible. I am grateful for their time and expertise. I am also grateful to Joe McCartin for introducing me to women's history early in my college career, and to Maureen Fitzgerald for teaching me how to think critically about gender and power. I had the good fortune to attend the University of Arizona, where members of a rich and supportive graduate community offered moral support and insightful critiques of my work. Laura Shelton, Jodie Kreider, Cherstin Lyon, Mike Rembis, Jerry Pierce, H. Michael Gelfand, Lydia Otero, Sharon Bailey-Glasco, Michael Crawford, Denise Bates, Maritza de la Trinidad, Michelle Berry, and Clark Pomerleau have each read and commented on aspects of this book. I appreciate their insights. I thank Jodie Kreider, Cherstin Lyon, and Laura Shelton for their guidance and friendship.

Reviewers for the University of North Carolina Press provided suggestions and advice that greatly improved this manuscript. I thank them for the time and care they took in critiquing my work. The editing staff at UNC Press has been a pleasure to work with. I thank Chuck Grench for his patience and strong interest in this project.

Nebraska Wesleyan University has provided a productive environment in which to teach and conduct research. I thank John Montag, Janet Lu, and Irma Sarata at NWU's Cochrane-Woods Library for tracking down much-needed sources and information. The History Department funded students to assist in the preparation of the manuscript. Jennifer Nance, Ross Bergt, Blake Simpson, and Evan Knight added to this project at various stages. I owe a debt of gratitude to Melissa Friedler for transcribing hours of interviews, compiling demographic data, and preparing electronic images for publication. She has been a smart and gifted research assistant. This book has also benefited from Derek Carson's careful editing skills and commitment to detail. I am grateful for his patience and integrity. As department chair, Elaine Kruse has been a generous mentor and friend. My colleagues in the History Department, Staci Bell, Kevin Bower, Sandra Mathews, Ron Naugle, and Jim Hewitt, have always showed enthusiasm for my research. Patrick Hayden-Roy's good humor and steady advice kept me grounded as I finished the manuscript. He and Rick Cypert read several versions of this work. I thank them for their critiques.

I would like to thank my parents, Brenda Winchell and Wayne Winchell, for their encouragement and love. Finally, I am grateful to my husband, Guy Davenport; our son, Mackenzie; and our daughter, Kelsey, for always supporting this project and allowing me the time to complete it. Thank you.

Index

Page numbers in italic refer to illustrations.

Adams, Michael C. C., 29–30
Advertising. *See* Publicity campaigns of USO
African American servicemen: ages of men visiting USO clubs, 30, 187 (n. 87); attitudes of, toward USO, 7; in Australia, 215 (n. 89); and dancing, 53–54, 137, 152–57; dating by, 213 (n. 54); discrimination against, 8–9, 15–17, 93–94, 155–56; in Hawaii, 153; and integration of USO clubs, 8–9, 17, 47, 54, 55, 155; morale of, 81–82, 93–94; pinups for, 74–75; recreation for, 93–94; rudeness of, toward junior hostesses, 93; sexual encounters by, 112; as sexual threat to white women, 155–56; training camps for and location of, 9, 93–94; USO clubs for, 16–18, *36*, 53–56, 81–82, 93–94, 155; and venereal disease (VD), 129–31
African American women: arrest of, in Georgia, 10; beauty of, 45; and bourgeois standards of respectability and morality, 65, 137; as clubwomen, 56–57; employment of, as domestic servants, 18; pinups of, 74–75; as prostitutes, 130; racial justice work by, 56–58; sexuality of, 9–10, 48, 65; as USO junior hostesses, 10, 46–47, 53–58, 64–65, 153, 155; as USO senior hostesses, 16–17, *36*; and USOs for African American servicemen, 16–17; and venereal disease (VD), 129–31; wartime employment for, 18, 53
Afro-American News, 54
Age: of servicemen visiting USO clubs, 30–31, 35, 187 (n. 87); of USO junior hostesses, 32, 58–59

Airborne Angel Cadets of Texas, 174–75
Alabama clubs. *See specific cities*
Alcohol consumption, 28–30, 50, 78, 99, 186 (n. 83)
All Girl Orchestras, 142
Alsop, Gulielma, 162
American Bureau of Public Relations, 154
American Revolution, 42
American Social Hygiene Association (ASHA), 27, 106–11, 122, 205 (n. 11)
Anderson, Edgar B., 74
Anderson, Rosemary, 121
Anti-Semitism, 9, 166–67
Arizona clubs. *See specific cities*
Arms and the Girl (McBride), 15
Armstrong, Audrey, 80–81, 106, 121, 126, 133
Armstrong, Mildred, 106
Armstrong, William, 106
Army. *See* African American servicemen; Servicemen; Servicewomen
Army and Navy Special Services Division, 85, 184–85 (n. 53)
Army chaplains, 23
Army hostesses, 85–86, 199 (n. 46)
Army Service Clubs, 85–86, 184–85 (n. 53)
Asaff, Janis, 58–59
Asbury Park, N.J., club, 95, 149
ASHA. *See* American Social Hygiene Association
Asian Americans, 55, 65–66
Assyia, Sylvia, 70
Austin, Tex., club, 20
Australia, 215 (n. 89)

Back, Les, 154
Bailey, Beth, 114, 126
Balbo, Laura, 4, 12, 26

Baldridge, Don, 171–72
Baldridge, Larry, 135–36, 137, 171–72
Baltimore *Afro-American News*, 54
Baltimore clubs: African American hostesses at, 54; during Christmas season, 38;
  dances at, 38, 139, 141, 148, 152; dress
  code for junior hostesses at, 68, 71;
  friendliness of junior hostesses at, 85; and
  Girls Service Organization (GSO), 49,
  102; junior captains at, 101; junior host-
  esses at, 47; marital status of hostesses at,
  59; and merchant marines, 180 (n. 4); and
  outings to private homes, 200 (n. 64); and
  rule against hostesses leaving club with
  servicemen, 119; selection of junior host-
  esses at, 49
Banner, Lois, 32
Beauty. *See* Femininity and beauty
Beauty contests, 72–73, 173, *174*
Becktell, Russell, 87–88, 118–19
Bentley, Amy, 37
Berlin, Irving, 38
Bill, William Y., Jr., 157
Birmingham, Ala., club, 103, 125, 146
Birth control. *See* Contraceptives
Birthday parties, 37, 187 (n. 105)
Birth rates, 168
Blacks. *See* African American servicemen;
  African American women
Blanding, Sarah, 199 (n. 46)
Bliss, Anna, 37
Blough, Pearl Case, 62, 63
Boston clubs: African American hostesses
  at, 55–58; for African American service-
  men, 55–56; awards for hostesses at, 104;
  chaperones for dances at, 147; dances at,
  77–78, 147, 149, 156–57; dress code for
  junior hostesses at, 69–70; games at, 97;
  segregation of, 55–57; for servicewomen,
  217 (n. 122); sex ratio at, 149, 157
Brandt, Allan, 110
Brawley, Calif., club, 163
Bristow, Nancy, 111
Britain, 154–55, 165, 218 (n. 134)

Brooks, Carol, 147
Brothels. *See* Prostitution
Brown, Nancy, 1, 45, 46, 67–68, 75, 83, 96
Brumberg, Joan Jacobs, 66
Bryant, Ozell E., 74–75
Burbank, Calif., club, 80–81, 106, 121
Burris, Norma, 163
Bush, Prescott S., 84–85
Byko, Barbara, 77

California clubs. *See specific cities*
Campbell, D'Ann, 13, 84
Campbell, Helen, 20
Campbell, Peggy, 103, 125, 133, *169*, 170
Carey, Drew, 176
Carroll, Helen, 151
Carson, Norma, 124
Catholic Church, 47–48, 103, 131, 166. *See
  also* National Catholic Community Service
CDHC. *See* Concord Dance Hostess
  Committee
Chaperoning: at dances, 120, 121, 133,
  146–48, 147–48, 213 (n. 46); as patriotic
  duty, 147; servicemen's attitude toward,
  147; and sexual reputation of junior host-
  esses, 108, 124–25, 127; at USO clubs
  generally, 12, 20, 124–25, 127
Chaplains. *See* Army chaplains
Chapman, Toni, 126–27, 131
Charleston, S.C., club, 65
Charlotte News, 28–29
Charm schools, 63–66, 99. *See also* Femininity and beauty
Chattanooga, Tenn., club, 161
Cheers for Volunteers, 35
"Cheesecake" pinups. *See* Pinup girls
Chicago clubs: food at, 187 (n. 101); games
  at, 87; junior hostesses at, 12, 47, 126;
  and morale building by junior hostesses,
  86; no-dating rule at, 120; positive lifelong consequences for work at, 103;
  senior hostesses at, 12; sewing for soldiers at, 41; visits to veterans at hospitals
  by junior hostesses at, 100–101

Children's Aid Society, 122–23
Chinese Americans, 65–66
Chinese Young Women's Society, 65
Christmas, 37–39, 148, 149, 188 (n. 119)
Churches. *See* Religion; *and specific churches*
Cigarettes. *See* Smoking and cigarettes
Cincinnati club: during Christmas season,
      188 (n. 119); dances at, 149; femininity and
      beauty of junior hostesses at, 60; rules for
      junior hostesses at, 208 (n. 83); sex ratio
      at, 149; socializing role of, 82–83; spirit of
      unity of junior hostesses at, 203 (n. 116);
      value of junior hostesses' work at, 84
Citizenship. *See* Patriotic duty
Civil rights movement, 172
Civil War, 42
Class. *See* Middle class; Working class
Cleanliness. *See* Hygiene habits of hostesses
Cleveland club, 61–62
Clothing: for dances, 69–70; of employed
      women, 71–72; enforcement of dress
      code for junior hostesses, 71–72, 195–96
      (n. 129); and good girl/bad girl image, 71;
      stockings or leg makeup, 70–71, 195
      (nn. 124–25); uniforms of servicemen,
      41, 135, 136, 138, 163–64, 170, 218
      (n. 134); of USO junior hostesses, 44, 45,
      53, 54, 60, 68–72, 69; of USO senior
      hostesses, 69
Cloyed, Doretta, 44–45, 75, 84
Cohen, Lizabeth, 13
Cold War films, 24
Columbus, Ga., club, 130
Concord Dance Hostess Committee
      (CDHC): age of junior hostesses in, 32,
      58; chaperones at, 147, 208 (n. 78); and
      Christmas Eve party, 149; and food for
      servicemen, 158–59, 200 (n. 64); resigna-
      tion of junior hostess from, 80; selection
      of junior hostesses for, 49, 117–18; and
      sexual reputation of junior hostesses,
      117–18
Conference of the Alcoholic Beverage
      Industries, 28

Contraceptives, 131, 173
Cooperman, Aileen, 103, 126, 131–32, 167
Cosmetics. *See* Makeup for junior hostesses
Costello, John, 112–13
Courtship, 124–25, 150, 158–59
Cowan, Ruth Schwartz, 34
Coyle, Grace, 199 (n. 46)
Craig, Maxine Leeds, 65
Crosby, Bing, 38
Currie, Julia, 104

Dallas USO, 47, 146
Dance for Defense program, 139
Dances: ballroom dancing to big-band
      music, 135, 139–44; benefits of, for ser-
      vicemen, 139–40; chaperoning of, 120,
      121, 133, 146–48; Christmas dances, 38;
      clothing of junior hostesses at, 69–70; at
      clubs for African American servicemen,
      156–57; at colleges, 137–38; communal
      availability of women at, 150–51; compe-
      tition for male attention at, 159–61; and
      dance classes for servicemen, 152; and
      dating between servicemen and USO
      junior hostesses, 135–36, 162–68; debu-
      tante balls, 70; democratic nature of, and
      USO senior hostesses, 138; and discom-
      fort of partners, 151–52; food for, 35–37;
      fox-trot, 142, 144, 145; guest tickets for
      women at, 159–60; interracial dancing,
      53–54, 137, 146, 152–56, 170; jitterbug,
      136–37, 144–46, *145*, 152, 154; junior
      hostesses asking servicemen to dance,
      77–78, 148–50, 164–65; Lindy Hop,
      144; and morale of servicemen, 81; music
      for, 135, 141–42; as patriotic service,
      138–39, 150; "Paul Jones" as mixer at,
      141; photographs of, *140, 142, 143, 145*;
      as positive activity for junior hostesses,
      151; racial connotations of, 136–37, 144–
      46; religious views on, 140–41; segrega-
      tion of dance halls, 56, 137; senior host-
      esses' role at, 147–48; servicewomen at,
      160–62; sex ratio at, 149, 150, 157, 213

(n. 62), 214 (n. 66); sexuality of dancing, 81, 112, 136–37, 139–40; square dancing, 139, 141, *142*; waltz, 144, 145; during World War I, 124

Dancing Masters of America, 139

Dating: by African American servicemen, 213 (n. 54); box lunch dates, 158–59; dances as gateway to, 135–36; interracial dating, 157–58, 170; and lies of servicemen, 164–65; and "lure of the uniform," 163–64, 170, 218 (n. 134); no-dating rule, 106, 118–21, 134, 162, 168, 208 (n. 78); religion as obstacle in, 166–67; risks of, 162–68; of servicemen by junior hostesses, 121–22, 135–36, 158–59, 162–68, 170, 172; by servicewomen, 161; and tensions over class and region, 165–68

Dayton, Ohio, club, 168

De Barril, Virginia, 25

Debutante balls, 70

Delano, Page Dougherty, 67

Del Rio, Tex., club, 157–58

Desegregation. *See* Integration

Detroit club, 16

Dieting, 66

Dietrich, Marlene, 45, 83

Discrimination: against African Americans, 8–10, 15–17, 93–94, 155–56, 167–68, 172; against Hispanics, 9, 157–58, 170; against Jews, 9, 166–67. *See also* Segregation

Dorsey, Tommy, 135, 142

Double V Campaign, 172

Douglas Aircraft, 45

Dress codes. *See* Clothing

Driver, Ian, 144

Dunaway, Mrs., 163

Ebony, 74

Edwards, James, 45

Ellington, Duke, 142

El Paso club, 37

Ely, Mrs. Van Horn, Jr., 79–80

Emmons, Barbara, 163

Emotional work, 4, 12–13, 22–25, 38–39, 43, 173–75

Employment of women. *See* Women in the labor force

Eng, Dorothy, 65

England. *See* Britain

Enloe, Cynthia, 173

Erenberg, Lewis, 144

Esquire, 74, 113

Face makeup. *See* Makeup for junior hostesses

Factory work, 1, 11, 74

Farber, David, 114

Farley, E. E., 130–31

Favorite, Mrs. Upton, 72, 154

Fawkes, W. F., 157

Fayetteville, N.C., clubs: advertising for, 59; African American hostesses at, 64; and African American servicemen, 81–82; and anti-Semitism, 166–67; interracial cooperation in, 18

Federal Security Administration, 22, 86

Female soldiers. *See* Servicewomen

Femininity and beauty: of African American women, 10, 45–47, 53–58, 64–65, 74–75; and age of junior hostesses, 58–59; and beauty contests, 72–73, 173, *174*; charm schools and advice manuals for USO junior hostesses, 63–67, 90–92, 99; of Chinese American hostesses, 65–66; and clothing of USO junior hostesses, 44, 45, 53, *54*, 60, 68–72, *69*, 195–96 (n. 129); and dieting, 66; and face makeup, 67; and hairstyle, 67–68; and hygiene habits, 66–67, 97, 99; and marital status of junior hostesses, 59; marketing of, by USO clubs, 59–60; middle-class values of, 45, 48–49, 75; and physical bodies of junior hostesses, 66; and pinup girls, 6, 66, 68, 73–74, 113–14; *Saturday Evening Post* image of USO junior hostesses, 52–53, *54*; selection criteria and selection process for junior hostesses, 10, 46–47; of servicewomen, 44, 45, 60–63, 75; and stockings or leg makeup, 70–71, 195 (nn. 124–25); and whiteness, 45, 52–53, 56, 75; of working-class women, 48

Films, 24, 88–89, 162, 200 (n. 61)

Florida clubs. *See specific clubs*

Food: and box lunch dates, 158–59; and dieting for women, 66; free food for ser-vicemen versus nominal fee for, 35–36, 187 (n. 101); hostesses not allowed to eat at USO clubs, 66; for parties, 35–37; and Rockwell's image of USO hostesses, 53, 54; and senior hostesses at USO clubs, 12, 20, 25–26, 28, 33–38, 34, 36, 42; and sweets, 35–37, 53, 54, 200 (n. 64)

Foote, Julie Anne, 117

Foster, Marjorie, 151–52

Fox-trot, 142, 144, 145. *See also* Dances

Fredrich, Margaret and Roger, 169, 170

Fund-raising campaigns for USO, 5, 7, 8, 79

Games, 60, 87–88, 90, 91, 97, 100, 200 (n. 64), 210–11 (n. 1)

Gavin, James M., 81–82

Gender roles: and Christmas shopping and wrapping, 39, 188 (n. 119); emotional work of women, 4, 12–13, 22–25, 38–39, 43, 173–75; and games, 87–89; in Great Depression, 14; and masculinity issues of servicemen, 23–24, 73, 77, 82, 87–88, 95, 96, 105, 112, 125; and morale building, 87–88; respectable women's roles in war-time, 1, 3–4, 13–14, 185 (n. 58); and ser-vicewomen, 60–63; and sewing, 12, 21, 39–43, 40; and sexual double standard, 6; women's responsibility for preserving and boosting male egos, 87–88, 92. *See also* Femininity and beauty; Food; Good girl/bad girl dichotomy; Motherhood

Generation of Vipers (Wylie), 24

Georgia, 10, 130

Gevov, Sophie, 101

Girls Service Organization (GSO), 49, 77, 102–3, 122

Goldstein, Dot, 68, 72, 81, 103–4

Goldstein, Mrs. Israel, 25

Good girl/bad girl dichotomy: and class sta-tus, 5–6; and clothing, 71; and makeup, 67; and Miss America beauty pageant, 173, 174; and sexuality, 106–8, 111–12, 115–17, 123–24, 126; and socializing with servicemen, 103; and USO, 123–25, 133–34, 151, 172–73, 176. *See also* Pickups; Prostitution; Sexuality

Goodman, Benny, 142

Goodson, Mary Agnes, 32–33

Goodwin, Katherine R., 161

Gorham, Ethel, 21

Gosnell, Helen, 70, 133

Granger, Lester B., 129

Great Britain. *See* Britain

Great Depression, 13, 14, 35, 48, 66, 70, 77

Greenman, Eleanor, 117

GSO. *See* Girls Service Organization

Gubar, Susan, 96, 114

Guild, Ray, 56–57

Gum chewing, 99

Gushue, Ann, 77–78, 197 (n. 15)

Gwinn, Alene, 95–96

Hairstyle of junior hostesses, 67–68

Hale, Marilyn, 50–51, 61–62, 161

Halsey, Margaret, 92–93, 155–56

Hamon, Martha, 62

Hamsher, Rev. M. R., 86

Hatheway, Jay, 3

Hattiesburg, Miss., club: dances at, 139, 140–41, 149, 160, 213 (n. 58); and dating between servicemen and junior hostesses, 122; dress code for junior hostesses at, 69; entertainment for servicemen at, 89; femininity and beauty of junior hostesses at, 59–60; game nights at, 60; member-ship statistics for, 79; morale building by junior hostesses at, 87; movie night at,

162; reprimands for junior hostesses at, 79; and resignations by junior hostesses due to spiritual revival, 140–41; selection of junior hostesses at, 49; senior hostesses at, 15; sex ratio at, 149

Hawaii clubs: and African American servicemen, 153; dances at, *143*; hostesses of Japanese descent in, 55; interracial contact in, 153; marital status of hostesses at, 59

Hawaii prostitutes, 114–15, 206 (n. 52)

Hawkins, Marjorie, 77, 78

Hayworth, Rita, 113

Heagan, Mary E., 162

Hefner, Hugh, 219 (n. 2)

Hegarty, Marilyn, 115, 127

Hendrickson, Donna, 99

Hennig, Victor, 170, 219 (n. 156)

Hill, Ruth, 147

Hispanics, 9, 157–58, 170, 216 (n. 104)

Hobson, William H., 130

Hochschid, Arlie, 12

Holiday Inn, 38

Hollywood clubs, 45, 67–68, 83, 96

Hollywood pinups. *See* Pinup girls

Homesickness of servicemen, 23–25

Homosexuality, 114

Hope, Bob, 176

Horn, Mrs. Hugh B., 37

Hosmer, Mrs., 162

Hospitals, 100–101, 154

Hostesses. *See* USO junior hostesses; USO senior hostesses

Hoza, John, 41

Hutchinson, Ethel, 49

Hutchinson, Kans., clubs, 201 (n. 84)

Hygiene habits of hostesses, 66–67, 97, 99

Illinois clubs. *See specific cities*

Immorality. *See* Alcohol consumption; Prostitution

Integration: of military, 172; of USO clubs, 8–9, 17, 47, 54, 55, 155, 157, 172

Interracial cooperation, 16–18

Interracial dancing, 53–54, 137, 146, 152–56, 170. *See also* Dances

Interracial marriage, 154–55

Interracial sex, 48

Iraq War, 174–75

Irvin, Clara, 54

Jackson, W. W., 158

Jacksonville, N.C., club, 16

James, Harry, 142

JANCWR. *See* Joint Army and Navy Committee on Welfare and Recreation

Japanese Americans, 55

Jeanson, Lena, 58

Jennings, Gordon, 29

Jewish hostesses, 9, 47, 79, 99, 166–67

Jewish Welfare Board, 2, 79, 99

Jitterbug, 136–37, 144–46, *145*, 152, 154. *See also* Dances

Johnson, Bascom, 109

Joint Army and Navy Committee on Welfare and Recreation (JANCWR), 23, 29, 62, 86

Junior hostesses. *See* USO junior hostesses

Junior League, 20

Kane, Norma, 166

Kansas City clubs: African American hostesses at, 74; conversations between junior hostesses and servicemen at, 95; and Girls Service Organization (GSO), 102–3; ladylike behavior of junior hostesses at, 99; no-alcohol rule at, 78

Kansas clubs. *See specific cities*

Kaye, Sammy, 142

Kelley, Shannon, 103

Kelly, John, 33–34

Kelly, John S., Sr., 120

Keppel, Francis, 62

Kerber, Linda, 13, 193 (n. 81)

Kimball, Lindsley, 109

King, Pinky, 195 (n. 125)

Korean War, 172–73

Kryder, Daniel, 130
Kurtz, William Fulton, 155

Labor force. *See* Women in the labor force
Ladies' Home Journal, 14, 15
Leadership training for USO junior host-
  esses, 101–2
Lebanon, Mo., 63–64
Legion Auxiliary, 138
Leg makeup or stockings, 70–71, 195
  (nn. 124–25)
Life magazine, 74, 154, 195 (n. 124)
Lill, Gertrude, 37
Linden, N.J., club, 77
Lindy Hop, 144
Lipstick. *See* Makeup for junior hostesses
Liquor. *See* Alcohol consumption
Littlejohn, Beverly, 47, 104, 146
Loneliness of servicemen, 23–25, 35, 74
Los Angeles clubs, identification card from,
  50–51
Louisiana. *See* New Orleans club
Lovelace, Maryann, 74, 133, 189 (n. 2), 191
  (n. 48)
Luckow, Anne, 48, 51, 78

Machado, Doris, 103, 150–51
Madison, Wisc., clubs, 66, 67, 87
Makeup for junior hostesses, 67
Manhattan, Kans., club, 77
Marines, 63
Marital status: of USO junior hostesses, 59;
  of USO senior hostesses, 12, 20–21
Markle Foundation, 109
Marling, Karal Ann, 39
Marriage: interracial, 154–55; statistics on,
  168; of USO junior hostesses, 80–81,
  136, 162, 168–71, 169, 219 (n. 156); and
  War Brides Act, 219 (n. 152)
Marshall, George C., 26
Maryland clubs. *See specific cities*
Masculinity. *See* Gender roles
Massachusetts clubs. *See specific cities*
Mathewson, F. S., 147

May Act, 110, 186 (n. 73), 206 (n. 52)
Mayfield, Phyllis, 52, 70, 135, 137, 171–72,
  176
McBride, Mary F., 15, 162
McComb, Miss., club, 58–59
McCormick, Ada, 17–18
McKnight, Alene, 59
McNutt, Paul, 22, 81
Memphis, Tenn., club: dances at, 151; dat-
  ing between servicemen and junior host-
  esses at, 163–64; dress code for junior
  hostesses at, 71; sexual activity by junior
  hostesses at, 126
Menopause, 31–32
Men's roles. *See* Gender roles
Merchant marines, 180 (n. 4)
Merrill, Joan, 142
Mexican Americans, 157–58, 170, 216
  (n. 104)
Meyer, Leisa, 60, 125, 193 (n. 82)
Meyerowitz, Joanne, 74
Miami club: dances at, 133, *140*, *145*; director of, 51, 52; dress code for junior hostesses at, 70; games at, *90*, *91*; selection of
  junior hostesses for, 51
Michigan clubs. *See specific cities*
Middle class: femininity and beauty stan-
  dards of, 45, 48–49, 75; philanthropic
  work of middle- and upper-income white
  women, 17–18; racial uplift by middle-
  income African Americans, 10; and sex-
  ual respectability, 5–6, 49, 52, 106–8,
  114, 123; USO and values of, 2–3, 10, 34,
  48–49, 59, 78
Military personnel. *See* African American
  servicemen; Servicemen; Servicewomen
Miller, Barbara, 149
Miller, Glenn, 135, 141–42
Miller, Joella, 19–20
Milwaukee, Wisc., club, 161
Minneapolis club, 147
Miscegenation, 154–55, 156, 170
Miss America beauty pageant, 173, *174*
Mississippi. *See* Hattiesburg, Miss., club

Missouri clubs. *See specific cities*

Momism, 24

Monaco, Dolly, 100–101

Monroe, Marilyn, 176

Monroe, Vaughn, 164

Montgomery, Ala., club: age of junior hostesses at, 58; dances at, 146; and dating between servicemen and junior hostesses, 122, 159; senior hostess of, 25

Moore, Elizabeth Luce, 22–23, 84–85

Moore, Mrs. Maurice T., 3, 4, 128, 139, 185 (n. 58)

Moore, Stella, 85, 86–87

Morale: of African American servicemen, 81–82, 93–94; of servicemen, 15, 73, 76–77, 81–88, 105, 111, 133; of USO junior hostesses, 101–2, 151, 203 (n. 116)

Mormon Church, 20

Motherhood: and food at USO clubs, 12, 20, 25–26, 28, 33–38, *34, 36*, 42; style of, during 1920s and 1930s, 28; suspicion and blame of mothers for servicemen's problems, 24; USO senior hostesses' motherly attention to servicemen, 22–26, 28, 31, 33–37, 42–43

Movies. *See* Films

Muller, Reba, 146

Mullin, Carolyn, 80, 85, 101, 102

Murray, Arthur, 142, 144

Music. *See* Dances

NAACP. *See* National Association for the Advancement of Colored People

Nacogdoches, Tex., club, 161–62

National Association for the Advancement of Colored People (NAACP), 16, 74, 94, 201 (n. 84)

National Catholic Community Service (NCCS): and creation of USO, 2; and Fayetteville, N.C., USO club, 81–82; and hostesses' wartime problems, 97; on listening skills of women, 23; moral stance of, against nonmarital sex, 111; on recreation for servicemen, 50; and San Francisco USO club, 200 (n. 64); on spirituality of women, 15; training for junior hostesses by, 99; and women as men's moral guardians, 111; on wrapping and mailing Christmas packages, 39

National Economy Act (1932), 14

National Opinion Research Center, 30

National Urban League, 10, 18, 93, 129, 157

National Woman Suffrage Association, 42

National Women's Committee of USO, 3, 49, 84–85, 139

Navy. *See* Servicemen; Servicewomen; Waves (female sailors)

Navy Ship's Service Clubs, 85–86, 184–85 (n. 53)

Nazi Party, 154

NCCS. *See* National Catholic Community Service

Nebraska club. *See* Omaha, Nebr., club

Ness, Elliot, 110

Newark, N.J., club, 94

New Deal, 35

New Jersey clubs. *See specific cities*

New Orleans club, 93

New York City clubs: African American hostesses at, 55; dances at, 164–65; dress code for junior hostesses at, 70, 195 (n. 128); Music Box Canteen, 73, 164–65, 196 (n. 137); pinup photographs of junior hostesses of, 73; selection of junior hostesses for, 45

Nisei soldiers, 55

North Carolina, 186 (n. 73). *See also specific cities*

Nyack, N.Y., club, 55

Oakland, Calif., club, 64, 65

OCWS. *See* Office of Community War Services

Office of Civilian Defense, 139

Office of Community War Services (OCWS), 26–27, 94, 107, 108–9, 111

Office of Price Administration (OPA), 13–14, 36–37

Office of Production Management, 6
Ohio clubs. *See specific clubs*
Omaha, Nebr., club, 52
O'Neill, Helen G., 63
OPA. *See* Office of Price Administration
Optimism of junior hostesses, 92
Orientation period for USO junior hostesses, 49
Osborn, Frederick, 28, 86

Parties: birthday, 37, 187 (n. 105); food for, 35–37
Patriotic duty: of African American hostesses, 57–58; chaperoning as, 147; dances as, 138–39, 150; of servicewomen, 62; and USO junior hostesses, 62, 76, 83–84, 86–87, 105, 138–39, 150; and USO senior hostesses, 13–14, 17, 57
Patterson, Robert P., 3
Peebler, Peggy Jane, 38, 97, 99, 127, 141
Peiss, Kathy, 67
Penicillin, 6, 26–27, 107
Pennsylvania clubs. *See* Philadelphia clubs
Personal hygiene. *See* Hygiene habits of hostesses
Personality of junior hostesses, 90–92
Phi Beta Phi, 20
Philadelphia clubs: absences and tardiness of junior hostesses at, 79–80; African American hostesses at, 53–55, 64, 153, 155; African American servicemen at, 53–55, 148, 152–53; age of junior hostesses at, 58; chaperones of dances at, 148; charm classes for junior hostesses at, 99; conversations between junior hostesses and servicemen at, 96; dances at, 148, 149, 150, 151, 153, 155, 157, 159 60, 164; dismissals of junior hostesses from, 79–80, 197 (n. 23); dress code for junior hostesses at, 71–72; friendliness of junior hostesses at, 85; hygiene of junior hostesses at, 66; and interracial contact, 152, 155–56; and interracial growth, 16–17; Jewish hostesses at, 166; junior captains

at, 101; junior hostesses not allowed to eat at, 66; leadership training for junior hostesses at, 101–2; morale building by hostesses at, 85, 86–87; motherly attention of senior hostesses in, 25, 148; no-alcohol policy of, 78; no-dating rule at, 119, 208 (n. 78); nonhostess dates of servicemen at USO Labor Plaza, 123–24; orientation for junior hostesses at, 49; "pinup girl" contests at, 74, 113–14; prizes for "Millionth serviceman" at, 159; reprimands for junior hostesses at, 79–80, 101; rudeness of servicemen toward junior hostesses at, 92–93, 152; selection of junior hostesses for, 45, 46, 47, 49, 80; selection of senior hostesses for, 19; and servicewomen, 61; socialization among junior hostesses at, 79
Phillips, Maria, 32
Phoebus, Va., 63, 159
Phoenix, Ariz., club: dances at, 141; and needs of junior hostesses, 97, 99, 127; socializing with servicemen at, 127
Pickups, 67, 103, 106–7, 110, 111, 112, 114, 115, *129*
Pinup girls, 6, 66, 68, 73–74, 106–7, 112–14, 214 (n. 70)
Playboy Bunny, 219 (n. 2)
Pleck, Elizabeth, 39
Population shifts, 6–7
Pregnancy outside marriage, 131–32
Prentiss, Vera Ruth, 25, 122, 146, 159
Prostitution: African American prostitutes, 130; arrest of prostitutes, 6, 110; ASHA's attempt to control, 108–10, 205 (n. 11); definition of, 106, 109; in Hawaii, 114–15, 206 (n. 52); May Act on criminalization of, 110, 186 (n. 73), 206 (n. 52); and servicemen, 26–29, 31, 50, 82–83, 107–11, 114; and venereal disease (VD), 6, 26–28, 50, 82–83, 107–10, 114–15, *129*, 130; and working-class women, 123
Publicity campaigns of USO, 5, 7, *8*, 59, 151

Race. *See* African American servicemen;
African American women; Asian Ameri-
cans; Discrimination; Hispanics; Integra-
tion; Segregation; *and headings beginning
with* Interracial
Racial justice work, 56–58, 94. *See also*
National Association for the Advance-
ment of Colored People
Radcliffe College, 47
Rationing, 13–14, 36–37
Reca, Mildred, 78
Red Cross, 13, 23, 42, 54, 93
The Red Shield, 28, 34–35, 37
Religion, 19–20, 47–48, 103, 140–41, 166–
67
Revolutionary War. *See* American
Revolution
Reynolds, John L., 82
Richardson, Marian, 52
Richmond, Va., club, 16
Robertson, Nora O., 150
Roby, Alice, 71, 120–21, 126, 132, 133,
151, 163–66
Rockefeller, John D., Jr., 7, 29, 82, 109, 185
(n. 58), 205 (n. 11), 216 (n. 105)
Rockford, Ill., club: no-alcohol rule at, 78;
selection of junior hostesses at, 48; sew-
ing for soldiers at, 41–42
Rockwell, Norman, 52–53, *54*
Rodriguez, Anne, 59, *143*
Rogin, Michael, 24
Roosevelt, Franklin, 1, 35
Rose, V. F., 158
Rosie the Riveter, 1, 11
Ross, Muriel, 73, 164
Ruiz, Vicki, 216 (n. 104)

Sailors. *See* Servicemen
Salinas, Calif., club, 151, 201 (n. 84)
Salvation Army: and charm lessons for
junior hostesses, 90; and Cincinnati USO
club, 82–83; and creation of USO, 2; on
food preparation by USO senior hostesses, 34–35, 37; and friendliness of
junior hostesses, 82–83; on hygiene of
junior hostesses, 66; moral stance of,
against nonmarital sex, 110–11; on
motherly role of senior hostesses, 24, 25,
28, 34–35; opposition to dances by, 140;
and servicewomen, 62; and temperance,
28; training for junior hostesses by, 90, 99
San Bernardino, Calif., club, 102
San Diego clubs: attractiveness of servicemen at, 163; chaperones at, 124; charm
lessons for junior hostesses at, 63; dances
at, 149; food at, 36–37; sex ratio at, 149
San Francisco clubs: dress code for junior
hostesses at, 72; food at, *34*; memorial
service commemorating Navy Day, 200
(n. 64); motivation of junior hostesses at,
83, 105; resignation of junior hostess
from, 81; rudeness of servicemen toward
junior hostesses at, 94–95; selection of
junior hostesses at, 45, 47
San Rafael, Calif., club, 126–27
Saturday Evening Post, 52–53, *54*
Scheidel, Helen, 12, 13, 47, 87
Scheidel, Marge, 12, 13, 47
Schlosberg, Mrs. Leon, 138
Scott, Mrs. Alfred, *36*
SDCs. *See* Stage Door Canteens
Security issues, 96–97, *98*
Segregation: of dance halls, 56, 137; military, 55, 154; in North versus South, 56;
of USO clubs, 9, 16, 17, 47, 94, 157, 172,
201 (n. 84). *See also* Discrimination
Senior, Theodore R., 74
Senior hostesses. *See* USO senior hostesses
Servais, Laura P., 49, 58, 117–18
Servicemen: activities for, at USO clubs,
200 (n. 64); ages of men visiting USO
clubs, 30–31, 35; alcohol consumption
by, 28–30, 50, 186 (n. 83); attitudes of,
toward USO, 7, 26, 85, 104, 208 (n. 88);
chain of command for, 23–24; characteristics of men visiting USO clubs, 30–
31, 197 (n. 10); at Christmas season, 37–
39, 148, 188 (n. 119); correspondence

between USO junior hostesses and, 73–74, 105; counseling for, from army chaplains, 23; dance classes for, 152; dancing as beneficial for, 139–40; dating of junior hostesses by, 121–22, 135–36, 158–59, 162–68, 170, 172; homesickness and loneliness of, 23–25, 35, 74; hometown girlfriends of, 88; hostesses' responsibility for preserving and boosting egos of, 87–88, 92; Japanese American soldiers, 55, lies of, to junior hostesses, 164–65; masculinity issues of, 23–24, 73, 77, 82, 87–88, 95, 96, 105, 112, 125; and military segregation, 55; morale of, 15, 73, 76–77, 81–88, 92–93, 105, 111, 133; and moral prohibitions against nonmarital sex, 108–12; motherly attention and informal counseling for, by USO senior hostesses, 12, 22–26, 28, 31, 33–37, 42–43, 184 (n. 52); mothers blamed for problems of, 24; news of deaths of, 105; no-dating rule regarding, 106, 118–21, 134, 162, 168; and pinup girls, 6, 66, 68, 73–74, 106–7, 112–14, 214 (n. 70); and prostitutes, 26–29, 31, 50, 82–83, 108–11, 114; public perceptions of, 7; recreation for generally, 50–51, 59, 86, 93–94; rudeness of, toward junior hostesses, 92–95, 152; sewing for, 12, 21, 39–43, 40; sex education for, to control venereal disease, 112, 115; sexual encounters by, 111–12, 165; statistics on, 7, 14; uniforms of, 41, 135, 136, 138, 163–64, 170, 218 (n. 134); and venereal disease (VD), 6, 26–28, 50, 82–83, 107–10, 112, 114–15, 127–28; wartime contributions of, compared with servicewomen, 84. *See also* African American servicemen; Dances; Servicewomen; USO

Servicewomen: as challenge to masculine structure of military, 125; compared with USO junior hostesses, 60–63; competition between junior hostesses and, 160–62, 170; at dances, 160–62; dating by,

161; femininity and beauty of, 44, 45, 60–63, 75, 162; public opinion of, 193 (n. 81); sexuality of, 125; and USO, 44, 45, 60–63, 75, 161–62, 217 (n. 122); wartime contributions of, compared with servicemen, 84

Sewing, 12, 21, 39–43, *40*

Sex education for servicemen, 112, 115

Sexuality: African American men as sexual threat to white women, 155–56; of African American women, 9–10, 48, 65; and clothing of junior hostesses, 71; connection between combat, sex, and death, 112–13; cultural assumptions about, for women, 116; and dancing, 81, 112, 136–37, 139–40; double standard in, 6, 114–15, 173; emotional costs of nonmarital sex for women, 116–17; homosexuality, 114; interracial sex, 48; junior hostesses' sexual services, 107–8, 112, 115–34; of married women, 59; middle-class notions of sexual respectability, 5–6, 49, 52, 106–8, 114, 123; military's view of, 112–16; moral stance on nonmarital sex, 108–12, 116–17; of older women, 31–32; of paid army hostesses, 85–86; of pickups, 67, 103, 106–7, 110, 111, 112, 114, 115, *129*; and pinup girls, 106–7, 112–14; and Playboy Bunny, 219 (n. 2); and rule on "no side-line petting," 119; servicemen's sexual encounters, 111–12, 165; of servicewomen, 125; and sexual reputation of USO hostesses, 107–8, 115–21, 124–27, 133–34; in *Stage Door Canteen* (film), 88–89; of USO junior hostesses, 31, 32, 81, 119–21, 126–28, 131–33, 172; of USO senior hostesses, 31–33; Victorian beliefs on, 116; whiteness and sexual respectability, 137, 144–46, 153, 157; and women's responsibility for sexual control, 111, 118–19, 156; women's sexual pleasure, 116–17; and working-class women, 5–6, 115, 122–23. *See also* Good girl/bad girl dichotomy; Prostitution; Venereal disease

Sexually transmitted diseases. *See* Venereal
disease
Sheehan, Cindy, 175
Shields, Mrs., 65
Shirley, Mass., club, 119, 210–11 (n. 1)
Shockley, Megan Taylor, 16
Shore, Dinah, 142
Sibley, Harper, 3
Simson, Marjorie, 71–72
Sinatra, Nancy, 176
Smith, Donna, 95
Smoking and cigarettes, 99, 210–11 (n. 1)
Snow, Dr., 27
Snowden, George "Shorty," 144
Social class. *See* Middle class; Working class
Socializing: and absences and tardiness of
USO junior hostesses, 79–80; at Army
Service Clubs, 85–86, 184–85 (n. 53);
and awards and honors for hostesses,
103–4, *104*; and conversations between
junior hostesses and servicemen, 95; at
hospitals, 100–101, 154; and ladylike
behavior of junior hostesses, 99–100; and
morale of servicemen, 81–88, 92–93; as
motivation of USO junior hostesses, 76–
78, 105; at Navy Ship's Service Clubs,
85–86, 184–85 (n. 53); and needs of
junior hostesses, 97, 99; and optimism of
junior hostesses, 92; and overcoming
shyness, 77–78; and paid army hostesses,
85–86; and patriotic value of hostessing
work, 83–84, 86–87, 105; and personality
of junior hostesses, 90–92; and playing
games, 60, 87–89, *90*, *91*, 97, 200 (n. 64),
210–11 (n. 1); positive lifelong consequences of, for junior hostesses, 103; and
recreation for servicemen, 86; and resignations of USO junior hostesses due to
engagements and marriages, 80–81; and
rudeness of servicemen toward junior
hostesses, 92–95, 152; rule against junior
hostesses socializing among themselves
at USO clubs, 78–79, 119; and security
issues, 96–97, *98*. *See also* Dances

Social Protection Division, 110, 127
Soldiers. *See* Servicemen; Servicewomen
Soldiers' Angels, 174–75
South Carolina clubs. *See specific cities*
Spartanburg, S.C., club, 159
Special Services Branch, 23
Spokane, Wash., club, 38
Spongberg, Mary, 109
Sprague, Horace, 23
Square dancing, 139, 141, *142*. *See also*
Dances
Stage Door Canteen (film), 88–89, 162, 200
(n. 61)
Stage Door Canteens (SDCs): African
American junior hostesses in, 53–54,
153; African American servicemen at,
152–53; conversations between junior
hostesses and servicemen at, 96; dances
at, 77–78, 148, 150, 153, 157; dress code
for junior hostesses at, 71–72, 195
(n. 128); junior captains at, 101; junior
hostesses in, 44, 46–47, 53–54, 66;
morale building by hostesses at, 85; no-
dating rule at, 119; "pinup girl" contests
at, 74, 113–14; popularity of, 61; reprimands of junior hostesses at, 79–80;
senior hostesses in, 19, 22, 148; and servicewomen, 60–62
Stansbery, Geraldine, 76
Sternberg, Colonel, 26–27
Stix, Barbara, 54–55
Stockings or leg makeup, 70–71, 195
(nn. 124–25)
Strecker, William, 24
Szuhay, Irene, 77, 144, 168, 170, 219
(n. 156)

Taft, Charles, 4–5, 111
Tennessee, 186 (n. 73). *See also specific cities*
TePoorten, Betty, 95, 149
Texas clubs. *See specific cities*
Thomas, Nadine, 47
Tivoli club, 25
Tommy Dorsey Orchestra, 135

Traveler's Aid Society, 2
Truman, Harry, 172
Tucson, Ariz., clubs, 17–18, 32–33

Uniforms of servicemen, 41, 135, 136, 138, 163–64, 170, 218 (n. 134)
USO: after V-J Day, 171, 172, 219 (n. 2); attendance statistics at USO clubs, 7; criticisms of, 28–29; decisions on open- ing USO clubs, 6–7; Field Plans Com- mittee of, 6, formation of, 2; fund-raising campaigns for, 5, 7, 8, 29; future research on, 175–76; integration policy of, 8–9, 17, 47, 54, 55, 155, 157, 172; and interra- cial cooperation, 16–18; middle-class propriety of, 2–3, 10, 34, 48–49, 59, 78; National Sponsoring Committee of, 7; publicity campaigns of, 5, 7, 8, 59, 151; purposes of, 4–5, 9, 26, 51, 61, 107–8, 109, 176; research approach to hostesses of, 11, 177–78, 182 (n. 32); segregation of USO clubs, 9, 16, 17, 47, 94, 157, 172; servicemen's attitudes on, 7, 26, 85, 104, 208 (n. 88); and servicewomen, 44, 45, 60–63, 75, 161–62, 217 (n. 122); statis- tics on, 2, 3, 7. See also Servicemen; Ser- vicewomen; USO junior hostesses; USO senior hostesses; and specific cities
USO Bulletin, 15, 21, 73, 123
USO Camp Shows, Inc., 3, 176
USO junior hostesses: absences and tardi- ness of, 79–80; African American women as, 10, 46–47, 53–58, 64–65, 153; age limits of, 32, 58–59; awards and honors for, 103–4, 104; captains for, 101; charac- teristics of, 48–49, 76; Chinese American hostesses, 65–66; clothing of and dress codes for, 44, 45, 53, 54, 60, 68–72, 69, 195–96 (n. 129); as college students, 47; compared with servicewomen, 60–63; competition between servicewomen and, 160–62, 170; and competition for male attention, 159–61; correspondence between servicemen and, 73–75, 105;

dating of servicemen by, 121–22, 135– 36, 158–59, 162–68, 170, 172; dismissals of, from USO clubs, 79–80, 120, 121, 197 (n. 23); duties of, 89, 116; eating by, not allowed at USO club, 66; friendliness of, 77–78, 85, 92, 118; and goal of USO clubs, 61, 107–8, 116; in labor force, 44– 49, 52, 68, 70, 123, 168, 190 (n. 19), 197 (n. 15); ladylike behavior of, 99–100; marital status of, 59; marriage of, 80–81, 136, 162, 168–71, 169, 219 (n. 156); morale of, 101–2, 151, 203 (n. 116); and morale of servicemen, 73, 76–77, 81–88, 92–93, 105, 111, 133; motivations of, 76– 78, 83, 105, 108, 132–33, 168, 170, 173– 74; movie portrayal of, 88–89, 162; and news of servicemen's deaths, 105; and no- dating rule, 106, 118–21, 134, 162, 168; optimism of, 92; orientation period for, 49; parents of, 48, 49, 125, 190 (n. 19), 197 (n. 15); and patriotic duty, 62, 76, 83–84, 86–87, 105, 138–39, 150; person- ality of, 90–92; photographs of, 46, 64, 69, 126, 140, 142, 143, 145; pinup photo- graphs of, sent to servicemen, 73–75, 113–14; and playing games with service- men, 60, 87–89, 90, 91, 97; positive life- long consequences for USO work by, 103–5; pride in work by, 104–5; prob- lems of, 97, 99; and protection of service- men from prostitutes and venereal dis- ease (VD), 82–83, 107, 112; references for, 48, 49; and religion, 47–48, 103; res- ignations of, due to engagements and marriages, 80–81; rudeness of service- men toward, 92–95, 152; and safety and respectability of USO clubs, 78, 121, 123, 127, 133–34, 150–51; Saturday Evening Post image of, 52–53, 54; selection crite- ria and selection process for, 44–52, 61, 117–18; servicemen's attitudes on, 85, 104; servicewomen's interest in becom- ing, 61; sexuality of, 31, 32, 119–21, 126– 28, 131–33, 172; sexual reputation of,

107–8, 115–21, 124–27, 133–34; sexual services of, 107–8, 112, 115–34; supervision of and reprimands for, by senior hostesses, 19, 59, 65, 72, 79–80; training for, 99–102; and venereal disease (VD), 127–31; visits to hospitals by, 100–101, 154; and wartime anxiety, 97, 99, 105; as working class, 48. *See also* Chaperoning; Dances; Femininity and beauty; Socializing; *and specific hostesses*

USO Manual, 18, 19

USO National Women's Committee, 3, 49, 84–85, 139

USO senior hostesses: African American women as, 16–17; age of, 12; and ages of servicemen visiting USO clubs, 30–31, 35; and alcohol consumption by servicemen, 28–30; as asexual women, 31–33; awards and honors for, 103; as chaperones at dances, 120, 121, 133, 146–48; characteristics of, 12, 19–20, 31; and charm and grooming lessons for junior hostesses, 63, 66, 67; at Christmas season, 37–39, 148, 188 (n. 119); citizenship obligation of, 13–14, 17; clothing of, 69; dancing by, 148; and dating between servicemen and junior hostesses, 121–22, 159, 213 (n. 54); and dress code for junior hostesses, 71–72; duties of, 12, 20; emotional work by, 12–13, 22–25, 38–39, 43; food prepared and served by, 12, 20, 25–26, 28, 33–38, *34, 36*, 42; gratitude of servicemen's mothers toward, 37, 42; and interracial contact, 152–53; jitterbug viewed with discomfort by, 136–37, 144–46; in labor force, 20; marital status of, 12, 20–21; as members of religious organizations or women's clubs, 19–20; and morale of servicemen, 15; motherly attention and informal counseling by, for servicemen, 12, 22–26, 28, 31, 33–37, 42–43, 148, 184 (n. 52); motivations of, 21–22, *22*, 173–74; and no-dating rule for junior hostesses, 120, 121; photographs of, *34, 36, 40*; and protection of servicemen from prostitutes, 26–29, 31; and rudeness of servicemen toward junior hostesses, 95, 152; *Saturday Evening Post* image of, 53, *54*; screening of junior hostesses by, 48; selection criteria and selection process for, 18–21; selection of junior hostesses by, 48, 49, 52; sewing by, 12, 21, 39–43, *40*; sexuality of, 31–33; social control in relationship between servicemen and, 27–28; statistics on, 15; supervision of reprimands for junior hostesses by, 19, 59, 65, 72, 79–80; training for, 23; on venereal disease (VD), 128. *See also* Chaperoning; *and specific hostesses*

USO Services for Women and Girls, 62

Valdosta, N.J., club, 37

Vargas, Alberto, 113

VD. *See* Venereal disease

Venereal disease (VD): and African Americans, 129–31; and health cards for working-class women, 115; penicillin for, 6, 26–27, 107; and pickup girls, 6, 107, 110, 112, 114, 115, 117, *129*; police actions for control of, 6, 110, 115, 124; poster on, *129*; and prostitutes, 6, 26–28, 50, 82–83, 107–10, 114–15, *129*, 130; reporting of sexual contacts by servicemen, 115; sex education for control of, 112, 115; USO hostesses as servicemen's protection from, 82–83, 107, 112; and USO junior hostesses, 127–31; during World War I, 26, 50, 107, 109

Victory girls. *See* Pickups

Vietnam War, 172–73

Virginia clubs. *See specific cities*

Volunteerism, 15. *See also* USO junior hostesses; USO senior hostesses

WAC (Women's Army Corps)/Wacs (female soldiers): as challenge to masculine structure of military, 125; compared with USO junior hostesses, 60–63; competition between USO junior hostesses and, 160–61, 170; father's forbidding daughter to join, 125, 170; femininity and beauty of, 44, 45, 60–63; recruitment for, 123; and USO, 44, 45, 160–62; wartime contributions of, 84

Wakefield, Larry, 26, 27

Walker, Frank C., 113

Wall, Marie, 159

Walla Walla, Wash., club, 59, 95–96

Waltz, 144, 145. See also Dances

War Brides Act, 219 (n. 152)

Ward, Betty, 51, 52

War Department, U.S., 26–27, 114

War Production Board, 6

Washington, George, 42

Washington, D.C., clubs: junior hostesses at, 44; selection of junior hostesses for, 44, 45, 52; and servicewomen, 60–61, 62; value of junior hostesses' work at, 84

Washington state clubs. See specific cities

Watrous, Livingston, 23

Waukegan, Ill., club, 65, 102

WAVES (Women Accepted for Volunteer Emergency Service)/Waves (female sailors), 45, 58, 60–63, 160, 161, 170

Weinstock, Warren, 61, 81

Westbrook, Robert, 73, 113, 214 (n. 70)

"White Christmas" (Berlin), 38

Williams, Mrs. Mallie B., 16

Williams, Norma, 101, 103

Williams, Robert, 33, 41, 114–15, 121

Wilmington, N.C., club, 64–65

Wilson, Margery, 90

Wisconsin clubs. See specific cities

Woman's Christian Temperance Union, 28

Women in the labor force: African Americans' work as domestic servants, 18; African Americans' work in factories, 74; clothing of, 71–72; factory work by, during World War II, 1, 11, 74; in Great Depression, 14–15; health cards for working-class women, 115; as sales clerks, 46; as secretaries, 45–46; statistics on, 19; and USO junior hostesses, 44–49, 52, 68, 70, 123, 168, 190 (n. 19), 197 (n. 15); and USO senior hostesses, 20; and working-class women, 34, 46, 122–23

Women in the military. See Servicewomen

Women of color. See African American women

Women's Army Corps (WAC). See WAC/ Wacs.

Women's clubs, 19–20

Women's magazines, 14, 15

Women's roles. See Gender roles

Working class: alcohol consumption of, 78; health cards for working-class women, 115; and interracial dancing, 154; sexuality and working-class women, 5–6, 115, 122–23; as USO junior hostesses, 48; women of, in labor force, 34, 115, 122–23

World War I: attitudes during, of women as men's moral guardians, 111; dances for servicemen during, 124; morale of servicemen during, 85; organizations providing assistance to U.S. troops during, 2; venereal disease (VD) during, 26, 50, 107, 109; women's contributions during, 42

Wylie, Philip, 24

Yank, 112–13

YMCA, 2, 47, 77, 102, 110–11, 119, 130, 139

YWCA, 2, 47, 92, 97, 99, 102, 111, 127, 160

Zahn, Bettelee, 47, 58, 75, 83, 94–95, 105

Zoot Suit riots, 157